english
defence

by Daniel King

EVERYMAN CHESS

Published by Everyman Publishers plc, London

First published in 1999 by Gloucester Publishers plc, (formerly Everyman Publishers plc), Northburgh House, 10 Northburgh Street, London, EC1V 0AT

Copyright © 1999 Daniel King

The right of Daniel King be identified as the author of this work has been asserted in accordance with the Copyrights, Designs and Patents Act 1988.

All rights reserved. No part of this publication may be reproduced, stored in a retrieval system or transmitted in any form or by any means, electronic, electrostatic, magnetic tape, photocopying, recording or otherwise, without prior permission of the publisher.

British Library Cataloguing-in-Publication Data
A catalogue record for this book is available from the British Library.

ISBN 1 85744 295 4

Distributed in North America by The Globe Pequot Press, P.O Box 480, 246 Goose Lane, Guilford, CT 06437-0480.

All other sales enquiries should be directed to Gloucester Publishers plc, Northburgh House, 10 Northburgh Street, London, EC1V 0AT
tel: 020 7253 7887 fax: 020 7490 3708
email: info@everymanchess.com
website: www.everymanchess.com

Everyman is the registered trade mark of Random House Inc. and is used in this work under license from Random House Inc.

EVERYMAN CHESS SERIES (formerly Cadogan Chess)

Commissioning Editor: Byron Jacobs

Typeset and edited by First Rank Publishing, Brighton.
Production by Navigator Guides.
Cover Design by Horatio Monteverde.
Printed in the U.K. by Lightning Source

CONTENTS

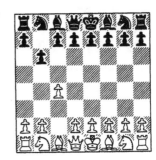

1 c4 b6

BIBLIOGRAPHY

Books
Encyclopaedia of Chess Openings volume A, second edition (Sahovski Informator, 1996)
The English Defence, Keene, Plaskett and Tisdall (Batsford, 1987)
Jon Speelman's Best Games, Speelman (Batsford, 1997)
Nunn's Chess Openings, Nunn, Burgess, Emms and Gallagher (Everyman Chess, 1999)

Periodicals
Informator
New in Chess Yearbook
New in Chess Magazine
ChessBase Megabase CD-ROM
Chess Monthly
British Chess Magazine

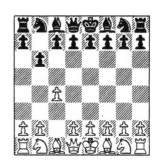

Whenever I am faced with an opponent who opens 1 d4 or 1 c4, I always get the feeling that I am up against a different breed of player to someone who starts with the e-pawn. 1 e4 players tend to want to 'have a go' at you in an open fight, sleeves already rolled up, quite prepared to give as good as they get. My impression of 1 d4 and flank opening players is different. They prefer to defer the struggle until they have brought out their pieces and rather like to stay on well-worn tramlines of development, a bit like carrying a comfort blanket around. (I won't be taking this cod chess psychology too far – it is too dangerous for me: depending on the day of the week I open 1 c4, or 1 d4, 1 ♘f3, 1 g3 and 1 e4. At the very least I am quite confused!)

That said, assuming there is a grain of truth in my view, then the English Defence is the perfect weapon against these kind of players. From the outset White cannot stick to his usual moves; he actually has to think for himself as standard responses are often not good enough. Before we get into looking at some of the typical strategies that Black employs, the question must be asked, 'What exactly is the English Defence?'

1 c4 Move Order

1 c4 b6

This is the pure starting position of the English Defence. Black invites his opponent to occupy the centre with his pawns, so that he can then shoot them down in flames.

2 d4 e6

2...♗b7 is also possible, but I want to show how Black can reach the English Defence via different move orders. This is crucial if White plays 1 d4.

1 d4 Move Order
Supposing your opponent opens with...
1 d4

...and you would still like to play the English Defence. I would recommend that you play...

1...e6!

It is true that this gives White the opportunity to transpose into a French Defence with 2 e4, but in my experience few players who open with 1 d4 like to do this (though you should have something up your sleeve just in case).

2 c4

2 ♘f3 is also common. After the text move Black can safely play...

2...b6!

and we are back to the English Defence. If you check out the move orders in the main games of this book you will begin to understand the best way to get into the opening according to your own overall repertoire.

Not Owen's Defence

By the way, I would not recommend that you answer...

1 d4

...with...

1...b6

In that case White plays...

2 e4!

...and if...

2...♗b7 3 ♗d3 e6

...White should not move the c-pawn, but just develop a piece, for instance.

4 ♘f3

Here White's centre is far more secure than in many of the games we will be considering, where the c-pawn is already on c4. I won't be examining this so-called Owen's Defence.

The English Defence in Practice

Since the 19th century various Englishmen had dabbled with 1...b6 from time to time, to little effect. However, the English Defence really only began to 'earn' its name in the early 1970s, when Michael Basman and Tony Miles began experimenting with the fianchetto of the queen's bishop. Miles in particular was able to pioneer the system at the highest levels of international chess – with great success. Over the years he has contributed so many remarkable ideas to the opening that he deserves the chief credit for its current cult status in the repertoire of some of the more imaginative players on the tournament circuit.

To help explain some of the main concepts of the English Defence, we could do worse than look at one of Miles's early games with the opening. It features three crucial concepts which have recurred in many games.

Farago-Miles
Hastings 1976/77

1 c4 b6 2 d4 e6

Note Miles's move order. Instead of preventing e2-e4 with 2...♗b7, he positively invites White to play it, and you would be amazed at how many players like to take up the challenge. Although this is probably the best course, it is very tricky – Grandmaster Farago doesn't make it past move 20.

3 e4

Game on. Black's task is to knock down the centre.

3...♗b7

A good start.

4 ♘c3

White protects the e-pawn, but...

4...♗b4

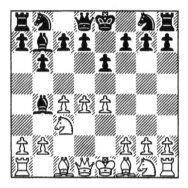

...Black pins the knight and renews the attack on the e-pawn. This is *Concept No.1*. The pin is an extremely useful weapon for Black: not only does he increase the pressure on the centre, but he also has the positional threat of doubling the c-pawns, intending to attack them later on, very much as in the Nimzo-Indian Defence.

5 ♕c2

White defends the e-pawn...

5...♕h4

...and Black attacks it again. *Concept No.2*: the early development of the queen to h4 to attack the pawn on e4 is an inte-

gral part of Black's system. It also creates some nasty threats on White's kingside. One of the bonuses of the queen move is that if White ever gets fed up and wants to boot it out with g2-g3, then serious weaknesses have been created on the long diagonal – remember that bishop sitting snugly and smugly in safety on b7.

At the time this game was played this kind of early queen placement would have come as quite a shock to someone like Farago. Nowadays it is commonplace, though no less difficult to handle.

6 ♗d3

White protects the pawn again...

6...f5!

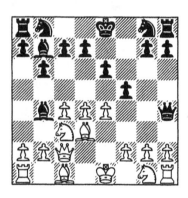

...Black attacks. *Concept No.3*: the advance of the f-pawn. This is a key part of Black's strategy in so many games. It is all very well attacking Black's centre with pieces, but that usually won't be enough to do the damage. A pawn break must come, and this fits the description perfectly. It is all about increasing the scope of that bishop on b7. (I once reached this position and my opponent captured on f5, so I took on g2 and that was a whole rook in the bag.)

7 g3 ♕h5

White relieves the pressure on his centre for a moment, but the move g2-g3 creates serious long-term weaknesses on the kingside and on the long diagonal.

8 ♗e2 ♕f7 9 f3 fxe4 10 fxe4 ♘f6 11 d5

The centre lurches forward, but this is just desperation. It isn't going anywhere.

11...0-0 12 ♘f3 ♕g6 13 ♗d3 ♕h5 14 0-0 ♘a6! 15 a3 ♗xc3 16 bxc3

It is interesting to see how Miles waited to be pushed by a2-a3 before he captured on c3: the knight wasn't running away and it was possible that the bishop could have been used elsewhere. 16 ♕xc3 ♘c5 17 e5 ♘g4 would also have been very good for Black.

16...♘c5 17 ♗e3 ♘xd3 18 ♕xd3 exd5 19 exd5 ♘xd5! 20 cxd5 ♖xf3 0-1

Here White resigned, clearly demoralised by his disastrous start. He could have struggled on with 21 ♖xf3 ♕xf3 22 ♖d1 c6, though clearly the situation is grim. (If you would like a more detailed analysis of this variation, then turn to Game 49.)

Webster-King
British Championship, Eastbourne 1990

As well as the three main attacking ideas I mentioned in the Farago-Miles game, there are a couple of other important themes that you should be aware of. Often, when Black plays ...f7-f5 the kingside can look a bit of a mess. Although this is not a critical problem, as in return White's centre has collapsed, it can mean that castling on the kingside is inadvisable.

A few moves before I had decided to castle on the queenside. There my king is well protected by four pawns – safer than White's king. This is an extremely common scenario in the English Defence. Chances at this point are about equal. Although Black is a pawn down I was reasonably optimistic in view of White's shattered kingside pawns; and that brings me on to the other theme I want to mention. After the confusion of the opening 10-15 moves, Black often emerges with a healthier pawn structure than his opponent. Let me show you the position we reached a few moves further on:

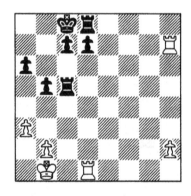

After a little good fortune and a little persuasion, I managed to reach this endgame. As you can see, several of those loose pawns have dropped off (well, they tend to) leaving me with my mass of four pawns supported and protected by my king. The ending is technically winning.

Rahman-Speelman
Calcutta 1998

Here is another example of Black's superior pawn structure making the difference between the two positions. Black has challenged the centre in the standard way, with ...f7-f5. White should probably try to hold the structure with 7 f3, but the tension was too great, and he captured:

7 exf5?! exd5!

Creating an imbalance in the structure rather similar to the last example.

8 ♘gf3 ♘e7 9 g4

If White could maintain the pawns like this then the position would be rather unclear. However...

9...h5!

...wrecks them.

10 ♖g1 dxc4 11 ♗xc4 hxg4 12 ♖xg4 ♘bc6 13 ♗d3 0-0-0

see following diagram

Having created chaos on the kingside, the king evacuates swiftly behind the four pawns and is perfectly safe. Now Black's task is to mop up the broken pawns.

14 b4 ♖df8 15 b5 ♘d8 16 ♘h4 ♘f7 17 f4 ♘d6 18 0-0-0 ♘dxf5

And Black was on the way to capturing the whole kingside. I'll be pointing out

more themes as we go along.

How this Book is Organised

The first five chapters of the book deal with positions where White accepts the challenge and occupies the centre with pawns. The sixth chapter contains games where White plays an early a2-a3, preventing ...♗b4, and thereby gives himself more control over the centre. Chapters 7 and 8 include games where White attempts to divert the game into the more familiar patterns of the English Opening and the Réti. We have ways of avoiding that tedious outcome – that's the reason we play 1...b6 in the first place!

As ever when learning an opening, I would recommend that you pick one of its greatest exponents and study what they do. Tony Miles still plays the system regularly and continues to produce highly imaginative ideas; and currently the other practitioner who has enjoyed success with 1...b6 is the Latvian Grandmaster Edvins Kengis. You'll find plenty of games by both these players in the book.

And finally, on a personal note, of all the openings that I play, the English Defence is the one which has given me perhaps the greatest sense of fun, and even some reasonable results, when I have tried it. One thing I can guarantee: play it in the right spirit and you'll never be bored.

CHAPTER ONE

Main Line with 3 e4 ♗b7 4 ♗d3: The 'new' 4...♘c6

Let us begin with what has evolved in recent years as the main line of the English Defence.

1 d4 e6 2 c4 b6 3 e4

White places three pawns in the centre and in so doing displays a metaphorical two-fingered salute to Black's opening strategy. The battle is on. If Black is unable to counter White's central domination then he could be driven off the edge of the board.

3...♗b7

The counterattack begins. The bishop snipes at the centre from the edge of the board, reminding White that when he assumes such an imposing central stance he also takes on great responsibility. After White's centre had been chopped down in various ways in the early years of the opening, it gradually became clear that the most solid and reliable method of defending the e-pawn was...

4 ♗d3

The alternatives, 4 ♘c3, 4 d5, 4 f3, 4 ♕c2 and 4 ♘d2, all allow Black more chances of attacking the centre (see Chapters 3-5). After 4 ♗d3 Black faces something of a dilemma. How should he go about undermining White's centre? The natural move to meet the early development of the bishop is 4...f5!? as the g2-pawn has been left undefended, but while this is great fun, it has been shown to be risky. I suppose it is a matter of taste. If you are prepared to go for it then I would direct you to Chapter 2, Games 12-19. Of the other alternatives, 4...♗b4+ is a bit wet, but sound, while 4...♕h4 is mad. Again, check out Chapter 2.

In this chapter we shall concentrate on a fourth possibility, 4...♘c6, which has become established as Black's most popular move in recent years.

Game 1
Ruzele-Kengis
Bad Godesburg 1996

---

1 d4 e6 2 c4 b6 3 e4 ♗b7 4 ♗d3

When the English Defence began its resurgence in the late seventies and eighties, 4...f5 was the move Black relied on. When experience proved that it was risky, the search was on for alternatives, and that is when...

4...♘c6

...became popular. To my knowledge it was first tried at top level in Sosonko-Miles, Tunis Interzonal 1985. Although that nine-move draw did not reveal much,

4...♘c6 has nevertheless proved since then to be a durable and reliable method of coping with White's system. Black does not seek to destroy the pawn centre straight away, as in so many other lines of this opening, but rather seeks to grab the bishop on d3 with his knight. Surprisingly, this takes the sting out of White's entire set-up. First White must think how he is to deal with the threat to his d-pawn.

5 ♘f3

This and 5 ♘e2 (Games 6-10) are the most popular moves, whereas 5 d5 is the move which Black would really like to provoke (Game 11).

5...♘b4

This is the idea of bringing the knight out so early, to force an exchange for the bishop. The bishop cannot retreat as the e-pawn would be en prise.

6 0-0 ♘xd3

Take the bishop quickly! Otherwise the knight might have had a wasted journey.

7 ♕xd3

Black is a long way behind in development and is quite seriously cramped. However, he is able to survive (more than survive, I believe that Black's chances are no worse than his opponent's) as the position is still closed. Since there are no open files Black is able to shuffle his pieces onto the right squares while White is only an onlooker.

7...♘e7

I favour this method of development, even though it is fairly slow. The straightforward development of the knight to f6 would be asking a little too much of the position: it would be kicked around by the white pawn advancing to e5. However, it is possible to develop the knight to f6 with a couple of preparatory moves (see Game 4).

8 ♘c3 ♘g6

The knight arrives at a square where it is not going to be hassled by an advancing pawn.

9 d5

This is a common move for White in these kinds of position. He feels he should be using his lead in development to 'do something', though it isn't clear to me what that something is. At least the d-pawn is now blocking the bishop on b7, though that piece is still the pride of Black's position – it has no opponent, so if it ever finds the right diagonal it will be a great asset. White's alternatives here are considered in Games 2 and 3.

9...♗e7 10 ♗e3 0-0 11 ♖ad1 e5

It might not seem to make sense to close the position when Black has the two bishops, but they will emerge later!

12 ♘e2 d6

The blocked pawn structure is reminiscent of a King's Indian. Black would love to get in the pawn break ...f7-f5 to attack on the kingside. Normally White counters this with play on the queenside (via b2-b4 and c4-c5) but that would be far too slow in this case (it is quite handy for Black that the pawn is already on b6, covering the c5-square). Instead White attempts to thwart Black's kingside play:

13 ♘g3 ♗c8

Bringing the bishop back to life.

14 h3

I don't quite see the point of this move. If White had played ♘f5 we would have arrived at a position similar to the next game.

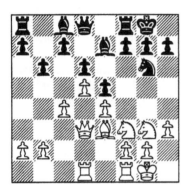

14...♞h4

To relieve a little of the congestion in his position Black seeks exchanges. 14...♞f4 would have been more ambitious, for instance:

a) 15 ♗xf4 exf4 16 ♞e2 (not 16 ♞h5 ♗g5 and the knight on h5 is stranded) 16...♗f6 17 b3 g5 18 ♞ed4 ♗d7 with chances for both sides.

b) 15 ♕d2 ♗g5 16 ♞xg5 ♕xg5 and Black is on the attack.

15 ♞xh4 ♗xh4 16 ♞f5

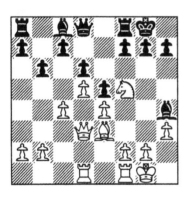

16...g6

This is fine, but afterwards the game simplifies very quickly. Black had a couple of alternatives which would have kept a bit more tension in the position: 16...♗g5!? or 16...♗f6!?, threatening to

either capture on f5 and break out with ...e5-e4; or to kick the knight out with ...g7-g6, retreat the bishop to g7 again and play for ...f7-f5.

17 ♞xh4 ♕xh4 18 b3 ♗d7 19 f3 f5 20 exf5 gxf5 21 f4 exf4 22 ♕d4 ♖ae8 23 ♕xf4 ♕xf4 24 ♗xf4 ½-½

Fair enough. There is not too much to play for now, but both sides could have played more ambitiously earlier – as the next game illustrates.

Game 2
Magerramov-Ehlvest
Moscow 1992

---

1 d4 e6 2 c4 b6 3 e4 ♗b7 4 ♗d3 ♞c6 5 ♞f3 ♞b4 6 0-0 ♞e7 7 ♞c3 ♞xd3 8 ♕xd3 ♞g6 9 b3 ♗e7 10 d5 e5 11 ♞e2 0-0 12 ♞g3 d6 13 ♞f5 ♗c8

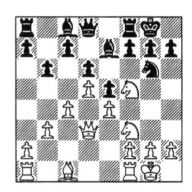

We have virtually the same position as the last game, though White has played more purposefully. The knight looks very fine on f5, but the question is, can he make use of it?

14 ♗d2 ♖e8 15 ♖ae1 ♗d7 16 ♔h1 ♗f8

Ehlvest has defended very coolly, withdrawing the bishop out of the knight's range. The bishop is also well placed on d7 and White must always be careful that the knight on f5 doesn't get exchanged off at a bad moment.

17 g3 ♕c8

Now there is the possibility of capturing on f5, playing ...e5-e4, and taking with the queen on f5. So the knight retreats.

18 ♘e3 h6 19 ♘g1 ♗e7 20 f4

Dangerous? Well, yes, but Black has organised his forces efficiently so that he can cope. In fact White's pawns look more exposed than threatening.

20...exf4 21 gxf4 ♗h4 22 ♖e2 ♗f6 23 ♘g2

If 23 f5 then the knight gets a fantastic square on e5. In other words, it is going to be difficult to advance the pawns further, and in the game they prove to be more of a liability than an asset. But Black still lacks space; so what does he do? Create some:

23...b5!

A smart pawn sacrifice ensuring that the light-squared bishop (the one without an opponent) will be able to get into the game.

24 c5

If White had captured the pawn Black would have had plenty of play: 24 cxb5 ♕b7 (or 24...a6 25 bxa6 ♕xa6 26 ♕xa6 ♖xa6 27 a4 ♖b8 and Black recovers the pawn) 25 a4 a6 26 bxa6 ♖xa6 to be followed by ...c7-c6; then just imagine that bishop on the long diagonal...

24...dxc5 25 e5

The pawns appear impressive, but Black has it all under control.

25...♗f5 26 ♕xb5 c6! 27 dxc6

27 ♕xc6 ♕xc6 28 dxc6 ♗d3 picks up the exchange.

27...♗e7

The point behind Black's pawn sacrifice was to break up White's pawns...

28 ♖e3 ♖b8 29 ♕a4 ♖b6 30 c7 ♖a6 31 ♗a5 ♗d7 32 ♕a3 ♗c6

...and get that bishop to the long diagonal. White is in desperate trouble.

33 ♘f3 ♕g4 34 e6 fxe6 35 b4 cxb4 36 ♕c1 ♗b7 0-1

The bishop on a5 is about to drop, among other things, so White resigned. For me, there was poetic justice in this game: White was punished for overextending his centre and the black light-squared bishop (which had reigned supreme since its opposite number was nabbed at the start of the game) played a significant part in its downfall.

I once had a game myself which also arrived at the same pawn structure, though in this case I was allowed to develop an attack on the kingside.

Game 3
Mednis-King
Stavanger 1989

---

1 c4 b6 2 d4 e6 3 e4 ♗b7 4 ♗d3 ♘c6 5 ♘f3 ♘b4 6 0-0 ♘e7 7 ♘c3 ♘xd3 8 ♕xd3 ♘g6 9 ♖e1

To be honest, I don't see the point of this move. When the centre becomes locked the rook is no better on e1 than on f1.

9...♗e7 10 d5

White invariably plays this move sooner or later. Otherwise Black can consider ...0-0 and ...f7-f5.

10...0-0

11 ♗e3 e5

The familiar closing of the position.

12 ♖ac1 ♗c8

I played this before ...d7-d6 to try to hold up White's pawn advance on the queenside. I only succeeded in doing so temporarily, but by that time my own play was in motion.

13 ♘d2 a5 14 a3 d6 15 b4

White has carried out a different plan to the first two games. Instead of containing Black's play on the kingside, he concentrates on his own attack on the queenside. His intention is to force through c4-c5. This is fine, but Black can also develop some play by opening the a-file – at least that's what I should have done.

15...f5 16 f3

16 exf5 allows that beautiful bishop into the game: 16...♗xf5 17 ♘de4 ♘f4 (or 17...♘h4!? with the idea of ...♕e8-g6) 18 ♗xf4 exf4 and then the other bishop will come into play via f6. Now I went for a straightforward attack with...

16...♘h4

...though, with hindsight, I have several stronger alternatives. Looking at the position again, 16...♘f4 would be my choice. It would be painful for White to leave the knight on f4, but if it is captured the bishops are going to fly: 17 ♗xf4 exf4 18 exf5 ♗xf5 with a similar position to the variation above – the other bishop will come in via f6. Similarly, 16...fxe4 17 fxe4 ♘f4 gives Black a pleasant initiative (17...♗g5!? is also strong, and only after the exchange ...♘f4).

17 ♔h1

17...♖f6

It would have been stronger to play 17...axb4!? 18 axb4 and only then 18...♖f6, and if 19 ♖a1 ♗d7. That way White is kept busy on the a-file and on the kingside too.

18 c5 bxc5

Unfortunately, opening the a-file doesn't work as well now: 18...axb4?! 19 cxd6 cxd6 20 axb4 followed by ♘c4, attacking the b6-pawn.

19 bxc5

Black still has some attack, but it is not as strong without an open file for the rook on the queenside.

19...♖g6 20 ♖g1 ♗a6 21 ♕c2 f4 22 ♗f2 ♖h6 23 a4 ♕e8 24 ♘b5 ♘f5

24...♗xb5 25 axb5 ♕xb5 is stronger.

25 h3

Not 25 exf5?? ♖xh2+ 26 ♔xh2 ♕h5+.

25...♗xb5 26 axb5 ♘e3 ½-½

I offered a draw here and was lucky that it was accepted (my opponent was in time pressure). After 27 ♗xe3 fxe3 28 ♘c4 ♕xb5 29 cxd6 cxd6 30 ♘xe3 the attack is all but over, but Black's rook is stuck out on the edge of the board, cut off from the queenside. The a-pawn gives me some counterplay, but there is no doubt that White stands better. For me, a disappointing conclusion after a successful opening. I repeat, I don't think that Black should have any difficulties if White plays in such a 'normal' fashion.

It is worth seeing how two of the greatest exponents of the English Defence have played this system. First, in this game, Edvins Kengis, and in the next, Tony Miles.

Game 4
Barkhagen-Kengis
Gausdal 1991

---

1 d4 e6 2 c4 b6 3 e4 ♗b7 4 ♗d3 ♘c6 5 ♘f3 ♘b4 6 0-0 ♘xd3 7 ♕xd3 d6

A divergence from the usual 7...♘g6, which we saw in the first three games.

8 ♘c3 ♗e7

see following diagram

9 b3

Kengis has faced two other moves here:

a) In Cmiel-Kengis, German Bundesliga 1992, White tried 9 ♕e2 ♘f6 10 e5, but I think this is a fundamental error as it opens up the diagonal for that wonderful bishop on b7. Black reached a superior ending after 10...dxe5 11 dxe5 ♘d7 12 ♘e4 0-0 13 ♗f4 ♘c5 14 ♘xc5 ♗xc5 15 ♘g5 h6 16 ♖ad1 ♕e8! 17 ♘e4 ♕c6! 18 ♖de1 ♕xe4 19 ♕xe4 ♗xe4 20 ♖xe4 ♖ad8. Black controls the only open file.

b) The most challenging move for Black at this point is 9 d5!? e5 10 c5! ♘f6 11 ♕b5+ ♔f8 12 c6 ♗c8. It takes a bit of time for Black to sort out his king, and from White's point of view it is a definite plus to have forced the pawn to c6, as Black is more cramped. Nevertheless, Kengis proved that his system is still viable after 13 a4 a5 14 ♕e2 g6 15 ♘e1 ♔g7 16 ♘d3 ♗a6 17 f4 exf4 18 ♖xf4 h5 19 h3 h4 20 ♗e3 ♘h5 21 ♗d4+ ♔g8 22 ♖f2 ♖h7 23 ♘b5 ♘g3 24 ♕f3 ♗g5 25 ♖e1 ♗xb5 26 axb5 ♕e7 27 e5 ♖e8 28 ♗c3 (28 e6!? ♘f5 29 ♗c3 fxe6 30 ♖xe6 ♕f7 31 ♖fe2 ♖xe6 32 ♖xe6 ♘g3 offers Black sufficient counterplay) 28...♕d8 29 ♕g4 dxe5 30 ♘xe5 f5 31 ♕d1 ♖he7 32 ♘c4 ♖xe1+ 33 ♗xe1 ♔h7 34 ♗c3 ♘e4 35 ♖f3 ♗e7 36 ♗e5 ♗c5+ 37 ♔h2 ♖xe5 38 ♘xe5 ♕d6 39 ♖xf5 gxf5 40 ♕h5+ ♔g7 41 ♕f7+ ♔h6 42 ♕xf5 ♕xe5+ 0-1 Shirov-Kengis, Gausdal (Arnold Cup) 1991.

9...♘f6

As can be seen from these games, Kengis likes to develop his knight to f6. I don't think it greatly changes the assessment of the position (I believe chances are balanced) but it demonstrates another sound option for Black.

10 ♗b2 0-0 11 d5 e5

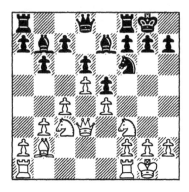

12 b4

Perhaps because Black appears cramped, White underestimates the potential of his opponent's position. For instance, the bishop is sitting on b2 – but it is now just biting on the solid pawn on e5; it would be stronger on c1 where it covers the f4-square. And this last move has actually created a serious weakness in White's position. As we are about to discover, the monster bishop on b7 is about to enter the game. First Black establishes some pressure on the a-file:

12...a5!

White cannot contemplate capturing on a5 as it would leave the a-pawn isolated, and the c5-square available for a knight.

13 a3 ♘h5

The knight heads for the outpost on f4 and makes way for the f-pawn...

14 ♖fe1 ♘f4 15 ♕c2 f5 16 ♘d1

16 exf5 would bring the light-squared bishop into the game, as White is unable to hold onto the pawn: 16...♗c8! 17 g4?! h5 and the kingside breaks up.

16...fxe4 17 ♖xe4 axb4 18 axb4 ♖xa1 19 ♗xa1

19...b5!

Undermining the pawn chain. White is lucky to scrape out of this position with just the loss of the exchange, though he does go down eventually anyway.

20 ♘e3 ♕a8 21 ♗b2 c6 22 c5 cxd5 23 cxd6 dxe4 24 dxe7 ♖c8 25 e8♕+ ♖xe8 26 ♘xe5 ♕a2 27 h3 ♖c8 28 ♕d2 ♕b1+ 29 ♔h2 ♘d3 30 ♘xd3 ♕xd3 31 ♕e1

In spite of the clear material advantage Black has great difficulty in winning this position as White is able to construct a kind of fortress. It takes great patience to crack it, but Kengis succeeds in the end by concentrating on White's weaknesses, notably the b-pawn, and thereby forces the exchange of queens; thereafter it isn't too difficult.

31...♖f8 32 ♔g1 ♗d5 33 ♗e5 ♗c4 34 ♕c1 ♕e2 35 ♗g3 ♖d8 36 ♕a1 ♕d2 37 ♕a5 ♖f8 38 ♔h2 ♕d7 39 ♕b6 ♗d3 40 ♕c5 ♖c8 41 ♕e5 ♖e8 42 ♕c5 h6 43 ♕b6 ♕e6 44 ♕c5 ♔h7 45 ♕d4 ♖f8 46 ♕c5 ♖f7 47 ♔g1 ♕a2 48 ♕d4 ♕a7 49 ♕e5 ♕e7 50 ♕d4 ♕f6 51 ♕c5 ♕b2 52 ♕d5 ♕a1+ 53 ♔h2 ♕a7 54 ♔g1 ♕d7 55 ♕c5 ♕e6 56 ♕d4 ♕c6 57 ♔h2 ♖d7 58 ♕e5 ♕f6 59 ♕c5 ♕e6 60 ♔g1 ♗c4 61 ♔h2 ♖f7 62 ♕d4 ♕c6 63 ♕e5 ♗e6 64 ♕b2 ♖a7 65 ♕d4 ♖d7 66 ♕b2 ♖d3 67 ♗e5 ♕d7 68 ♗c3 ♕a7 69 ♗e1 ♕d4 70

♕c1 ♗c4 71 ♔g1 ♖b3 72 ♘f5 ♕e5 73 ♘e3 ♕b2

Mission half-accomplished.

74 ♕xb2 ♖xb2 75 ♗c3 ♖b3 76 ♗d2 ♖b1+ 77 ♔h2 ♖b2 78 ♗e1 ♖e2 79 ♗c3 ♖xf2 80 ♔g3 ♖f7 81 ♗d4 ♗e6 82 ♗b6 ♔g6 83 ♔h4 ♖d7 84 ♔g3 ♔g5 85 ♗c5 ♖f7 86 ♗b6 ♔h5 87 h4 ♖d7 88 ♗c5 ♖d3 89 ♔f4 ♔xh4 90 ♔xe4 ♖d2 91 ♗f8 ♖d7 92 ♔e5 ♗g4 0-1

Mission accomplished.

> ### Game 5
> ### Polovodin-Miles
> *Los Angeles 1991*

1 e4 b6 2 d4 ♗b7 3 ♗d3 e6 4 c4 ♘c6 5 ♘f3 ♗b4 6 ♘c3 ♘xd3+ 7 ♕xd3 ♗b4

I remember looking at this variation over ten years ago and coming to the conclusion that if Black were given the chance to pin then he should do it. An exchange of the bishop for knight clears more space for Black (he is manoeuvring behind three ranks for the moment) and puts more pressure on White's centre. It is worth noting that if White wishes to avoid this pin then he could castle on move six instead of playing the knight to c3. Of course if he does castle kingside quickly then White somewhat reduces his own options – in the note below the king goes left instead of right with success.

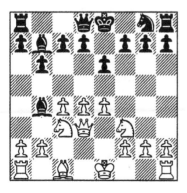

8 d5

White has also tried 8 ♗d2, indicating a desire to castle queenside. After 8...♘e7 9 a3 ♗xc3 10 ♗xc3 0-0 11 d5 Black has:

a) A safe option for Black is 11...f6, closing the diagonal. After 12 0-0-0 e5 (12...exd5!?) Black not only has a very solid position, but there are also chances to attack on the queenside.

b) Also playable is 11...c6, not fearing 12 d6 ♘g6 13 c5 b5. In the game Sherbakov-Bischoff, Linares 1996, White tried 13 h4!?, and after 13...cxd5 14 cxd5 (or 14 exd5 b5!) 14...exd5 15 e5 ♘g6 a very unclear position had arisen.

c) In the game Levin-Teske, Bad Wörishofen open 1998, Black tried the rather risky 11...f5? and suffered on the long diagonal after 12 ♕d4 ♖f6 13 0-0-0 fxe4 14 ♕xe4 exd5 15 cxd5 ♖d6 16 ♕e5 ♕f8 17 ♗b4 winning the exchange.

8...♘e7 9 a3 ♗xc3+ 10 ♕xc3 0-0 11 0-0

White's centre is ripe. In classic style Miles hits out with the f-pawn.

11...f5!

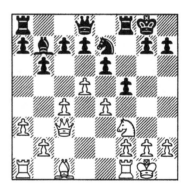

12 dxe6

12 exf5 would have been a more dynamic way of playing the position:

a) 12...♘xf5 is a solid option, when after 13 dxe6 (13 ♗g5 ♕e8 14 ♖ae1 ♕g6 just swings the queen to a good attacking square) 13...dxe6 Black's active pieces compensate for the weak pawn on e6.

b) 12...exd5 would be more daring for Black (he might just win a pawn) but after 13 ♗g5 White has good development and free lines for his rooks.

12...fxe4 13 ♘g5 ♕e8 14 ♖e1 ♕g6 15 exd7 ♖ad8 16 ♕e5

White could have tried 16 ♖d1 ♕f5 17 ♗e3 ♖xd7, though the position of the knight on g5 is still unfortunate.

16...♖xd7 17 ♕e6+ ♕xe6 18 ♘xe6 ♖f6 19 ♘f4 ♘f5 20 ♘e2

White runs into trouble if he plays a 'normal' move, e.g. 20 ♗e3 ♘xe3 21 fxe3 ♖d2 and Black controls the file.

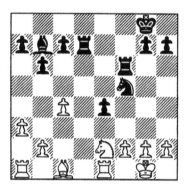

20...e3!

A pleasing sacrifice to open the line of the bishop on b7.

21 fxe3 ♘h4 22 e4 ♗xe4 23 ♘g3 ♗xg2 24 ♗g5 ♘f3+ 25 ♔xg2 ♘xg5

With an extra pawn Black should have won, but he blows it right at the end.

26 ♖ad1 ♖df7 27 ♖e8+ ♖f8 28 ♖xf8+ ♔xf8 29 ♖d8+ ♔e7 30 ♖a8 a5 31 c5 ♖c6 32 ♘f5+ ♔f6 33 cxb6 ♖c2+ 34 ♔g3 cxb6 35 ♖f8+ ♔e5 36 ♘xg7 ♘e4+ 37 ♔h3 ♖xb2 38 ♖f5+ ♔d4 39 ♘e6+ ♔c4 40 ♘f8 ♖b3+ 41 ♔g4 ♖xa3 42 ♘xh7 ♖a1 43 ♖f4 ♔d3 44 h4 a4 45 ♘g5 ♘c3 46 ♖f3+ ♔c4 47 h5 ♖g1+ 48 ♔h4 a3 49 h6 a2 50 h7 a1♕ 51 h8♕ ♖xg5 52 ♖f4+ ♔b3 53 ♕f6 ♖b5 54 ♕e6+ ♔a3

54...♔b2! 55 ♖f2+ ♔a3 56 ♕d6+ ♖b4+ would have won for Black.

55 ♕e7+ ♔b3 56 ♕e6+ ♘d5 57 ♕h3+ ♘e3 58 ♕e6+ ♔b2 59 ♕f6+ ♔b1 60 ♕g6+ ♘f5+ ½-½

The conclusion is that Black has a comfortable game if he is able to pin the knight on c3 – but White need not allow it.

Game 6
Arlandi-Yefimov
Asti 1995

---

1 d4 e6 2 c4 b6 3 e4 ♗b7 4 ♗d3 ♘c6

Black faces a sterner test if instead of 5 ♘f3 White replies...

5 ♘e2

At first glance it is hard to imagine that playing the knight to e2 rather than f3 can make such a great difference. However, with the knight on e2 White has an extra option: he can use the f-pawn as a battering ram to open Black's position. We can see straightaway in this game how this affects the way in which Black is able to develop. (By the way, I should add that in practice most players of the white pieces have preferred 5 ♘f3.)

5...♘b4

Not the only legal move. Speelman has tried 5...e5 and Kengis has experimented with 5...g6. For these options, see Games 9 and 10 respectively.

6 0-0

The continuation of the game Anastasian-Dausch, Cappelle la Grande open 1996, is a good example of the f-pawn in action: 6 ♘bc3 ♘xd3+ 7 ♕xd3 g6 (for 7...♗b4!? see Game 8) 8 0-0 ♗g7 9 f4 f5?! (9...♘e7 strikes me as more sensible) 10 exf5 gxf5 11 d5 ♕h4 12 ♘b5 0-0-0 13 d6 ♕g4 14 ♖f2 c6 15 ♘xa7+ ♔b8 16 ♗e3 and White already had a winning attack.

6...♘xd3 7 ♕xd3 ♘e7

For 7...d6, see the next main game.

8 ♘bc3 g6

Black must change his method of defence. If the knight were on f3, then instead 8...♘g6 would be quite acceptable here, as we have seen. However, in this position 8...♘g6 would be met by 9 f4!, when Black is in danger of being overrun. Note, however, that 8...d6 transposes to the next game.

9 ♗g5

9 ♕h3 is an interesting alternative, hoping to exchange bishops on h6: 9...♗g7 (9...d6 is more flexible. Black can go for ...♕d7 and ...0-0-0, or revert back to castling kingside, depending upon how White reacts) 10 ♗h6 0-0 11 ♗xg7 (11 ♖ad1! would have prevented Black's defensive manoeuvre) 11...♔xg7 12 ♖ad1 d6 13 ♘f4 ♘g8 and even here White enjoyed a pleasant space advantage in Kohlweyer-Gulko, Geneva 1997.

9...♗g7

10 f4

There it goes again. The f-pawn spells danger, though Black constructs a sturdy defence.

10...f6 11 ♗h4 0-0 12 d5

If White were to be entirely consistent, then 12 f5!? is the move, with an exchange sacrifice in mind: 12...exf5 13 exf5 ♘xf5 14 ♖xf5 gxf5 15 ♘g3. However it does not look sound to me; for instance, 15...♗e4!, getting rid of one of the knights and using the bishop before it gets locked out of the game with d4-d5.

12...♗a6 13 ♖ad1

13 b3 looks stronger to me, so that if Black continues as in the game with 13...♕e8 White can play 14 d6! cxd6 15 ♕xd6 with a clear advantage. Likewise, 13...exd5 14 ♘xd5 ♘xd5 15 ♕xd5+ ♖f7 is obviously more pleasant for White than his opponent.

13...♕e8 14 ♘d4 exd5 15 exd5 ♕f7 16 b3 c5 17 ♘db5

17 dxc6!? dxc6 18 f5 (18 ♕f3 ♗b7 19 f5 is also strong) 18...♖fd8 19 ♕f3 gives White some advantage.

17...♗xb5 18 ♘xb5

With a series of accurate moves Black now manages to equalise the position, but I feel that White has had the better of the opening.

18...♘f5 19 ♗f2 d6 20 g4 a6 21 ♘c3 ♘h6 22 h3 ♕d7 23 ♖de1 ♖ae8 24 ♖xe8

♖xe8 25 ♖e1 f5 26 g5 ♘f7 27 ♖xe8+
♕xe8 28 ♕e2 ♔f8 29 ♕xe8+ ♔xe8 30
♗e1 ½-½

Game 7
Gelfand-Short
Novgorod 1997

**1 d4 e6 2 c4 b6 3 e4 ♗b7 4 ♗d3 ♘c6 5
♘e2 ♘b4 6 ♘bc3**

Not the most accurate continuation as
it gives Black the chance to pin the knight
on c3 if he wishes to with 6...♘xd3+ 7
♕xd3 ♗b4 (see Game 8). To avoid that
possibility White could simply castle kingside straightaway.

6...♘xd3+ 7 ♕xd3 d6

Since 7...♘e7 and 8...g6 is lacking, this
has taken over as the move of choice for
the those in the know.

8 0-0 ♘e7!?

8...♘f6 has also been played, though it
is less dynamic: 9 d5 ♗e7 10 ♘d4 ♕d7 11
f4! (11 b3, as in Epishin-Ehlvest, Novo-
sibirsk 1993, is playable but obviously less
critical) 11...c5 12 ♘de2 exd5 13 cxd5 h5
14 a4 h4 15 h3 0-0 16 b3 ♘e8 17 ♗b2 ♘c7
18 f5 ♗f6 19 ♖f4 ♕e7 20 ♖g4 ♔h7 21 ♕d2
♘e8 22 ♔h1 g5 23 ♘g1 ♖g8 24 ♘f3 ♖g7
25 ♖f1 ♔g8 26 e5! dxe5 27 ♘e4 with a
lethal attack in Anastasian-Kengis, Katowice open 1993.

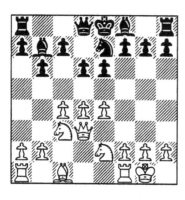

9 d5

9 ♕h3 was tried in Bareev-Kengis, Pula
1997, but the queen manoeuvre can be
immediately countered by 9...♕d7! (the
queen is good on a light square when
White has no bishop to challenge it) 10
♗e3 g6 11 d5 ♗a6 12 dxe6 ♕xe6 13 ♕h4
♗g7 14 b3 0-0 15 ♗d4 f6 16 ♖ad1 ♖ae8 17
♖fe1 c5 18 ♗e3 f5 19 ♗h6 ♗xh6 20 ♕xh6
fxe4 21 ♘g3 ♘f5 22 ♘xf5 ♕xf5 23 ♕e3
when a draw was agreed as 23...♗e6 24
♘xe4 ♗b7 25 f3 ♗xe4 26 fxe4 leads to an
equal position.

9...♕d7!

Black retains flexibility. He still might
castle on the kingside, but he is also prepared to go queenside; and the queen covers the sensitive e6-square. Black could
close the centre with 9...e5, but I would be
concerned about a direct assault with 10
f4.

10 f4!

Although White's strategy rebounds in
the end, I feel that if he is to get anything
from this variation he must play aggres-
sively, so this one gets my approval. Alternatively, 10 ♗e3 ♘g6 (10...g6!?) 11 f4
♗e7 12 ♗d4 0-0 13 dxe6 fxe6 14 f5 e5
(14...exf5!? 15 exf5 ♘h4 is good fun: 16
♕g3 ♗d8 17 f6 c5 18 fxg7 ♖f5 19 ♗e3
♕xg7 20 ♕xg7+ ♔xg7 is a bizarre variation. Okay I admit it, I used the computer
to check this one out but I don't see how
White can improve – Black is doing fine in
this position.) 15 ♗e3 ♘h8 16 ♘d5 ♗d8
17 ♖ad1 ♘f7 18 b4 c6 19 ♘dc3 ♕e8 20
♘g3 ♗f6 21 ♔h1 ♖d8 22 a4 ♖d7 23 ♕e2
♔h8 24 ♖d2 ♕e7 25 b5 and White was a
bit better in Dautov-Kengis, Hockenheim
rapidplay 1997, though the game was
drawn in 44 moves.

10...g6 11 ♘d4

11 ♕d4 ♖g8 is satisfactory for Black,
but in his annotations in *Informator 70*
Short suggests that the continuation 11
♗e3 ♗g7 12 ♗d4 would have slightly favoured White.

11...0-0-0

Advisable. At first I thought it might be preferable to delay castling for a move with 11...♗g7, but White can stir up enough trouble with 12 f5! gxf5 13 exf5, and now after either 13...♗xd4+ 14 ♕xd4 0-0-0 (14...e5 15 ♕f2) 15 fxe6 fxe6 16 ♗g5 or 13...♘xf5 14 ♘xf5 exf5 15 ♗g5 White has taken control.

12 b4

After 12 dxe6 fxe6 13 ♕h3 ♗g7!? (after 13...e5 14 ♘e6 ♖e8 15 ♘d5 White has an attack) 14 ♘xe6 ♗xc3 15 bxc3 (not 15 ♘xd8?? ♗d4+ 16 ♔h1 ♕xh3 and wins) 15...♖de8 Black has excellent compensation for the pawn – the pawns on e4 and c4 are extremely weak.

However, the move which concerns me here is 12 a4. White's attack is potentially lethal. For instance:

a) 12...a5 13 b4 axb4 14 ♘cb5 followed by a4-a5 and a big explosion on the queenside. Black is so cramped that it is extremely difficult to bring his pieces across to defend the king.

b) 12...♗g7 is stronger, e.g. 13 a5 exd5 14 exd5! (14 cxd5 f5! 15 ♘e6 fxe4 16 ♘xe4 ♘xd5 17 ♘xd8 ♖xd8 18 axb6 axb6 with good compensation for the exchange) 14...♘f5 and now White can go in for insane complications with 15 ♘db5 a6 or play for an endgame advantage based on Black's weak pawns after 15 ♘xf5 ♕xf5 16

♕xf5 gxf5.

c) Finally, Short suggests 12...c5!? 13 dxc6 ♘xc6 with an unclear position.

12...♗g7 13 b5?

All very fine if White could land the knight on c6, but...

13...♗xd4+!

...stops that idea, and then it just looks like pushing the b-pawn has wasted two moves.

14 ♕xd4 f5

Once again the f-pawn saves the day, undermining White's centre and letting Black's bishop breathe again. Without this move Black has no play.

15 ♖e1

If 15 exf5 then Stohl recommends 15...♘xf5 (I prefer 15...exd5 16 cxd5 ♕xf5 17 ♖d1 ♖he8 18 a4 ♘g8! 19 a5 ♘f6 20 axb6 axb6 21 ♖a7 ♘e4 with good counterplay) 16 ♕d3 ♕g7 17 ♖d1 ♖he8, which he assesses as unclear.

15...♖he8

Black has to build up first before dissolving the centre. For instance, 15...exd5 16 exd5 and the bishop on b7 is permanently locked in, while 15...fxe4 16 ♕xe4 loses the pawn on e6.

16 ♗b2

16 ♕g7 fxe4 17 ♘xe4 ♘g8! covers everything.

16...fxe4 17 ♘xe4 ♘g8 18 ♘c3 ♕f7 19 ♖e3

I would still be concerned about White going for an attack on the queenside with 19 a4, though in this case Black has enough counterplay after 19...♘f6!

19...exd5

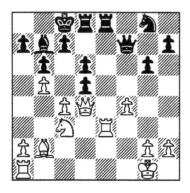

20 ♘xd5

Black has good counterplay whatever White decides to capture, e.g. 20 cxd5 ♖xe3 21 ♕xe3 ♗xd5, winning a pawn, or 20 ♖xe8 ♖xe8 and now:

a) 21 cxd5 ♘e7 22 ♖d1 (22 ♖e1 ♘xd5!) 22...♘f5 and an invasion on e3.

b) 21 ♘xd5 ♘e7 (21...♖e2!?) 22 ♘xe7+ ♖xe7. White has a couple of vulnerable points in his position (g2 and c4) whereas Black has no real weaknesses. The opposite-coloured bishops make life difficult for White as he will be unable to dampen the attack with exchanges.

20...♖xe3 21 ♕xe3

Understandably, Gelfand decides to ditch a pawn rather than lose the initiative. If 21 ♘xe3 then 21...♖e8 and the balance is shifting in Black's favour.

21...♗xd5 22 cxd5 ♕xd5 23 a4 ♔b8 24 a5?

This offer of a second pawn is just too much. Black would still have had some work to do to convert his extra pawn if White had played 24 ♖c1, reminding Black that c7 is vulnerable. Everything would be fine for Black if the knight could just find a decent square, but it is not easy

to re-deploy it.

24...♕xb5 25 axb6 axb6 26 ♗d4 ♕c6 27 ♖c1 ♕b7

Now Black is winning.

28 f5 gxf5 29 ♕g5 ♖e8 30 ♕h5

Or 30 ♕xf5 ♕e4 and wins.

30...♕e4 31 ♗f2 ♘f6 32 ♕f7 ♕e7 33 ♕a2 ♘g4 34 ♖a1

34 ♗d4? ♕e1+! 35 ♖xe1 ♖xe1 is mate.

34...♕e4 35 ♕a7+ ♔c8 36 ♖c1 ♕b7 37 ♕a4 ♖e7 38 ♕b3 0-1

White gave up here. There's not much hope, e.g. 38...♘xf2 39 ♕g8+ ♔d7 40 ♔xf2 ♕e4. An excellent game by Short. He played with great accuracy, but I feel that this whole line needs checking. White's queenside attack concerns me.

Game 8
Franco-Teske
Havana 1998

1 d4 e6 2 c4 b6 3 e4 ♗b7 4 ♗d3 ♘c6 5 ♘e2 ♘b4 6 ♘bc3

6 0-0 is more accurate as it avoids the pin, though in approximately half the games I've seen White plays his knight out first, as in the text game.

6...♘xd3+ 7 ♕xd3 ♗b4

This isn't quite as effective compared to when White has the knight on f3 (the knight on e2 is ready to recapture). Nevertheless, the exchange still helps Black to free his game.

8 0-0 ♘e7 9 a3

9 ♘d1!? is worth considering, intending to trap the bishop. Here are a few possibilities:

a) 9...f5 10 e5 ♘g6 11 c5 bxc5 12 a3 ♗a5, when it is messy but Black should be fine.

b) 9...♘g6 10 c5 (10 ♘e3!?) 10...bxc5 11 a3 ♗a5 12 dxc5 c6 13 b4 ♗c7 and I prefer White's position.

c) 9...c5 10 a3 ♗a5 11 ♖b1 and Black has not solved his problems.

9...♗xc3 10 ♘xc3 0-0 11 d5 d6 12 ♗g5

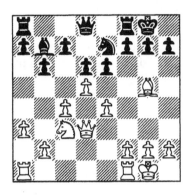

12...♕d7

Why not 12...f6...? The bishop retreats, 13 ♗e3, and after 13...e5 Black gets ready for ...f6-f5.

13 ♖ad1 ♖ae8 14 ♘b5 a6 15 ♘d4 ½-½

After 15 ♘d4 Black has no difficulties. For example, 15...e5 16 ♗xe7 ♕xe7 17 ♘f5 ♕g5 followed by ...♗c8; when the knight retreats, ...f7-f5 comes. 7...♗b4, pinning the knight on c3, is a sensible continuation which gives Black good chances to equalise; though if White is canny he can avoid the debate altogether just by castling before developing the knight.

Game 9
Lobron-Speelman
German Bundesliga 1997

---

1 d4 e6 2 c4 b6 3 e4 ♗b7 4 ♗d3 ♘c6 5 ♘e2 e5

'This invites White to shut the b7-bishop out of the game for the foreseeable future. But it does at least stop White from rolling Black up in the centre with a quick f2-f4.' – Jon Speelman. Speelman goes his own way, as usual. No one else has tried this idea before, or since. I'm grateful to him for supplying notes to this game and where the comments are his, I have said so. Black forces his opponent's hand in the centre, arriving at a closed

pawn structure familiar from the first few games in this chapter. This is the only reasonable method of getting this structure, since playing the knight to g6 straightaway runs into the path of White's f-pawn (see the notes to Game 6). All this is possible because of the knight's modest placement on e2. Now let's see whether it is any good or not.

6 d5

White must close the centre if he is to hope for anything from the opening. 6 dxe5 ♘xe5 gives Black free and easy development.

6...♘b4

It is possible to flick the check in first, but the position is too easy for White to play, e.g. 6...♗b4+ 7 ♘d2 ♘ce7 8 0-0 ♘g6 9 a3 ♗xd2 10 ♗xd2 and White can play on both sides of the board. Forget the closed pawn structure – with a space advantage the two bishops are extremely powerful.

7 0-0 ♘e7 8 ♘bc3

The question that must be asked is whether or not White can use the f-pawn attack to disrupt Black's system. Let's try: 8 f4 ♘xd3 9 ♕xd3 exf4 10 ♗xf4 ♘g6. Black should be able to develop satisfactorily as he has a check on c5 for his bishop to speed the process – a big advantage of omitting ...d7-d6.

8...♘xd3 9 ♕xd3 ♘g6

10 ♘g3

White makes a virtue out of the knight on e2, which heads straight towards the dangerous outpost on f5. Instead of that, we should check out the f-pawn attack: 10 f4 exf4 11 ♘xf4 ♗d6 and once again Black has the situation under control.

10...♗e7

10...♗c5!? would have been more enterprising. The bishop can be distinctly irritating on that diagonal, and White must always watch out that the bishop doesn't find a secure home on d4.

11 ♘f5! 0-0 12 g3

Speelman says that 12 d6 ♗xd6 13 ♘xd6 cxd6 14 ♕xd6 may be good for White, 'but it would be hugely anti-positional to open up the b7-bishop's diagonal; and Black has possible counterplay with ...f7-f5.'

12...d6 13 h4

White's kingside initiative develops quickly and it is difficult to find meaningful counterplay. Speelman aims for a policy of containment on the kingside combined with a pawn break on the queenside. Strong nerves are required.

13...♗f6 14 ♔g2 ♗c8 15 ♖h1 ♖e8 16 ♗d2 a6 17 a4 ♗d7 18 ♖ag1

Perhaps 18 ♖af1!? (Speelman). The significance of the rook's position will become apparent later on.

18...♖b8

If White becomes too preoccupied with his kingside attack, then Black can open up the queenside with ...b6-b5.

19 h5

'I was much more concerned about a semi-waiting move on the queenside, 19 b4 say, when I would have to decide whether to carry out my "threat" to initiate queenside action – or much more likely find a waiting move myself.' – Speelman.

19...♘f8 20 h6

Lobron must keep going forward or Black will establish a blockade. For instance, 20 g4 h6 followed by ...♘h7.

20...g6

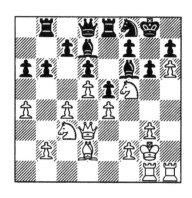

21 ♘g7

White sacrifices a pawn to open some lines, but he doesn't quite manage to make a decisive breakthrough. It is close though.

21...♗xg7 22 hxg7 ♔xg7 23 ♗h6+ ♔g8 24 f4

'Now we can see why the rook would have been better on f1 than g1.' – Speelman.

24...f6 25 f5 ♖e7 26 ♘d1 ♗xa4 27 ♘e3 ♗e8 28 ♘g4

After 28 ♗xf8 ♔xf8 29 ♘g4 ♖g7 30 ♖f1 gxf5 31 ♘xf6 f4 Black wins (Speelman).

28...♘d7 29 ♖f1 g5 30 ♗xg5 ♖g7 31 ♗h6

Instead, Speelman recommends 31 ♘h6+ ♔f8 32 ♗h4 b5 33 b3! with the long-term plan of ♔h3, g3-g4, ♖hg1 and g4-g5.

31...♖xg4 32 ♕f3 ♖g5 33 ♗xg5 fxg5 34 ♖h6 ♘f6 35 ♖fh1 c5

So as to defend along the second rank with the rook if necessary.

36 ♕a3 a5

37 b4!?

An ingenious 'randomiser' in his own time pressure, though it still fails.

37...♕e7!

37...cxb4? 38 ♕c1! breaks the defence.

38 bxa5 bxa5 39 ♕xa5 ♖b2+ 40 ♔g1 ♕b7 41 ♖6h2 ♖b1+ 42 ♔g2 ♕b2+ 43 ♔h3 g4+ 44 ♔h4 h6 0-1

Speelman's system was successful against Lobron's rhinoceros attacking style, but with a steadier approach I would say that White is doing well. He has a space advantage and Black has no clear method of counterplay. Nevertheless, I hope that we haven't seen the last of this system. I would recommend 10...♗c5!? as an improvement. At least it is active.

Game 10
Yrjola-Kengis
Yerevan 1996

---

1 d4 e6 2 c4 b6 3 e4 ♗b7 4 ♗d3 ♘c6 5 ♘e2 g6

Another invention of the Latvian Grandmaster Edvins Kengis. Black doesn't go for the bishop on d3 with the knight, but aims at a curious double-fianchetto.

6 ♘bc3

Orthodox development has to be White's best policy – leave it to Black to sort out the mess he has put his pieces in. For that reason I'm not too keen on White's strategy in Kaunas-Kengis, Riga 1995: 6 h4 ♗g7 7 ♗e3 h5 8 ♘bc3 ♘ge7 9 ♕d2 d5 10 0-0-0 ♘b4 11 cxd5 ♘xd3+ 12 ♕xd3 exd5 13 f3 ♕d7, when Black had a promising position (two bishops and pressure on White's centre) and his opening has been completely justified (Black won in 27 moves). However, there was no need for White to give up the bishops and castle on the queenside.

6...♗g7 7 ♗e3 ♘ge7 8 ♖c1

8 a3 is a good alternative. Kachiani Gersinska-Freckmann, Baden Baden open 1993, continued 8...a5 (8...d5!? 9 cxd5 exd5 10 e5 ♕d7 would have been more true to the Kengis method of playing the opening) 9 f4 f5 10 e5 d6 11 0-0 dxe5 12 fxe5 0-0 13 ♗c2 ♕d7 14 ♗a4 ♖ad8 15 ♕e1 ♕c8 16 ♖d1 and White had a dominating position and went on to win.

8...d5

I would love to play 8...e5 here but, sadly, it just loses a pawn: 9 d5 ♘d4 10 ♗xd4 exd4 11 ♘b5. 8...0-0 could be considered instead, though, keeping Black's options open for a moment. If White castles, 9 0-0, then 9...e5!? 10 d5 ♘d4 is possible as 11 ♗xd4 exd4 12 ♘b5 c5 saves the pawn. 11 f4 is stronger, when after 11...c5 (11...d6 12 f5 gives White a strong attack) 12 ♕d2 White has the better prospects, though Black's knight in the middle gives him some counter-chances.

9 cxd5 exd5 10 e5 ♕d7 11 0-0 0-0

12 ♘f4

Here a draw was agreed in Budnikov-Kengis, Reykjavik open 1984.

Instead 12 f4 is critical:

a) 12...♘f5? 13 ♗xf5 gxf5 (or 13...♕xf5 14 ♘g3 ♕d7 15 f5 with a powerful attack) 14 ♘g3.

b) 12...f5! 13 exf6 (or 13 a3 ♘a5!? with chances for both sides) 13...♖xf6 14 ♕d2 when I prefer White's chances (I like his three to two pawn majority on the kingside), though having said that Black's pieces are not too badly placed.

12...a6

I don't know how necessary this move is. As Black moves the knight on c6 on the next turn, why not move it straightaway? For instance, 12...♘d8 13 ♗e2 (13 ♘b5 ♗c6 is satisfactory for Black) 13...♘e6 14 ♗g4 ♖ad8 is a slight improvement on the game, but I still prefer White's position – he has pressure on the c-file and a juicy pin.

13 ♗e2 ♘d8 14 ♗g4 ♘e6 15 b4 ♖ad8 16 ♘ce2

This allows Black to free his game at the small cost of a pawn. 16 a4! would have kept Black's bishop locked in behind its own pawns and guaranteed White a good game.

16...♗c6! 17 ♕c2 ♗b5 18 ♘xe6 fxe6 19 ♕xc7 ♘f5 20 ♕xd7

20 ♕xb6 ♖b8 21 ♕a5 ♘xe3 22 fxe3 h5 23 ♖xf8+ ♖xf8 24 ♗f3 ♖xf3 25 gxf3 ♗xe2 26 ♖c7 ♕e8 is okay for Black – he will get enough counterplay on the kingside with his queen.

20...♖xd7

It is difficult to make anything of the extra pawn in the ending, and Black holds the draw comfortably.

21 ♖fe1 ♗c4 22 ♘f4 ♔f7 23 a3 ♖a8 24 ♗e2 b5 25 ♘d3 a5 26 ♘c5 ♖da7 27 a4 ♗xe2 28 ♖xe2 axb4 29 axb5 ♖b8 30 ♖b2 ♖xb5 31 ♔f1 ♖c7 32 ♖cb1 ♗xe5 33 ♘a6 ♖a7 34 dxe5 ♖xa6 35 ♖xb4 ♖xb4 36 ♖xb4 ♘xe3+ 37 fxe3 g5 38 g4 ♔g6 39 h3 h5 40 ♔f2 ♖c6 41 ♔f3 ½-½

Kengis's idea is interesting (and certainly different) though I have to say I remain sceptical. To my eyes the knight does not belong on c6 when Black plays a double fianchetto.

Game 11
Ahundov-Bagirov
Yerevan 1996

1 d4 e6 2 c4 b6 3 e4 ♗b7 4 ♗d3 ♘c6 5 d5

This is the only game that I have come across where White plays this blunt push. This advance is really what you are hoping for if you are playing Black – it is easier to get to grips with the centre if it lurches forward.

5...♘e5 6 ♗e2

Provocative! White could still compromise with 6 ♘f3, when after Black whips off the bishop chances are balanced.

6...f5

I am a little surprised by this one. Black exchanges off the e-pawn, but I would like to attack it! For instance, 6...♕h4 is more in the spirit of the English Defence as played by the English, and now 7 ♘c3 ♗b4 (7...♗c5 8 g3 ♕e7 is also possible) 8 ♕d4 d6 9 ♘f3 ♗xc3+ (9...♘xf3+!? 10 ♗xf3 e5) 10 bxc3 ♘xf3+ 11 ♗xf3 e5 12 ♕d3 ♘f6 is about equal.

Apart from 6...♕h4, Black also has 6...♗b4+ 7 ♗d2 ♕e7 and 6...exd5 7 cxd5 ♘f6. In both cases White's centre is under some pressure.

7 exf5 exf5 8 ♘h3

Why not 8 ♘f3...? After 8...♗b4+ the position looks about equal, but White certainly isn't in any danger. In the game Black is given more chances than he deserves.

8...♗b4+ 9 ♘d2

9 ♗d2 is more sensible. Black uses his dark-squared bishop to good effect in the game.

9...♘f6 10 a3 ♗d6 11 0-0 0-0 12 ♘f3 ♘e4!

Black assumes the initiative, or at least White is convinced enough to fall on the defensive, and his position begins to take a turn for the worse.

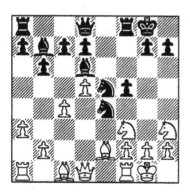

13 ♘xe5 ♗xe5 14 ♗d3?!

14 f3 ♘d6 (14...♘c5 is also fine) 15 ♗g5 ♗f6 16 ♕d2 is about equal.

14...♕f6 15 ♖a2 c6!

That's a crucial move. If the bishop doesn't break out from behind the pawn chain then Black won't stand a chance of getting an advantage.

16 f3 ♘c5 17 ♗b1 cxd5 18 ♗g5 ♕f7 19 b4 ♘e6 20 cxd5 ♘xg5 21 ♘xg5 ♕h5 22 ♘h3 ♗d6 23 ♖e1 ♕h4 24 ♖ae2

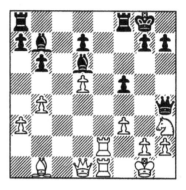

This is a classic demonstration of the power of the two bishops. White can do very little with his pieces because of the monstrous piece on d6.

24...a5!

Increasing the scope of said monster.

25 b5 ♖ac8 26 ♗a2 h6 27 f4 ♔h7 28 a4 ♖c3 29 ♔h1 ♖f6 30 ♖e3 ♖xe3 31 ♖xe3 ♖f8 32 ♘g5+ ♔h8 33 g3 ♕g4 34 ♕xg4 fxg4 35 ♘e4 ♗b4 36 ♘f2 ♖c8 37 ♗b3 ♗c5 38 ♖e2 ♗xf2 39 ♖xf2 ♖c3 40 ♗a2 ♖a3 41 ♔g1 ♖xa4 42 ♖c2 ♖d4 43 ♔f2 ♗xd5

...and there goes the final remnant of White's lovely centre.

44 ♖c8+ ♔h7 45 ♗b1+ g6 46 f5 gxf5 47 ♗xf5+ ♔g7 48 ♗xd7 a4 49 ♖c7 ♔f6 50 ♖a7 ♔e5 51 ♖a6 ♔d6 52 ♗c6 ♗xc6 53 ♖xb6 ♔c5 54 ♖xc6+ ♔xb5 55 ♖xh6 a3 56 ♖e6 a2 57 ♖e1 ♖a4 58 ♔e3 a1♕ 0-1

Although Black won smoothly I didn't find his treatment of the opening too convincing. Nevertheless, 5 d5 does not pose a threat to Black. Quite the opposite in fact – I would be delighted to face it over the board.

Summary

4...♘c6 has rightly taken over as the main response to 4 ♗d3. Against 5 ♘f3 Black should not encounter any difficulties, as the first five games of this chapter demonstrate – and that is still the most commonly played move. 5 ♘e2 is a more severe test, and in particular Game 7, Gelfand-Short, is worthy of close examination. Even though he got an uncomfortable position, I liked Speelman's treatment of the opening in Game 9; I hope someone else tries it. Kengis's double fianchetto in Game 10 is dubious; and 5 d5 as in Game 11 is exactly what Black wants.

1 d4 e6 2 c4 b6 3 e4 ♗b7 4 ♗d3 ♘c6 *(D)*

5 ♘f3
    5 ♘e2
        5...♘b4 *(D)*
            6 0-0 ♘xd3 7 ♕xd3 ♘e7 8 ♘bc3
                8...g6 – *Game 6*
                8...d6 – *Game 7*
            6 ♘bc3 ♘xd3+ 7 ♕xd3 ♗b4 – *Game 8*
        5...e5 – *Game 9*
        5...g6 – *Game 10*
      5 d5 – *Game 11*
5...♘b4 *(D)* **6 0-0**
      6 ♘c3 ♘xd3+ 7 ♕xd3 ♗b4 – *Game 5*
6...♘xd3 7 ♕xd3 ♘e7
      7...d6 – *Game 4*
8 ♘c3 ♘g6 *(D)* **9 d5**
      9 b3 – *Game 2*
      9 ♖e1 – *Game 3*
9...♗e7 – *Game 1*

    4...♘c6

    5...♘b4

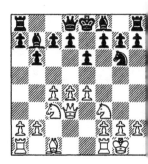
    8...♘g6

CHAPTER TWO

Main Line with 3 e4 ♗b7 4 ♗d3: Other Fourth Moves for Black

1 d4 e6 2 c4 b6 3 e4 ♗b7 4 ♗d3

Let me remind you what I said in the first chapter about Black's options after 4 ♗d3: 4...f5 is risky but fun (and is the subject of Games 12-19); 4...♗b4+ is a bit wet but sound (you'll find that in Games 20-23); and 4...♕h4 is just mad – see Game 24. Having considered 4...♘c6 in the first chapter, we can move on to look at these alternatives. First of all:

Game 12
Beliavsky-Short
Groningen 1997

---

1 d4 e6 2 c4 b6 3 e4 ♗b7 4 ♗d3 f5!?

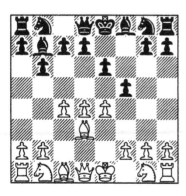

This is the consistent move. Black ex-

ploits weaknesses on the long diagonal and immediately attacks White's centre. In the early days of the resurgence of the English Defence (the seventies and early eighties) theoretical attention centred on this move following investigations and games from Miles, Plaskett and, originally, Basman. When the variation proved to be dubious (at least at international level) then alternatives were explored, notably 4...♘c6. Nevertheless, the complexities of 4...f5 were never fully resolved – there are still many uncharted branches to explore, and it is partially a measure of the success of 4...♘c6 that the pawn push has fallen into disuse – though of course it might just be because it is unsound. It is interesting to see Short returning to the move in this game, particularly against such an illustrious opponent, though the game was, I believe, played at a fast time control, so there were 'tactical' reasons for his choice.

5 exf5

The general feeling is that if White is to get anything from the opening then he must capture the pawn. In the early days of the English Defence, when this move often came as a shock, White players would often 'decline' the offer of complications, preferring a continuation such as

5 ♘c3 (Chapter 3, Games 25-33), 5 ♕h5+ g6 6 ♕e2 (Game 18) or 5 d5 (Game 19). They do not offer White anything special. Nowadays if you see 4 ♗d3 in front of you, you can be fairly sure that your opponent will be ready and willing to plunge into the mire – and he'll take you with him.

5...♗b4+

5...♗xg2 introduces random complications and is dealt with in Games 15-17.

6 ♔f1

Forced. The g-pawn must be protected. Black has certainly gained by displacing the king, though the bishop on b4 is out on a limb and this provides tactical comfort for White. If the check is blocked, then Black may capture on g2 with impunity. For instance, 6 ♘c3 ♗xg2 7 ♕h5+ ♔f8 8 fxe6 ♕e8 9 ♕f5+ ♘f6 10 d5 dxe6 11 dxe6 ♕g6 12 ♕xg6 hxg6 13 ♘ge2 ♗xh1 and the extra rook came good in Lopez Colon-Miles, Gran Canaria open 1996.

6...♘f6

To me, this developing move appears the most natural (there is no need to close the f-file with White's king at the end of it) though 6...exf5 has also been played – see Game 14.

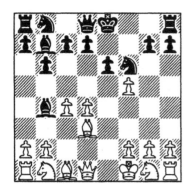

7 ♗e2!

'A very strong novelty that buries the whole line. White's idea is 7 c5 bxc5 8 a3, but it did not work yet because of 8...c4!,

so White prepares this deadly threat and combines it with moves such as 8 ♗h5 and 8 ♗f3.' – Alexander Beliavsky and his trainer Adrian Mikhalchishin writing in *New in Chess*. Sadly, from Black's point of view, I think their assessment of the position is correct – though it is interesting to note that Dreev declined to go in for this line in a later game at the Elista Olympiad (see the next game). Dreev subsequently wrote that he is not completely convinced by 7 ♗e2, but that leaves us none the wiser!

Prior to Beliavsky's innovation White had thrashed around with varying degrees of success, though opinion had not crystallised as to the strongest continuation. For alternatives to 7 ♗e2, see the next game.

7...0-0

7...exf5 8 c5 bxc5 9 a3 ♗a5 10 dxc5 c6 is good for White, though Black has grovelling chances: the bishop goes back to c7, followed by ...a7-a5, ...♗a6, and there is hope. If White's king were on a sensible square then he would simply stand beautifully, but on f1, it is enough to keep Black going.

I thought about 7...♗d6 to solve the problem of the misplaced bishop, but then one of the points of Beliavsky's idea is revealed: 8 ♗h5+! causes serious disruption:

a) 8...♔e7 9 ♗g5 with a clear plus for White.

b) 8...♘xh5 9 ♕xh5+ ♔f8 10 ♗g5.

c) 8...g6 9 fxg6 0-0 is an idea known from the King's Gambit, but here it is just too silly: 10 ♗h6 wins.

Since writing this analysis, the following game has come to light:

d) 8...♔f8 9 fxe6 dxe6 10 ♗f3 ♘c6 11 ♘c3 ♕e8 12 ♘ge2 ♖d8 13 ♕a4 ♔f7 14 ♘b5 ♖f8 15 ♘xd6+ cxd6 16 ♗g5 ♔g8 17 ♖e1 ♕g6 18 h4 ♘e4 19 ♖h3 ♘a5 20 d5 ♘xg5 21 hxg5 exd5 (21...♕xg5 22 ♘d4) 22 cxd5 ♕xg5 23 ♕e4 h6 24 b4 ♖de8 25 ♕d3

♗c8 26 ♖h5 ♖xf3 27 ♕xf3 ♕d2 28 ♕c3 and White was clearly better in Meessen-Bunzmann, Leuven 1998.

8 c5

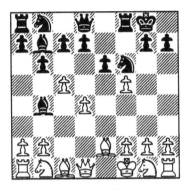

8...bxc5

Julian Hodgson made an interesting attempt at rehabilitating this whole variation when he played 8...♘c6!? in a recent game, and his opponent duly trapped the piece with 9 a3 (it would have been stronger to play 9 ♘f3!?, delaying the capture of the bishop for a move; in that case I have great doubts that Black will have enough for the piece: 9...bxc5 10 a3 ♗a5 11 dxc5 ♘e4 12 b4 ♘xb4 13 axb4 ♗xb4 14 fxe6 and wins). However, after the surprising sacrifice 9...♘xd4!? Black generated some play with 10 axb4 ♘xe2.

While I was working on this manuscript two other games have appeared with this line:

a) 11 ♕xe2 ♘d5 12 fxe6 dxe6 13 b5 (13 ♘f3!?) 13...a6 14 ♘f3 axb5 15 ♖xa8 ♕xa8 16 h4 ♕a1 17 ♕xe6+ ♔h8 18 ♘e5 ♘f6 19 ♘f7+ ♔g8 20 ♘e5+ ♔h8 21♘f7+ ♔g8 22 ♘d6+ ♔h8 23 ♕e7 ♔g8 24 ♕e6+ ♔h8 25 ♕e7 ♔g8 26 ♕e6+ ♔h8 27 ♘xb7 ♕xb1 28 ♕e1 ♘e4 29 ♖h3 (29 f3!?) 29...♖xf2+ 30 ♔g1 ♖c2 31♖f3 ♘f6 32 ♕e8+ ♘g8 33 ♘d8 ♖xc1+ 34 ♔h2 h6 35 cxb6 cxb6 36 h5 ♖e1 37 ♖e3 ♖h1+ 38 ♔g3 ♕f5 39 ♕g6 ♖f1 40 ♖e8 ♕f4+ 0-1 Dautov-Tischbierek, German Championship 1998. Mind boggling.

Obviously White could have taken a draw by repetition on a couple of occasions, but I suspect he was doing well anyway.

b) 11 ♘xe2 ♘g4 12 ♕d4 (much better is 12 ♘g3! ♕h4 13 ♕d2 exf5 14 ♕f4 ♖ae8 15 h3 ♕e7 16 ♗d2 ♘e5 17 ♖xa7 and White was on the way to consolidating his extra piece in Vaisser-Sulava, Corsica 1998) 12...♕h4 13 h3 ♖xf5 14 g3 ♕e7 15 hxg4 ♖d5 16 ♖h5 ♖xd4 17 ♘xd4 ♕f6 with a complicated struggle ahead in Ippolito-Hodgson, Mermaid Beach 1998. It will not be easy to contain Black's queen, particularly with the presence of opposite-coloured bishops.

9 a3 ♗a5

9...cxd4 10 axb4 e5 11 ♘f3 should be good for White as the pawns can't really advance.

10 dxc5 ♘d5

10...c6? saves the bishop, but 11 b4 ♗c7 'leads to a completely lost position' – Beliavsky/Mikhalchishin. Of course, it is not terribly good for Black, but he can fight on (as in a similar variation above) with ...a7-a5.

A burst of activity starting with 10...♘e4 does not reap rewards: 11 b4 ♖xf5 (or 11...♕f6 12 ♖a2 ♘xf2 13 ♔xf2 ♕xf5+ 14 ♘f3 ♕xb1 15 ♖b2) 12 ♘f3 ♕f6 13 ♖a2 ♗d5 14 ♖b2 and White has everything under control.

11 ♘f3

Fine, but Beliavsky actually considers 11 fxe6 to be even stronger. The idea is that if 11...♕f6 then 12 ♘f3 'with a huge advantage' – Beliavsky. At least Short now gains some compensation for the piece, though Beliavsky is still in control.

11...♖xf5 12 b4 ♘xb4 13 axb4 ♗xb4 14 ♗b2 a5!?

If 14...♗xc5 Stohl recommends 15 ♘bd2 with the idea of ♗d3 and ♕c2; whereas Beliavsky favours the attractive 15 ♖a4! and ♖g4. Black is going to be hard-pressed to defend on the kingside.

15 h4

Afterwards Beliavsky felt that it might have been stronger to play either 15 ♘a3 or 15 ♘bd2 followed by either ♘c2 or ♘c4.

15...♖d5 16 ♕b3 ♘a6 17 ♘c3 ♘xc5 18 ♕c2 ♖f5 19 ♖h3 ♕e7 20 ♔g1 ♖af8 21 ♖f1 d6 22 ♘g5 h6

Short makes a practical decision to give up more material so as to wrest the initiative away from White – and he almost succeeds in turning the game around. Objectively though, White must still be winning. A full examination of this tremendous game is beyond the scope of this book, though I've added a few light notes to indicate some of the major turning points.

23 g4 hxg5 24 gxf5 ♖xf5 25 ♗g4

Perhaps 25 f4!? gxf4 26 ♗g4 – Beliavsky.

25...♖f4 26 f3 gxh4 27 ♕h2

If 27 ♕g6 e5 28 ♕h5 g5 with compensation – Beliavsky.

27...♕g5 28 ♖xh4 ♘d3 29 ♖h8+ ♔f7

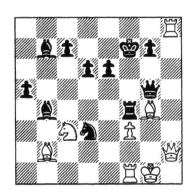

30 ♕g3!

30 ♕h5+ ♕xh5 31 ♗xh5+ g6 32 ♖h7+ ♔g8 33 ♗xg6 ♘xb2 34 ♖xc7 is equal – Beliavsky.

30...♕c5+ 31 ♔h2 ♗xc3 32 ♕h4!

Not 32 ♗h5+? ♔e7 33 ♗xc3 ♕xc3 and Black is on top.

32...♗f6 33 ♕h7 ♕c2+

33...♘xb2 34 ♕g8+ ♔g6 (or 34...♔e7 35 ♕e8 mate) 35 ♕e8+ ♔g5 36 ♕h5 is mate.

34 ♔h3!

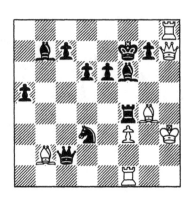

34...♖xf3 + ?

There was a debate in the magazine *New in Chess* over the following variation of Beliavsky's: 34...♖xg4 35 ♕g8+ ♔g6 36 ♕e8+ ♔f5 37 fxg4+ ♔e4 38 ♕xe6+ (38 ♗xf6 [Mikhalchishin] 38...♘f4+! 39 ♖xf4+ ♔xf4 and Black wins – Hebert in *New in Chess*) 38...♗e5 39 ♗xe5 dxe5 40 ♔g3 ♕c3 41 ♕f5+ ♔e3 42 ♖h2 and wins. This variation of Beliavsky and Mikhalchishin is, at the time of writing, the final word.

35 ♗xf3 ♘f4+ 36 ♔g3 ♕xb2 37 ♕g8+ ♔g6 38 ♕h7+ ♔f7 39 ♕g8+ ♔g6 40 ♕e8+ ♔f5 41 ♗xb7 g5

Or 41...♕c3+ 42 ♗f3 and White is winning.

42 ♖h6! ♕c3+ 43 ♗f3

43...♘e2+

Or 43...g4 44 ♖xf6+! ♕xf6 (44...♔xf6 45 ♕h8+) 45 ♗xg4+ ♔g5 46 ♕g8+ ♕g6 47 ♕d8+ and wins.

44 ♔g2 ♘f4+ 45 ♔h1 d5 46 ♕f7 1-0

46...a4 (or 46...g4 47 ♗g2) 47 ♖xf6+ ♕xf6 48 ♗g4+ ♔e5 49 ♖e1+ is terminal.

7 ♗e2 is undoubtedly a powerful new move. Objectively, I feel that White should emerge from the opening with a clear advantage. Nevertheless, there are certain factors which cloud the issue. First and foremost is the fact that White's king stands on a poor square. That gives Black additional time to develop his pieces and he may be able to go on the attack. Second, the position is highly unorthodox and more rigid players might not be able to get a grip on the position. Even Beliavsky almost lost this game. So has this entire variation been put out of business? I don't think so. My advice is to pick your opponent and situation carefully.

Game 13
Dreev-Shabalov
Elista Olympiad 1998

---

1 d4 e6 2 c4 b6 3 e4 ♗b7 4 ♗d3 f5!? 5 exf5 ♗b4+ 6 ♔f1 ♘f6 7 c5

The most popular move before Beliavsky's 7 ♗e2 turned up.

Other moves for White are less effective:

a) 7 ♗g5 0-0 8 a3 ♗d6 9 ♘c3 exf5!? (if 9...♘c6 10 ♘f3 ♘e7 11 fxe6 dxe6 12 ♕e2 ♕d7 13 ♖e1 h6 14 ♗xf6 ♖xf6 15 ♘e4 and White was clearly on top in Goldin-Gofshtein, Rishon Le Zion 1997) 10 d5 (what about 10 ♗xf5!? – it is counterintuitive to open the f-file, but I don't see what Black's response should be; White has opened useful diagonals towards Black's king) 10...h6 11 ♗d2 ♘a6 12 b4 c6 13 dxc6 dxc6 14 ♕b1 ♗xb4 15 axb4 ♘xb4 with a powerful initiative for Black in Brondum-

Plaskett, Copenhagen 1981.

b) 7 fxe6 dxe6 8 ♗e3 0-0 9 h3 ♘bd7 10 ♘f3 e5! 11 ♘xe5 ♘xe5 12 dxe5 ♘e4 13 ♔g1 ♘xf2 14 ♗xh7+ ♔xh7 15 ♕h5+ ♔g8 16 ♗xf2 ♖xf2 17 ♔xf2 ♕d4+ 0-1 Kleinplatz-Lempert, Hyeres open 1992.

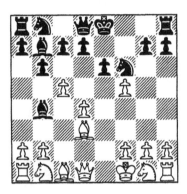

7...bxc5 8 a3 c4

8...♗a5? 9 dxc5 followed by b2-b4 is unpleasant.

9 ♗xc4 ♗a5

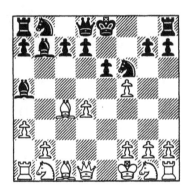

10 ♘f3

The critical test is 10 fxe6 dxe6 (10...♗b6 is too much after 11 exd7+ ♕xd7 12 ♘f3 ♘c6 13 ♕e2+ ♔f8 14 ♗e3 when White was clearly better and went on to win in Arlandi-Sulava, Asti open 1995) 11 ♕a4+ (11 ♗xe6?! ♕e7 12 d5 ♘xd5! 13 ♗xd5 ♗xd5 14 ♘e2 ♕f7 gave Black excellent compensation for the pawn in Sideif Zade-Lempert, Naberezhnye

Chelny 1993) 11...♘c6 12 ♘f3 (12 ♗b5?! is weaker: 12...♕d5 13 ♘c3 ♗xc3 14 bxc3 0-0 15 ♕c4 ♘e4 with an initiative for Black in Lauber-Czebe, Budapest 1997) 12...♕d6? (12...0-0 is stronger, when Black does have some compensation) 13 ♘c3 0-0-0 14 ♘b5 ♕d7 15 ♘xa7+ ♘xa7 16 ♕xa5 and White won quickly in Dautov-Teske, Vienna open 1996.

10...0-0 11 ♗d2

In *Informator 72* Dautov suggests 11 ♘c3 and if 11...d5 12 ♗d3 with a clear plus for White.

11...♘c6 12 ♗xa5 ♘xa5 13 ♗a2 ♘e4 14 b4

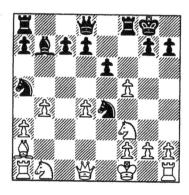

14...♖xf5!?

An enterprising piece sacrifice. In his annotations in *Informator 73* Dreev also suggests 14...♘c6!? 15 d5 ♘e7 with an unclear position.

15 bxa5 ♘xf2! 16 ♔xf2 ♕h4+ 17 ♔f1

17 ♔g1 would have been met by 17...♗xf3 18 gxf3 ♖b8! with a strong attack – Dreev.

17...♗a6+ 18 ♔g1 ♖xf3 19 gxf3 ♖f8 20 ♘d2 ♕g5+ ½-½

Game 14
Seirawan-Schussler
Malmo 1979

---

1 c4 b6 2 d4 e6 3 e4 ♗b7 4 ♗d3 f5!? 5 exf5 ♗b4+ 6 ♔f1 exf5!?

If Black is to play 5...♗b4+, then this i the main alternative to 6...♘f6. My per sonal view is that 6...♘f6 is a more dy namic continuation (it appears natural t keep the centre fluid when White's king i stuck there) but as that is under somethin of a cloud following Beliavsky's novelty c Game 12 it is perhaps worth examinin this older move again.

7 c5!

This ruse to misplace the bishop shoul be familiar by now from the last tw games. Alternatively, I cannot imagine to many players going in for 7 ♗xf5. If noth ing else, it would give Black considerabl encouragement to see the f-file opened.

7...bxc5 8 a3 c4!

8...♗a5 would be far worse accordin to Seirawan, and I believe him: 9 dxc5 c (or 9...♕f6 10 ♖a2 c6 11 b4 ♗d8 12 ♖e2-♘e7 13 ♗b2 with a big plus for White) 1 b4 ♗c7 11 ♗b2 ♘f6 12 ♕e2+ and Whit has a clear advantage.

9 ♗xc4 ♗d6

Black has managed to bring the bishop back to a sensible position, but White ha gained a great deal over the last few moves Most notably, the a2-g8 diagonal is wid open – if Black could retract one mov then he would pick up the f-pawn and pu it back on f7 – but passing over illega moves, we can say that Black is suffering from chronic weaknesses. Even White's displaced king (normally the straw to which Black clutches) is feeling happier with the f-file closed and the e-file open; a rook can suddenly land on e1 to join the attack.

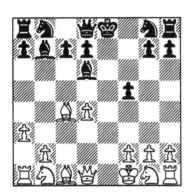

10 ♘c3

10 ♕b3 was tried in Christensen-Nielsen, Danish Championship 1992, and, while not as powerful as the game continuation, it does also have its merits: 10...♗a6 11 ♗xa6 ♘xa6 12 ♘f3 (if 12 ♕b5 ♕c8 13 ♕xf5 ♘f6 then Black has compensation for the pawn) 12...c6 (12...♘f6 did not fare well in Summerscale-Williams, British Championship, Torquay 1998: 13 ♘c3 c6 14 ♗g5 ♕b6 15 ♖e1+ ♔d8 16 ♗xf6+ gxf6 17 ♕c2 and White was clearly better) 13 ♘c3 ♕b6 14 ♕c4 ♘c7 15 g3 ♕a6 16 ♕xa6 ♘xa6 17 d5 ♘e7 18 dxc6 dxc6 19 ♔g2 and although the game was drawn, White does have a small but definite advantage here. By the way, 10 ♗xg8 doesn't bring any rewards: 10...♗a6+ 11 ♔e1 ♕e7+ and Black assumes the initiative.

10...♘f6 11 ♘f3

11 ♘h3!? also isn't bad: 11...♘c6 12 ♗f4 ♘a5 13 ♗a2 ♗a6+ 14 ♔g1 ♗c4 15 ♗xc4 ♘xc4 16 ♕e2+ 1-0 was a bit of a disaster for Black in Kaiser-Carton, German Bundesliga 1993.

11...♕e7

After this game Seirawan recommended

11...♘e4!?, but 12 ♕b3! is powerful. For instance, 12...♗a6 13 ♗xa6 ♘xa6 14 ♕b5 ♕c8 15 ♕xf5 and Black is a pawn down for nothing.

12 ♗g5! ♔d8

The king was never going to get to the kingside, so it nudges out of the line of fire on the e-file – but into the line of fire of the bishop on g5.

13 ♘h4!?

Crafty. Black is forced to play ...g7-g6 and so the diagonal is weakened, and the bishop on g5 gains in power. 13 ♘d5!? ♗xd5 14 ♗xd5 c6 15 ♕b3 is also strong.

13...g6 14 d5

It is difficult for Black to move any of his pieces after this one.

14...♗c5 15 ♘a4! ♗xf2

15...♗b6 is stronger, but that just shows the poor state of Black's position: 16 ♘xb6 axb6 17 d6 cxd6 18 ♕d4.

16 ♘f3 ♗b6 17 ♘xb6 axb6 18 d6 cxd6 19 ♕d4 ♖f8 20 ♖e1

White could have won immediately with 20 ♕xb6+ ♔c8 21 ♖e1 ♕d8 (or 21...♗e4 22 ♘d4 ♖e8 23 ♘b5 ♗d3+ 24 ♔f2 ♘g4+ 25 ♔g3) 22 ♕xd6 ♘c6 23 ♖e6!

20...♗e4 21 ♕xb6+ ♔e8 22 ♗f4 ♘c6 23 ♕c7 ♘e5 24 ♘xe5 dxe5 25 ♗xe5 d5 26 ♕c6+ ♔f7 27 ♗xf6 ♕xf6 28 ♗xd5+ ♗xd5 29 ♕xd5+ ♔g7

Black has survived at the small cost of a pawn. White steers for a draw before his own king lands in trouble.

30 ♕e5 ♕xe5 31 ♖xe5 ♖fb8 32 ♖e2 ♖b3
33 ♔f2 ♖ab8 34 ♖a1 ♖xb2 35 a4 ♔f6
36 a5 ♖2b5 37 ♖c2 ♖a8 38 ♖c6+ ♔e5
39 a6 ♖a7 40 ♖a3 ♔d5 41 ♖f6 ½-½

Unless a big improvement is found, then in my opinion 6...exf5 is even worse than 6...♘f6. Black regains a pawn but loses dynamism.

Game 15
Browne-Miles
Tilburg 1978

---

1 c4 b6 2 d4 e6 3 e4 ♗b7 4 ♗d3 f5!? 5 exf5 ♗xg2

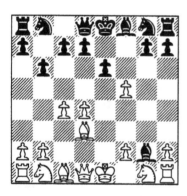

If 5...♗b4+ had some semblance of sanity, then this move strips all that away. The capture of the pawn leads the game into random and bizarre complications. It is difficult to get a handle on the positions that arise – they are so far away from anything that is 'normal' that reference to similar positions doesn't come into it; it simply isn't possible. In many variations White gives up a whole rook for the attack, while Black has a wobbly king and a pawn on the seventh rank to deal with. Great fun.

In recent years this variation has hardly been seen as attention has turned towards 4...♘c6. After games such as this one, many players felt it was simply too chancy to be subjected to such a violent attack. One false move and you get your head blown off. Nevertheless, I hope I will prove that there is still plenty of room for exploration, self-expression and discovery. And it is not only risky for Black: there are plenty of games where White has come to grief.

Incidentally, 5...♕h4 was suggested by Basman, but as Plaskett points out 6 ♘f3 is a good answer: 6...♕g4 7 0-0 and White is simply better.

6 ♕h5+ g6

6...♔e7 would be a fine move if it weren't for 7 ♕g5+, winning the bishop on g2.

7 fxg6 ♗g7

Forced. 7...♘f6 isn't quite good enough: 8 g7+ ♘xh5 9 gxh8♕ ♘f6 (not 9...♗xh1 10 ♕xh7 and wins) 10 ♗h6 ♔f7 11 ♗xf8 ♕xf8 12 ♕xf8+ ♔xf8 13 ♘d2 ♗xh1 14 f3 ♘c6 15 ♔f2 ♘b4 16 ♗b1 ♔e7 17 ♘e2 ♖g8 18 ♘g3 ♗xf3 19 ♔xf3 and White was winning, although Black managed a swindle (0-1 in 39 moves!) in Jakobsen-Jepsen, Danish Team Championship 1990.

8 gxh7+ ♔f8

see following diagram

---

9 ♘e2!

This became established as the best move after this game (but note that 9

♗g5+ ♘f6 10 ♕h4 ♗xh1 11 ♘e2 comes to the same thing).

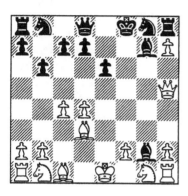

Prior to this game 9 hxg8♕+ was played, but Black had been doing well after 9...♔xg8 10 ♕g6 (10 ♕g4 ♗xh1 11 ♗g5 ♕e8! is clearly better for Black, e.g. 12 h4 ♘c6 13 ♘c3 ♘xd4! and Black won quickly in Lehmensick-Basman, British Championship, Brighton 1972) 10...♗xh1 11 ♗g5 ♕f8 when Black holds a clear plus. Nobody plays like this any more.

Alternatively, 9 ♘f3 was played in one obscure game in England (Hazel-Hardy, Peterborough 1979) but has never been repeated. Plaskett considers that the best continuation for both sides then is 9...♘f6 10 ♕h4 ♗xh1 11 ♘e5 d6 12 ♗h6 dxe5 13 dxe5 ♕xd3 14 ♕xf6+ ♔e8 15 ♕xe6+ ♔f8 16 ♕f6+ ♔e8 with a draw by repetition.

9...♗xh1 10 ♗g5!

10 hxg8♕+ ♔xg8 is still good for Black; and 10 ♘f4 is met by 10...♘e7.

10...♘f6

Not 10...♘e7? 11 ♘f4 ♕e8 12 ♘g6+ ♘xg6 13 ♗xg6 ♕c8 14 ♕h4! and wins; while 10...♗f6? 11 h4! looks good to me.

11 ♕h4 ♘c6

This natural developing move has been played in the vast majority of games, but there are two alternatives which are worth exploring: 11...♕e7!? and 11...♗f3!? For these, see Game 17.

12 ♘f4

For 12 ♘d2!, see the next main game.

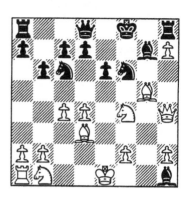

12...♔f7?

Black gets walloped after this one, but improvements were found later:

a) Not 12...♘b4? 13 ♗g6 ♕e7 14 ♘h5 ♘c2+ 15 ♗xc2 ♕b4+ 16 ♘d2 ♗xh5 17 0-0-0 1-0 Forintos-J.Fernandez, Capablanca memorial 1979, Havana 1979.

b) Basman recommends 12...e5! 13 ♘g6+ ♔f7 14 dxe5 ♖xh7 and this does look good for Black: 15 ♕f4 ♖h3 16 exf6 ♗xf6 17 ♗e2 ♔xg6 18 ♕g4 ♖h8 and wins – a very 'Fritzy' variation!

c) 12...♘xd4 is also playable: 13 ♘g6+ ♔e8 (or even 13...♔f7 14 ♘e5+ ♔f8 15 ♕xd4 [15 ♘g6+ ♔f7 16 ♘e5+ ♔f8 17 ♘g6+ ♔f7 is a draw by repetition] 15...d6 16 ♘g6+ ♔f7 17 ♘xh8+ ♕xh8 with an unclear position, e.g. 18 ♕h4?! ♖xh7 19 ♗xh7 ♗xb2 20 ♕h5+ ♔f8 21 ♕g6 ♗xa1 22 ♔f1 ♗c6 23 h4 ♖b8 24 ♘d2 ♗e8 25 ♕d3 ♗f7 26 ♗e4 ♕c3 27 ♕e2 a6 28 ♗d3 ♕e5 29 ♗e4 ♕h2 30 ♕f3 ♕e5 31 ♗f6 ♕xf6 0-1 Stassans-Sandler, Riga 1979) 14 ♕xd4 ♖xh7 15 ♘e5 and now John Nunn states that Black should play 15...♖xh2, since Miles's 15...♖h3 16 ♘g6+ ♔f8 17 ♘c3 d6 18 0-0-0 ♗b7 favours White according to Ftacnik.

13 ♗g6+ ♔e7 14 ♘h5 ♕f8 15 ♘d2

White's attack is now decisive.

15...e5

Alternatively, 15...d5 16 0-0-0 ♗e4 17

♘xe4! dxe4 18 ♘xg7 ♕xg7 19 ♗xe4; or 15...♘b8 16 0-0-0 ♗b7 17 ♖e1 (or even 17 d5) with a winning position for White in each case.

16 0-0-0 ♘xd4 17 ♖xh1 ♘e6 18 f4!

18 ♖e1 ♘xg5 19 ♕xg5 ♔d8? 20 ♖xe5 ♔c8 21 ♖f5. After the text White is winning.

18...d6 19 ♘e4 ♘xg5 20 ♕xg5 ♗h6 21 ♕h4! ♗g7 22 fxe5 dxe5 23 ♖f1 ♔d7 24 ♘exf6+ ♗xf6 25 ♘xf6+ ♔c8 26 ♗e4 c6 27 ♕h3+ ♔b7 28 ♗xc6+ 1-0

28...♔a6 (28...♔xc6 29 ♕d7+ ♔c5 30 ♕d5+ ♔b4 31 ♕b5 mate) 29 ♗b5+ ♔a5 30 a3 is hopeless for Black. A crushing victory, though not totally convincing. Improvements were later found – for White!

Game 16
Magerramov-Psakhis
Riga 1980

---

1 c4 b6 2 d4 e6 3 e4 ♗b7 4 ♗d3 f5!? 5 exf5 ♗xg2 6 ♕h5+ g6 7 fxg6 ♗g7 8 gxh7+ ♔f8 9 ♗g5 ♘f6 10 ♕h4 ♗xh1 11 ♘e2 ♘c6 12 ♘d2!

This is superior to the 12 ♘f4 of the previous game.

12...e5

Basman's 12...b5!? was the most interesting attempt to rehabilitate this variation. Black gains some control over the d5-square, which gives his minor pieces a

crucial foothold in the centre of the board 13 cxb5! ♘b4 14 ♗g6 ♗b7 15 ♘f4 ♔e7 16 ♘h5 ♕f8 17 d5 ♘bxd5 18 ♘e4 ♔d8 19 ♘exf6 ♔c8 20 ♘xg7 and the game Flear Plaskett, British Championship, Torquay 1982, was drawn in 62 eventful moves However, 20 ♘xd5 is stronger according to Hardy and Basman: 20...♗xd5 21 ♘xg7 ♕xg7 22 ♗d3 ♔b7 23 0-0-0 ♖hf8 24 ♗h6 ♕e5 25 ♗xf8 ♖xf8 when Black is fighting hard but that pawn on h7 endures.

13 0-0-0!

The best. 13 ♘g3?! runs into 13...e4! 14 ♗xe4 ♗xe4 15 ♘gxe4 ♖xh7 16 ♕f4 ♘xd (16...♕e7! – Nunn) 17 ♗xf6 (17 ♘xf6! – Nunn) 17...♗xf6 18 ♘xf6 ♕e7+ 19 ♘de ♖h4 20 ♘g4+ ♕f7 21 ♕g3 ♖e8 22 ♔f ♕xc4+ 23 ♔g2 ♘f5 24 ♕a3+ d6 0-1 Akes son-Short, World Junior Championship Dortmund 1980.

13...e4 14 ♗xe4 ♗xe4 15 ♘xe4 ♖xh7 16 ♕f4 ♔f7 17 ♘2c3

17 ♖g1 is also quite good: 17...♕h8 18 ♗xf6 ♗xf6 19 ♘g5+ ♔e7 20 ♕e4+ ♔d6 21 ♘xh7 ♗xd4 22 ♖g6+ ♔c5 23 ♕d5+ 1-0 D.Cramling-Gausel, Gausdal 1982.

17...♖h5 18 h4 ♘b4 19 a3 d5 20 ♘xf6 ♗xf6 21 axb4 ♕d6 22 ♕g4 ♖ah8 23 ♘xd5 ♗xg5+ 24 hxg5 ♖h1 25 ♕f3+ 1-0

It is this encounter, more than the previous main game, which has dampened enthusiasm for 5...♗xg2. But what about the next game...?

Game 17
Vegh-Zlatilov
St Augustin 1990

1 d4 e6 2 c4 b6 3 e4 ♗b7 4 ♗d3 f5!? 5 exf5 ♗xg2 6 ♕h5+ g6 7 fxg6 ♗g7 8 gxh7+ ♔f8 9 ♘e2 ♗xh1 10 ♗g5 ♘f6 11 ♕h4 ♕e7

New move! Most players have opted for 11...♘c6 instead (as in the previous two games) but Mr Zlatilov has had a little think about the position. 11...♗f3!? has been suggested by the English player Otto Hardy, but to my knowledge never tried in practice. It is well-motivated. The bishop comes back into play, threatening to exchange itself for one of White's main attacking pieces, and if the knight moves, then White is unable to castle on the queenside. Until we see a few games with it the jury remains out.

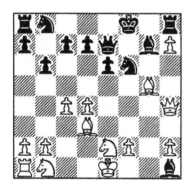

12 ♘f4

12 ♘d2!? followed by castling queenside is critical.

12...♕f7 13 ♘d2

Alternatively, 13 ♗g6 ♖xh7 14 ♗xh7 ♘xh7 15 ♕xh7 ♗xd4 looks okay for Black; and 13 ♘g6+ ♔e8 14 ♘e5 ♕e7 (or even 14...♕f8!? 15 ♗g6+ ♔d8 16 ♘g4 ♔c8) 15 ♗g6+ ♔d8 16 ♘g4 ♔c8 17 ♘xf6 ♕b4+ 18 ♘d2 ♕xb2 19 ♖b1 ♕c3 is totally unclear.

13...♘c6 14 ♗g6

14 0-0-0!? was perhaps an improvement.

14...♖xh7

This move, returning the rook, must have come as a shock to White:

15 ♗xh7 ♘xh7 16 ♕xh7 ♘xd4 17 ♘g6+ ♔e8 18 ♘h8 ♘f3+ 19 ♔f1

Or 19 ♘xf3 ♗c3+.

19...♘xg5 20 ♕h4 ♘f3 0-1

I do not present this as the answer to all Black's problems, but it is evidence that there is far more to the rook sacrifice than meets the eye. Hardy's 11...♗f3 must also be worth a try. Go on, be brave; and above all, pick the right opponent!

Game 18
Toth-Ornstein
Oslo 1978

1 d4 e6 2 c4 b6 3 e4 ♗b7 4 ♗d3 f5 5 ♕h5+

By flicking in the check White hopes to create a weakness on the kingside, but in this game Black makes a virtue out of it. 5 ♕e2 ♘f6 6 ♗g5 ♗b4+ (6...h6!?) 7 ♘c3 fxe4 8 ♗xe4 ♗xc3+ 9 bxc3 ♗xe4 10 ♗xf6 ♕xf6 11 ♕xe4 ♘c6, as in Sosonko-Keene, Haifa 1976, also leads to a satisfactory position for Black (the game was drawn in 26 moves).

5...g6 6 ♕e2 ♘f6 7 ♗g5 h6

More adventurous than 7...fxe4 8 ♗xe4

♗xe4 9 ♗xf6 ♕xf6 10 ♕xe4 ♘c6 11 ♘f3 ♗c5?! 12 ♘c3 ♗b4 13 ♕d3 ♕f5 ½-½ Muir-Carton, European Team Championship, Haifa 1989.

8 ♗xf6 ♕xf6 9 ♘f3 ♘c6! 10 e5 ♕f7

White's centre pawns are inflexible: the lack of a dark-squared bishop will soon be felt.

11 ♘c3 a6 12 a3 ♗g7!

The pawn on e5 is the target of Black's play.

13 ♖d1 0-0 14 0-0 ♖ae8 15 ♗c2 g5 16 ♖fe1 ♘e7 17 h3 ♘g6 18 g3 c5! 19 d5 exd5 20 ♘xd5 ♘xe5 21 ♘xe5 ♖xe5 22 ♕xe5 ♗xe5 23 ♖xe5 ♕g7 24 ♖de1 ♗xd5 25 cxd5 d6 26 ♖xf5 ♕xb2 27 ♖xf8+ ♔xf8 28 ♗f5 ♕d2 29 ♖e6 ♕xd5 30 g4 c4 31 ♖xh6 c3 32 ♖h8+ ♔e7 33 ♖h7+ ♔f6 34 ♖c7 ♕d2 35 ♖c6 ♔e5 36 a4 ♕d1+ 37 ♔h2 ♕f3 0-1

> ### Game 19
> ## Reuben-Basman
> ### *London 1982*

1 d4 e6 2 c4 b6 3 e4 ♗b7 4 ♗d3 f5!? 5 d5

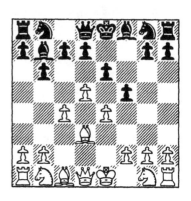

Not very strong. Instead of neutralising the pressure on the centre, this move merely intensifies it.

5...fxe4 6 ♗xe4 ♕h4! 7 ♕e2 ♘f6 8 ♗f3 ♗b4+ 9 ♗d2

9 ♘c3 transposes to Chapter 3, Games 27 and 28, while after 9 ♘d2 0-0 (9...♘a6!? is Basman's suggestion, e.g. 10 dxe6 0-0-0 11 exd7+ ♖xd7 12 ♗xb7+ ♔xb7 13 ♘gf3 ♕h5 with excellent compensation) 10 a3 exd5! 11 axb4 ♖e8 12 ♕xe8+ ♘xe8 and Black went on to win comfortably in Mednis-Psakhis, Amsterdam 1989.

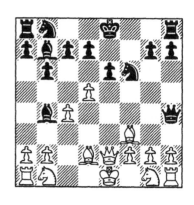

9...♗xd2+ 10 ♘xd2 0-0 11 dxe6 ♘c6 12

exd7 ♘xd7 13 0-0-0 ♘d4 14 ♕d3 ♘c5
15 ♕f1 ♖ad8 16 ♗xb7 ♖xf2 17 ♘gf3
♘xf3 18 ♘xf3 ♕f4+ 19 ♔b1 ♖xf1 0-1

Another one that didn't make it past move 20! This is typical of the mess that an unprepared White player can make of his position when faced with the shocking 4...f5!?

Game 20
Jo.Horvath-Gulko
Nova Gorica 1997

---

1 d4 e6 2 c4 b6 3 e4 ♗b7 4 ♗d3 ♗b4+

After the chaos of 4...f5!? it is almost a relief to return to tranquil waters with 4...♗b4+. Naturally, there are different interpretations of the move, but for the most part this is a solid option. By going for an exchange of bishops Black eases some of the congestion in his position. The danger with this approach is that it robs Black's position of some of its dynamism; and if he is unable to challenge White's centre successfully, he could find himself getting squashed.

5 ♗d2!

5 ♘c3 transposes to Chapter 3, Games 25-33; and 5 ♘d2, to my knowledge, has never been played. Both moves invite 5...f5! Finally, 5 ♔f1 is dealt with in Game 23.

5...♕e7

For me, this is the best option, but 5...♘c6 and 5...♗xd2+ are both possible – see Games 21 and 22.

6 ♘c3

At first I thought that White could count on some advantage if he simply went for exchanges with 6 ♗xb4!? ♕xb4+ 7 ♕d2 ♕xd2+ 8 ♘xd2, but 8...f5, as is often the case, nibbles away at the centre and gives Black enough counterplay to equalise: 9 ♘gf3 fxe4 10 ♘xe4 ♘c6! 11 ♔d2 (11 0-0-0 ♘b4) and now all three knight moves, 11...♘ge7, 11...♘f6 and

11...♘h6, give Black a reasonable game.

On the other hand, if 6 ♘e2 then Black should take the opportunity to get in 6...f5! (6...♗xd2+ 7 ♕xd2 ♘h6 8 ♘bc3 0-0 9 0-0 d6 10 f4 ♘d7 11 d5 e5 12 f5 f6 13 b4 gave White a massive space advantage in Avrukh-Speelman, Elista Olympiad 1998) with all the usual complications: 7 exf5 ♗xg2 8 ♖g1 ♗b7 (8...♗f3!? is worth considering; compare with Schneider-Forintos later on) 9 ♘bc3 ♘c6 10 fxe6 dxe6 11 a3 ♗xc3 (11...♗d6!?) 12 ♗xc3 ♘f6 13 ♕c2 0-0-0 14 0-0-0 is more comfortable for White, but Black effortlessly notched up a victory anyway in Vasiliev-Lempert, Moscow 1990.

Finally, 6 ♘f3 ♘f6 (but why not 6...f5...? If White captures then his king has an awkward check to deal with: 7 exf5 exf5+) 7 a3 ♗xd2+ 8 ♘bxd2 d6 9 0-0 e5 10 d5 0-0 11 b4 ♘bd7 12 ♕c2 and, although Black's position is solid enough, White, with his space advantage, had a small but comfortable advantage in Malisauskas-Litus, Katowice 1991.

6...f5!

Alternatively, 6...♗xc3 was tried in Pöltl-Ta.Horvath, Gleisdorf 1989, though I wouldn't be keen on giving up the bishop pair so readily: 7 ♗xc3 f5 8 ♕h5+! g6 9 ♕e2 ♘f6 10 d5 (I like the way Black has attacked the centre with ...f7-f5 but would be concerned about the bishop on c3) 10...♘a6 11 f3 (too tame; 11 exf5!) 11...fxe4 12 fxe4 0-0 13 0-0-0 ♘c5 14 ♘f3 exd5 15 exd5 ♕xe2 16 ♗xe2 ♘ce4 17 ♗d4 c5 18 dxc6 dxc6 19 ♖he1 c5 when Black has equalised and a draw was agreed.

7 ♘ge2 fxe4

A solid move, breaking down White's centre and trading pieces. Gulko equalises by precise play. 7...♘f6!? leads the game into more random territory, e.g. 8 exf5 ♗xg2 9 ♖g1 ♗f3 10 ♖g3 ♗b7 11 fxe6 dxe6 12 ♕a4+ ♗c6 13 ♕c2 ♗d6 ½-½ Schneider-Forintos, Hungarian Championship 1979. A pity. The game was just starting to warm up.

8 ♗xe4 ♗xe4 9 ♘xe4 ♘f6 10 ♘2g3

10 ♘xf6+ gxf6 would have unbalanced the position. Black would castle on the queenside and hope for the best, and White would do the same on the kingside.

10...♘xe4 11 ♘xe4 ♕h4!? 12 ♘g3

12 ♘f6+?! gxf6 13 ♗xb4 ♘c6 14 ♗c3 ♕e4+ is irritating.

12...♗d6 13 ♕h5+ ♕xh5 14 ♘xh5 0-0 15 ♘g3 ♘c6 16 ♗e3

The game is balanced – but not drawn. Gulko finds a way to create some chances.

16...♘b4 17 ♔d2

By keeping White's king in the middle there are more tactical possibilities open to Black.

17...♗f4 18 ♖hc1 ♖ae8 19 ♗xf4 ♖xf4 20 ♔e3 ♖h4 21 h3 d5 22 c5

After 22 a3 ♘c6 the king is caught in the crossfire of Black's rooks.

22...b5 23 c6 e5 24 a3 ♘a6 25 dxe5 ♖xe5+ 26 ♔d3 ♖c4 27 ♖xc4 dxc4+ 28 ♔d4 ♖e6 29 a4 ♖d6+ 30 ♔c3 ♖d3+ 31 ♔c2 ♘b4+

31...b4!? followed by ...b4-b3+ and ...♘b4 is dangerous.

32 ♔c1 c3 33 bxc3 ♖xc3+ 34 ♔b2 ♖c5 35 ♘e4 ♖c4 36 f3 ♘d3+ 37 ♔b3 ♘c1+ 38 ♔b2 bxa4 39 ♖a3 ♖xc6 40 ♖xa4 ♘d3+ 41 ♔a3 a6 42 g4 h6 43 ♖d4 ♘e1 44 ♖d8+ ♔h7 45 f4 ♖e6 46 ♘c5 ♖e3+ 47 ♔a2 ♔g6 48 ♖d7 ♖xh3 ½-½

After 49 ♘e4 White has enough counterplay to draw. Gulko's opening play was sound, and it was fascinating to watch him create something out of nothing in the ending, even though it wasn't quite enough to win.

Game 21
Nogueiras-Velez
Cienfuegos 1983

1 e4 e6 2 d4 b6 3 c4 ♗b7 4 ♗d3 ♗b4+ 5 ♗d2 ♘c6

This idea turns out well here, though I do harbour some doubts as to its effectiveness.

6 ♘f3 ♗xd2+ 7 ♘bxd2

After 7 ♕xd2 Black could play solidly with 7...d6 and ...e6-e5, but that doesn't challenge White's central position. Instead 7...♕f6!? is more interesting, e.g. 8 e5 (8 d5!?) 8...♕e7 9 ♘c3 f6 with some pressure on the centre.

7...♕f6 8 e5

8 d5 is more testing, e.g. 8...♘b4 (8...♘d4!?) 9 ♗e2 ♕xb2 10 0-0 ♘a6 (10...♘c2 11 ♖b1 ♕xa2 12 ♗d3 is clearly better for White, while after 10...♘xa2 11 ♖b1 ♕a3 12 ♖b3 ♕a4 13 c5 White has good compensation for the pawns) 11 ♘b3 when White has compensation for the pawn, though Black's position is playable.

8...♕f4!

A nice finesse, forcing White to weaken himself on the long diagonal.

9 g3 ♕h6 10 0-0 f5

I would prefer 10...f6 so that the f-file can be used.

11 d5 ♘ce7 12 ♖e1 exd5 13 cxd5 ♗xd5 14 ♖c1 ♘c6 15 ♗xf5 ♘ge7 16 ♗e4 ♗f7 17 h4

17 ♘c4! followed by ♘d6 would have given White a clear advantage according to Vilela in *Informator 35*.

17...0-0 18 ♘g5 ♗g6 19 ♗g2 ♔h8 20 e6

20 ♘de4! would still have been at least a little better for White.

20...d5 21 ♗xd5 ♘xd5 22 ♖xc6 ♗h5 23 ♕b3 ♕f6 24 ♘de4 ♕f5 25 ♖c2 h6 26 e7 ♘xe7 27 ♘e6 ♗f7 ½-½

I prefer Black's position. The pin is unpleasant for White, and there are chances to attack on the kingside.

Game 22
Petursson-Wauthier
San Bernardino open 1991

---

1 d4 e6 2 c4 b6 3 e4 ♗b7 4 ♗d3 ♗b4+ 5 ♗d2 ♗xd2+

I feel that this makes life too easy for White, but it isn't a bad move.

6 ♘xd2

After the solid 6 ♕xd2 f5 7 ♘c3 ♘f6 (I prefer 7...fxe4 8 ♗xe4 ♗xe4 9 ♘xe4 ♘f6 and Black is close to equalising) 8 f3 fxe4 9 fxe4 d6 10 ♘f3 ♘bd7 11 0-0 ♕e7 White had a slight plus in Kaufman-Mouzon, Atlantic open, Washington 1997.

6...♘h6

6...f5 is more forthright: 7 ♕h5+ g6 8 ♕e2 ♘h6 9 ♘gf3 ♕f6 10 0-0-0 ♘c6 11 e5 ♕e7 12 a3 ♘a5 13 h3 c5 14 ♖he1 0-0 15 ♔b1 ♖ac8 16 g3 ♔g7 17 ♔a2 ♖c7 18 ♖c1 ♖fc8 with a balanced position in Forintos-Chetverik, Zalakaros open 1996.

However, 6...d6 isn't terribly inspired: 7 ♘e2 e5 8 d5 ♘e7 9 0-0 ♘d7 10 b4 a5 11 a3 and White had a typical advantage for this opening in Van der Vliet-Ree, Amsterdam 1983.

7 ♕h5

If White develops normally, then 7 ♘gf3 0-0 8 0-0 f5 with the usual kind of play for Black, as in Byrne-Sandler, Australian Championship 1995.

7...♕f6!?

7...0-0 8 ♘gf3 f5 9 0-0 ♘c6 is also playable – the queen isn't too threatening on h5.

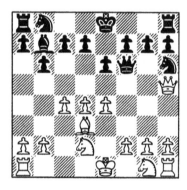

8 ♘gf3

Alternatively, 8 e5 ♕f4 9 ♘e2 ♕g4 10 ♕xg4 ♘xg4 11 f3 ♘h6, as in Flear-Wauthier, San Bernardino open 1991, is quite similar to the game, but here White played the outré 12 g4 creating profound weaknesses in his own kingside. Although he won the game, I don't think it was particularly convincing: 12...♘c6 13 0-0-0 0-0-0 14 ♖hg1 d6 (perhaps 14...f6!? 15 f4 fxe5 16 dxe5 g5) 15 g5 ♘g8 (or 15...♘f5!? 16 ♗xf5 exf5 17 exd6 ♖xd6) 16 exd6 ♖xd6 17 ♖g4 ♘e5 (17...♘ge7) 18 dxe5 ♖xd3 19

♖f4 ♘e7 20 ♖xf7 ♘f5 21 ♘f4 ♖d7 22 ♖xd7 ♔xd7 23 ♘e4+ ♔e7 24 ♖d3, and now if Black had played 24...♘h4! 25 ♘d2 ♖f8 26 ♘h5 ♘xf3 27 ♘xf3 ♖xf3 28 ♖xf3 ♗xf3 29 ♘f4 the game would have ended in a draw.

8...♘c6 9 e5 ♕f4 10 g3 ♕g4 11 ♕xg4 ♘xg4 12 0-0 f6 13 h3 ♘h6 14 exf6 gxf6 15 a3 ♘f7 16 b4 0-0-0 17 ♖fe1

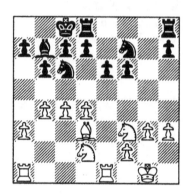

White has some space on the queenside, but Black's position is solid.

17...♘g5?

It was better to play 17...♖dg8! with chances for both sides.

18 ♘xg5 fxg5 19 d5 exd5 20 cxd5 ♘b8 21 d6 ♖de8 22 ♗xh7

White now has a clear advantage.

22...♖e6 23 ♖xe6 dxe6 24 ♗e4 ♗d5 25 dxc7 ♔xc7 26 ♗xd5 exd5 27 ♘f3 ♖xh3 28 ♘xg5 ♖h6 29 f4 ♔c6 30 ♖d1 ♖d6 31

♘f3 ♔d7 32 ♔f2 ♔e7 33 g4 a6 34 ♘h4
♔f7 35 ♘f5 ♖d8 36 ♖c1 ♖h8 37 ♖c7+
♔f6 38 ♘d4 ♖d8 39 ♔f3 ♔g6 40 ♖b7
♘d7 41 ♘f5 1-0

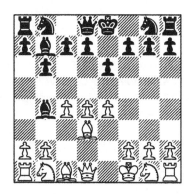

Game 23
Joyce-Speelman
Bunratty Masters 1998

**1 d4 e6 2 c4 b6 3 e4 ♗b7 4 ♗d3 ♗b4+
5 ♔f1**

I find it extraordinary that this move
has ever been played by White, but as I
have discovered several practical examples
of this move, I thought I ought to cover it.
I just don't see the point. Of course, it
takes a bit of time to re-deploy the bishop
from b4, but it has caused some disruption. I don't think White is worse, but I
still can't find a good answer to the question, 'Why?'
5...♘c6

Perhaps even 5...♗f8!? (the bishop is going round to g7) 6 ♘c3 d6 7 d5 e5 8 ♗e3
♘f6 9 g4 g6 10 h4 ♗c8 11 f3 h5 12 g5 ♘h7
13 b4 ♗e7 14 c5 with complications,
though White should be better as his
queenside attack is well advanced, in Jans-
sen-Rogers, Sonnevanck 1996.

But there is no need to play the bishop
all the way back to f8: 5...♗e7 is possible
(Speelman played in similar fashion in the
main game). Now after 6 ♘c3 d6 7 ♕g4

♗f6 8 ♘f3 ♘c6 9 ♗e3 e5 10 dxe5 h5!?
(both 10...dxe5 and 10...♘xe5 are sensible)
11 ♕g3 h4 (11...♘xe5!?) 12 ♕h3 ♗c8 13 g4
♘xe5 14 ♘xe5 instead of 14...dxe5 (Dan-
ner-Barle, Ljubljana 1981) I would prefer
14...♗xe5!? 15 ♖c1 c6 16 f3 ♕f6 with the
more promising position for Black.
6 ♘f3 ♗e7 7 a3

Black was threatening ...♘b4, bagging
the bishop.
7...d6

I imagine Speelman was considering
...♗f6, similar to the game in the note
above, but White leaps in first.
**8 d5 ♘e5 9 ♘xe5 dxe5 10 ♗e3 ♘f6 11
♘c3 0-0**

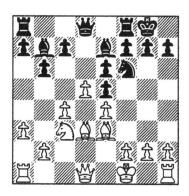

12 dxe6?!

There are too many holes in White's
position after this. 12 g3 should be about
level.
**12...fxe6 13 ♗c2 ♕e8 14 ♔g1 ♖d8 15
♕e1 ♘g4 16 h4 ♖d7 17 ♖d1 ♕d8 18
♖xd7 ♕xd7 19 ♕d1 ♕xd1+ 20 ♘xd1
♖d8 21 ♔f1 ♗xe4 22 ♗b3 ♖d3 0-1**

5 ♔f1 actually gives more trouble to
White than his opponent. Personally, I
like to pay my king more respect.

Game 24
Shirov-Prie
Val Maubuee 1990

1 d4 e6 2 c4 b6 3 e4 ♗b7 4 ♗d3 ♕h4

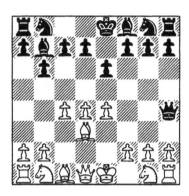

Mad. Although this move is seen regularly in the English Defence, in this particular position it isn't justified.

5 d5

This gives Black some hope. There are two alternatives which are stronger:

a) 5 ♘d2! ♗b4 6 ♘gf3 ♕g4 (or 6...♗xd2+ 7 ♗xd2 ♕g4 8 ♕e2 f5 9 h3 ♕xg2 10 0-0-0 ♘f6 11 ♘h4 ♕xh1 12 ♖xh1 fxe4 13 ♖g1 exd3 14 ♕e5 ♔f7 15 d5 ♘a6 16 ♗c3 ♖af8 17 dxe6+ dxe6 18 ♖xg7+ 1-0 Papacek-Prie, Clichy 1990; another setback for the former Paris Champion, Erik Prie, with his dubious 4...♕h4) 7 0-0 ♗xd2 8 ♘xd2 (8 h3!? ♕g6 9 ♘e5 ♕f6 10 ♗xd2 – two bishops, big centre, lead in development; sorted!) 8...♕xd1 9 ♖xd1 d6 10 b3 ♘d7 11 ♗b2 ♘e7 12 ♗c3 ♘g6 13 d5 e5 14 b4 0-0 15 ♘b3 and White soon won in Mortensen-Brondum, Copenhagen 1980.

b) 5 ♘f3!? ♕g4 6 0-0 (Keene, Plaskett and Tisdall point out that White can even force a draw with 6 h3 ♕xg2 7 ♖g1 ♕xh3 8 ♖g3 ♕h1+ 9 ♖g1 ♕h5 10 ♖g5 ♕h6 11 ♖g1 etc.) 6...♗xe4 7 ♗xe4 ♕xe4 8 ♘c3 ♕b7 has been played by the Hungarian grandmaster Gyözö Forintos as Black but, as yet, not by anyone else. White has big compensation for the pawn.

5...♗b4+ 6 ♔f1 ♗c5 7 g3 ♕e7 8 ♘f3 ♘f6

8...f5 is met by 9 ♗g5.

9 ♔g2 0-0 10 e5 ♘g4

10...♘e8? 11 ♗xh7+ ♔xh7 12 ♘g5+ ♔g8 13 ♕h5.

11 ♗xh7+ ♔xh7 12 ♘g5+ ♔g8 13 ♕xg4 f6 14 exf6 ♕xf6 15 ♘e4 ♕f7 16 ♘bc3 ♗d4 17 f3 ♗xc3 18 ♘xc3 exd5 19 cxd5 ♗xd5 20 ♘xd5 ♕xd5

Black has done remarkably well to get this far – but he still stands worse.

21 ♗f4 ♖f7 22 ♖hd1 ♕b5 23 ♖d2 ♘a6 24 ♖e1 d6 25 ♕g5 ♕c6 26 h4 ♖e8 27 ♕d5 ♕d7 28 ♖de2 ♖xe2+ 29 ♖xe2 ♘b4 30 ♕e4 a5 31 a3 ♘c6 32 h5 ♖e7 33 ♕d5+ ♔f8 34 ♖d2 ♖e6 35 ♖c2 ♘e5 36 ♖xc7 ♕xc7 37 ♕xe6 ♘f7 38 g4 ♕c2+ 39 ♔g3 ♕xb2 40 g5 ♕d4 41 ♗e3 ♕c3 42 ♕e4 ♕e1+ 43 ♔g4 ♘e5+ 44 ♔f5 ♕h1 45 ♕a8+ ♔e7 46 ♕b7+ ♘d7 47 ♔g6 ♕h3 48 ♗d4 d5 49 ♔xg7 ♕xf3 50 ♗f6+ ♔d6 51 h6 ♕e3 52 h7 ♘xf6 53 gxf6 ♕g5+ 54 ♔f7 ♕h5+ 55 ♔g8 1-0

Summary

Although the position after 4...f5 5 exf5 ♗b4+ is quite unstable and for many moves quite unclear, my feeling is that Black is suffering in Games 12-14. Even if improvements are found in Beliavsky-Short, the older lines in Game 13 aren't appealing anyway. The rook sacrifice 4...f5 5 exf5 ♗xg2 in Games 15-17 has not yet been fully explored. If you put the effort in here then you could be rewarded. On the other hand, attempts by White to run from the sacrifice in Games 18 and 19 are simply poor. I find 4...♗b4+ in Games 20-23 a bit tame; and, as I said before, 4...♕h4 is just daft.

1 d4 e6 2 c4 b6 3 e4 ♗b7 4 ♗d3

4...f5 *(D)*

    4...♗b4+

        5 ♗d2

            5...♕e7 – *Game 20*

            5...♘c6 – *Game 21*

            5...♗xd2+ – *Game 22*

        5 ♔f1 – *Game 23*

    4...♕h4 – *Game 24*

5 exf5

    5 ♘c3 – *Chapter 3, Games 25-33*

    5 ♕h5+ – *Game 18*

    5 d5 – *Game 19*

5...♗b4+

    5...♗xg2 6 ♕h5+ g6 7 fxg6 ♗g7 8 gxh7+ ♔f8 9 ♗g5 ♘f6 10 ♕h4 ♗xh1 11 ♘e2 *(D)*

        11...♘c6

            12 ♘f4 – *Game 15*; 12 ♘d2 – *Game 16*

        11...♕e7 – *Game 17*

6 ♔f1 ♘f6 *(D)*

    6...exf5 – *Game 14*

7 ♗e2

    7 c5 – *Game 13*

7...0-0 – *Game 12*

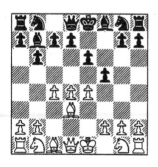

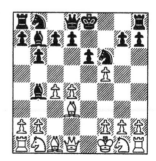

      4...f5   *11 ♘e2*   *6...♘f6*

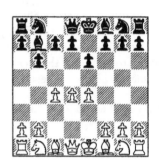

CHAPTER THREE

Main Line with 3 e4 ♗b7 4 d5, 4 ♘c3 ♗b4 5 d5 and 4 ♘c3 ♗b4 5 ♗d3

1 d4 e6 2 c4 b6 3 e4 ♗b7

In this section we shall deal with games where White puts his three pawns in the centre, and then supports it with either ♘c3 combined with ♗d3 (Games 25-33) or an early d4-d5 (Games 34-36). In the following two chapters we shall then move on to look at games where White plays the three pawns forward but chooses to protect the centre with f2-f3 (Chapter 4) or ♕c2 (Chapter 5).

Beliavsky used to play with both ♗d3 and ♘c3 before he realised that he could take the pawn on f5 (see Game 12 in the previous chapter). No wonder he felt he needed to try something new, for although Beliavsky gets the advantage in Game 25, Gulko didn't play the opening as vigorously as he might have. Incidentally, this common position can, and often is, reached via a different move order whereby the knight comes out to c3 and is pinned (4 ♘c3 ♗b4) before the bishop gets to d3 (5 ♗d3).

Game 25
Beliavsky-Gulko
Polanica Zdroj 1996

1 d4 e6 2 e4 b6 3 c4 ♗b7 4 ♗d3

4 d5 is quite a common alternative – see Games 35 and 36, while 4 ♘c3 f5 5 d5 is the subject of Game 4.

4...f5 5 ♘c3 ♗b4

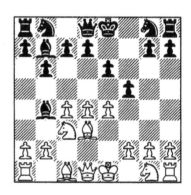

In principle this should present Black with few difficulties: White's centre is under enormous strain.

6 d5

For 6 ♕h5+ see Games 29–32; and for 6 ♕e2 see Game 33.

6...fxe4 7 ♗xe4 ♘f6

A solid treatment, but 7...♕h4!? is more ambitious – as Gulko himself later realised – see Games 27 and 28.

8 ♗f3

Beliavsky mentions 8 ♗g5!?, but the following game demonstrates that Black has few difficulties: 8...♗xc3+ 9 bxc3 ♘a6 10 ♘e2 ♘c5 (as is so often the case in this opening, once Black's queen's knight finds a decent square, then he has normally solved his opening problems) 11 ♗f3 0-0 12 0-0 ♕e8 13 ♘g3 ♕g6 14 ♗e3 ♘fe4 and Black already had the more active position in Bozic-Lempert, Bled 1994.

8...e5

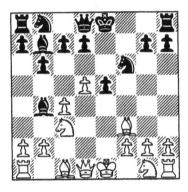

I do think it is a pity to close the centre like this: Black's bishop on b7 looks stupid. The next main game shows that Black does have better alternatives.

9 ♗d2

Not 9 ♘e2? e4, but 9 ♘h3 deserves a closer look: 9...0-0 10 0-0 ♗xc3 11 bxc3 ♘a6 12 ♗a3 d6 13 ♘g5 and although Black eventually won in Reyes-Yermolinsky, Seattle 1994, at this point I prefer White's chances.

9...0-0 10 ♘ge2

White has a solid position, his pieces harmoniously placed; while Black's opening has not been a great success. The idea of blocking the centre doesn't fit in with Black's set-up – at least not in this position. The bishop on b7 is blocked in and the knight on b8 has yet to find a good square. Conclusion: White has the advantage.

10...c6 11 0-0 cxd5 12 ♘xd5

see following diagram

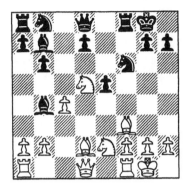

This turns out well, but Beliavsky mentions that 12 cxd5! is even stronger, with the idea that 12...♘a6 13 ♘g3 ♘c7? 14 d6 wins a piece.

12...♘xd5 13 ♗xd5+ ♗xd5 14 cxd5

I think I would have just taken the exchange here: 14 ♗xb4 ♗xc4 15 ♗xf8 ♕xf8 16 b3 ♗e6 17 f4 just looks good for White to me. Having said that, the game continuation is also strong.

14...♗xd2 15 ♕xd2 ♘a6

Normal moves don't help, e.g. 15...d6 16 ♖ac1 ♘d7 17 ♖c6 ♘b8 18 ♖c4 with a clear advantage.

16 d6 ♘c5 17 ♕d5+ ♔h8 18 b4 ♘e6 19 ♕xe5

White is a clear pawn up, but ... Gulko does well to get some play for it. The point is that finally Black's knight has found a stable square in the middle of the board, and it is hard for White to break through.

19...a5 20 b5?

Beliavsky believes that 20 a3 would have retained his advantage: 20...axb4 21 axb4 ♖xa1 22 ♖xa1 ♕h4 23 f4.

20...♕h4 21 ♕e3

Or 21 f4 ♖ae8 with compensation.

21...♕c4 22 ♖fc1

If 22 a4 ♘c5 and Black obviously again has compensation.

22...♕xb5 23 ♘d4 ♘xd4 24 ♕xd4 ♖f6 25 ♖ab1 ♕e2

26 ♖b2

If 26 ♕xb6 ♕xa2 is possible, e.g. 27 ♕b8+ ♖f8! with equality (but not 27...♖xb8? 28 ♖xb8+ ♕g8 29 ♖cc8 and wins).

26...♕e6 27 ♕xb6 ♕xd6 28 ♕xd6 ♖xd6 29 g3 ♔g8 30 ♖c4 ♖d5 31 h4 ♖a6 32 ♔g2 ♔f7 33 ♖e2 ♖e6 ½-½

7...♘f6 is a sound way of dealing with 6 d5 – if Black plays in the same fashion as Bagirov in the next game.

Game 26
Dgebuadze-Bagirov
Linares 1997

---

1 c4 b6 2 d4 e6 3 ♘c3 ♗b7 4 e4 ♗b4 5 ♗d3 f5 6 d5 fxe4 7 ♗xe4 ♘f6 8 ♗f3

This is the point where Gulko tried 8...e5. Bagirov's move is stronger:

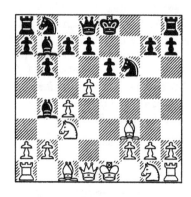

8...♗xc3+

This isn't the only decent option:

a) 8...exd5 9 cxd5 c6!? (9...♘a6 10 ♘ge2 ♘c5 11 0-0 ♗a6 12 ♕d4 ♗xc3 13 bxc3 0-0 14 c4 was slightly better for White in Minasian-Tratar, Cannes open 1995) 10 de ♗xc3+ 11 bxc3 0-0 12 ♘e2 ♘a6 13 0-0 ♘c5 14 ♕d4 ♗a6 15 c4 ♘e8 16 ♗e3 ♕f6 17 ♕g4 ♕f7 18 ♖fd1 ♗xc4 and Black was a clear pawn ahead in Lautier-David, Hameln Voba 1987.

b) 8...0-0 9 ♘ge2 b5!? 10 b3 bxc4 11 bxc4 ♘a6 12 0-0 ♖b8 13 ♗e3 ♗c5 14 ♗xc5 ♘xc5 15 ♘d4 ♗a6 16 ♘db5 e5 17 ♖e1 ♗xb5 18 cxb5 d6 19 a4 ♕d7 20 h3 g6 21 ♘e4 ♘fxe4 22 ♗xe4 a6 23 bxa6 ♖b4 24 ♗d3 ♖d4 0-1 Johansson-Bagirov, Jyvaskyla open 1996, was a successful experiment, but it is interesting to note that by the time he came to play this main game, Bagirov had thought better of this idea and essayed the safer 8...♗xc3+.

9 bxc3 0-0

Alternatively, 9...exd5 10 cxd5 0-0 11 ♘e2 ♘a6 12 0-0 ♘c5 13 c4 ♘e8 14 ♗b2 ♘d6 15 ♖c1 ♗a6 16 ♕d4 ♕g5, when although White has pressure on the long diagonal, Black has it covered, and his knights have found excellent squares. Chances were balanced in Sakalauskas-Gorbatow, Polanica Zdroj open 1996.

10 ♘e2 e5 11 ♘g3 d6 12 0-0 ♘bd7

The exchange of bishop for knight on

c3 means that Bagirov can aim to put a horse on the beautiful c5-square; or at least force White to give up the bishop pair to prevent this.

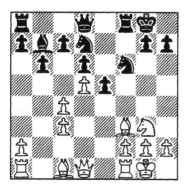

13 ♗e3 ♕e8 14 ♕c2 ♕f7 15 ♗e2 ♖ae8 16 ♗d3 ♗c8 17 ♖ae1 ♘c5 18 ♗xc5 bxc5 19 ♕a4 a6 20 ♕a5 g6 21 f3 ♕d7 ½-½

A curious move to offer a draw with! Bagirov has a plan: to play the queen back to d8, then swing the knight over from f6-d7-b6. That would secure the queenside (thereby releasing Black's queen) and put some pressure on c4. In that case I would prefer Black's position. The question is, can White prevent it? Let's continue the game a little further: 22 ♗c2 ♕d8 23 ♗a4 ♖e7 24 ♖b1 ♘d7 (24...e4!?) 25 ♗xd7 ♕xd7 26 ♖b8 ♖ef7 followed by ...♕e7 and chances are level.

---

1 d4 e6 2 c4 b6 3 ♘c3 ♗b7 4 e4 ♗b4 5 ♗d3 f5 6 d5 fxe4 7 ♗xe4 ♕h4!

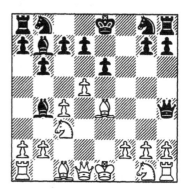

That's more in the spirit of the opening. Let's see if it is any good. 7...♘f6 was played in the previous two games.

8 ♕e2

White has two alternatives here:

a) 8 ♕d3?! is provocative:

a1) 8...♘f6 9 ♗f3 e5 (9...♘a6!? is also promising) 10 ♗e3? (10 ♘ge2 is playable) 10...e4 11 ♕d4 exf3 12 ♕xh4 fxg2 13 0-0-0 gxh1♕ with a winning position for Black in Simonsen-Nicolaisen, Hillerod 1979.

a2) 8...exd5 9 cxd5 ♘f6 10 ♗f3 ♗a6 11 ♕e3+ ♔f7 12 ♕f4 ♖e8+ 13 ♔d1 ♕xf4 14 ♗xf4 ♗xc3 15 bxc3 d6 16 ♘h3 (16 ♘e2 ♗c4!) 16...h6!, containing White's pieces before cashing in. Black duly converted the point in Whiteley-Keene, Cambridge 1976.

b) 8 ♕d4 ♘f6 9 ♗f4 ♗xc3+ 10 bxc3 ♘xe4 11 ♕xe4 0-0 12 g3 ♕f6 13 ♘e2 exd5 14 cxd5 ♘a6 15 0-0 ♘c5 and Black already had a powerful initiative in Bauer-Chetverik, Zalakaros open 1996.

8...♘f6 9 ♗f3

Alternatively, 9 ♗d3 ♘a6 (for the greedy among you, why not 9...0-0!? 10

♘f3 ♕g4 11 0-0 ♗xc3 12 bxc3 exd5) 10 ♘f3 ♕h5 11 ♗d2 0-0-0 12 0-0-0 ♖he8 and Black stood well in Kalantarian-Bricard, Cannes open 1995.

9...♗a6

If a defence is later discovered for White, then Black might also try 9...0-0 – see the next game.

10 dxe6 d5

Good move. White is struggling to get his king out of the middle, and in the game he immediately goes wrong.

11 a3?

White ought to play 11 ♕e5, though after 11...♕xc4 12 ♘ge2 0-0 chances are balanced

11...♗xc3+ 12 bxc3 ♗xc4 13 ♕c2 ♘e4 14 ♗e3

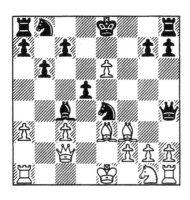

White has to defend f2 before developing the knight. If 14 g3 ♕f6 and the attack

rolls on, while 14 ♗xe4!? dxe4 15 ♘e2 0-0 16 0-0 ♘c6 is also miserable for White – he is going to come out a pawn down even if he does manage to avoid being checkmated.

14...♘c6 15 ♘e2 ♘e5 16 ♖d1 0-0 17 ♗xe4 dxe4 18 0-0 ♘f3+ 19 gxf3 exf3 20 e7 ♕g4+ 21 ♘g3 ♕h3 22 exf8♕+ ♖xf8 0-1

Can't argue with that; or the next game. 6 d5 is in trouble.

Game 28
Marchand-Gulko
Geneva 1997

---

1 d4 e6 2 c4 b6 3 e4 ♗b7 4 ♗d3 f5 5 ♘c3 ♗b4 6 d5 fxe4 7 ♗xe4 ♕h4 8 ♕e2 ♘f6 9 ♗f3 0-0

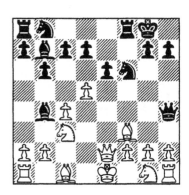

While 9...♗a6 was successful in the last game, I have to say that castling is the first move that would enter my head: the king exits, the rook enters and carnage is on the cards. From this position I have three games on my database, with White managing one measly half-point – and that with some luck.

10 dxe6

10 ♗e3 ♘e4 11 g3 was played in Spigel-Sutter, US open 1994, and now 11...♕f6 would have been powerful.

10...♘c6!

That's the trick. There is no need to exchange bishops (which would only help White develop) and at a stroke Black's rooks are connected.

11 g3

11 ♗e3 was played in Kaplan-Miles, Sao Paolo 1977. It is interesting to see that 7...♕h4 was played so long ago, which makes it all the more curious that players started experimenting with 7...♘f6. That game continued 11...♘e4 12 0-0-0 ♘xc3 13 bxc3 ♗a3+ 14 ♔b1 dxe6 15 ♕c2 ♗c5!? (an interesting decision; Miles allows his pawns to be shattered and in return gets tremendous piece play) 16 ♗xc5 bxc5 17 ♘e2 ♖ab8 18 ♔a1 ♕xc4 19 ♗e4 ♖xf2 20 ♗xh7+ ♔h8 21 ♖d2 ♕h4 22 ♗g6 ♖bf8 (22...♖xg2!?) 23 ♖b1. There is no doubt that Black is better here, but it is a difficult position to control and White eventually succeeded in scraping a draw.

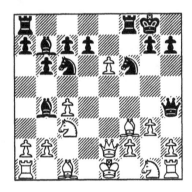

11...♕d4 12 ♗d2 ♗a6 13 exd7

The capture of another pawn does not really help matters. It would have been better to castle queenside at once.

13...♗xc4 14 ♕e3 ♕xd7 15 0-0-0 ♖ae8 16 ♕f4 ♘e5 17 ♕h4 ♕e6

see following diagram

What a picture. White could have resigned here with a clear conscience.

18 ♔b1 ♗xc3 19 ♗xc3 ♗xa2+ 20 ♔a1 ♗b3 21 ♖e1 b5 22 ♖xe5 ♕a6+ 23 ♔b1 ♕a2+ 24 ♔c1 ♖xe5 25 ♗xe5 ♖d8 26

♗d4 ♕a1+ 27 ♔d2 ♕xb2+ 28 ♔e3 ♕c1+ **0-1**

It is time to conclude our look at 6 d5 – and my advice to players of the white pieces would be: avoid it! 7...♘f6 is a solid response, but on the evidence of the last two games, there is every chance that White will be blown out of the water if Black goes in for 7...♕h4.

Game 29
Gärtner-Dey
Berlin 1994

---

1 d4 e6 2 c4 b6 3 e4 ♗b7 4 ♘c3 ♗b4 5 ♗d3 f5 6 ♕h5+

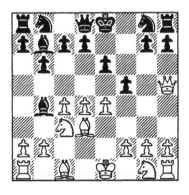

This check has been quite popular in practice. Instead of protecting the e-pawn straightaway, White forces one of Black's pawns forward on the kingside, creating a slight weakness, and only then drops back to e2. All very sophisticated; but in my opinion, it is not up to much (but keep it quiet!). The immediate 6 ♕e2 is considered in Game 33, while 6 ♕c2 is well met by 6...♕h4 with tremendous pressure on the white centre (see Chapter 5, Game 49).

6...g6 7 ♕e2 ♘f6 8 ♗g5

White still cannot move the e-pawn; or at least he ought not to, e.g. 8 e5 ♗xg2 9 exf6 ♕xf6 10 ♗f4 ♘c6 11 0-0-0 ♗xh1 12 d5 ♗xc3 13 dxc6 ♗xc6 14 bxc3 ♕xc3+ 15 ♔b1 0-0-0 16 ♘f3 d6 17 ♗c1 e5 and Black was well on the road to victory in Knott-Speelman, British Championship, Ayr 1978. However, it is possible to bolster the centre with 8 f3 – see Game 32.

8...fxe4

This is the most sound and safest way of handling White's system. Black should not encounter any difficulties if he plays accurately. However, a more enterprising choice is 8...h6, for which see Game 31.

9 ♗xe4

The correct move order. A couple of inattentive players have tried 9 ♗xf6 at this point, failing to spot the intermezzo 9...exd3! 10 ♕e5 (10 ♗xd8 dxe2 wins as the g2-pawn is en prise) 10...♘c6 11 ♕g5 ♗e7 12 ♗xe7 ♕xe7 13 ♕xe7+ ♔xe7 14 ♘f3 ♘a5 15 ♘d2 (or 15 b3 ♗xf3 16 gxf3 ♖af8) 15...♗xg2 16 ♖g1 ♗h3 17 ♖g3 ♗f5 with a winning ending for Black in Taz-

hieva-Chiburdanidze, Moscow Women's Olympiad 1994.

Finally 9 ♗c2?! (an unnecessary gambit) was tried in Rodriguez-Keene, Alicante 1977, but Black was up to the task: 9...♕e7 10 0-0-0 ♗xc3 11 bxc3 ♘c6 12 f3 ♕a3+ 13 ♔b1 0-0 14 ♗c1 ♗xc3 15 ♗b2 ♕a5 and after some complications White lost the game.

9...♗xe4

The speculative 9...♘xe4 is the subject of the next main game.

10 ♗xf6 ♕xf6 11 ♕xe4

11...♗xc3+

It isn't absolutely necessary to capture on c3 immediately, though the bishop isn't going to retreat either. In this kind of position Black is able to use the f-file to generate play, though in Sorin-Garbarino, St Martin 1995, he tried a different strategy: 11...♘c6 12 ♘f3 ♕f5!? (this is what is slightly unusual – normally there is a rook supporting the queen) 13 ♕xf5 ♗xc3+ 14 bxc3 exf5 (14...gxf5!? would have unbalanced the position) 15 ♔d2 0-0 16 h4 h6 17 ♔d3 ♖ae8 18 ♖ae1 d6 and the chances were even.

12 bxc3 ♘c6 13 ♘f3 0-0 14 0-0 ♕f4

see following diagram

15 ♖fe1

If the queen backs off then Black should not have too many problems. Here are a couple of examples, with Black employing differing strategies:

a) 15 ♕d3 ♕f5 16 ♕e2 ♖ae8 17 ♖ae1 ♖e7 18 ♕d2 ♘d8 19 ♖e3 d6 20 ♖fe1 ♖fe8 (it strikes me that Black should transfer his heavy pieces to the f-file 20...♖ef7, as the knight on d8 holds the e6-pawn comfortably; Black can follow up with ...g7-g5 and if necessary ...h7-h5, when Black's rooks attack and defend the king at the same time) 21 ♕b2 ♘f7 22 ♕b5 ♔g7 with equal chances in Elguezabal Varela-Yewdokimov, Madrid 1994.

b) 15 ♕e2 is similar, though Black played more boldly on the kingside in Iskusnyh-Lempert, Orel 1995 – and reaped the reward: 15...♖f5 16 ♘d2 ♕h6 17 ♘e4 ♖af8 18 ♖ad1 ♘e7 19 ♖d3 g5!? 20 ♖h3 ♕g7 21 ♕d1 ♘g6 22 ♖g3 h6 23 ♖e3 ♘f4 24 ♘g3 ♖5f7 25 ♘h5 ♕g6 26 ♘g3 ♔h7 27 ♕b1 ♕xb1 28 ♖xb1 ♔g6 29 ♖b5 ♘h5 30 ♘xh5 ♔xh5 31 f3 ♔g6 32 h3 ♖f5 33 ♖ee5 a6 34 ♖xf5 ♖xf5 35 ♖xf5 ♔xf5 (the ending is winning) 36 ♔f2 h5 37 g3 h4 38 gxh4 gxh4 39 ♔e3 d5 40 cxd5 exd5 41 a3 a5 42 f4 a4 43 ♔f3 c6 44 ♔e3 c5 0-1. A fine positional achievement.

15...♕xe4 16 ♖xe4 ♖f5 17 ♖d1

Compare this game with Game 33, where White does not bother to check on h5 and plays the immediate 6 ♕e2. The position is the same apart from the pawn on g6 which there stands on g7. Keene

played 17...♖a5 and held the draw comfortably. That's not to say the move in the game is a mistake.

17...♖af8 18 d5 exd5

I prefer 18...♘d8 – the knight does not stand badly, and it is a pity to undouble the c-pawns; moreover the knight can be re-deployed (after exchanging pawns) via b7 to d6 or c5.

19 cxd5 ♘a5 20 d6 cxd6 21 ♖xd6 ♘b7 22 ♖d2

Not 22 ♖xd7? ♘c5.

22...♘c5 23 ♖e3

It is unfortunate that Black's queenside pawns have been split, but his knight has found a good square on c5. But White is better thanks to his strongly placed rooks and his three beautiful kingside pawns.

23...♖f4

23...♖8f7 is probably stronger.

24 h3 ♖8f6 25 ♘e5 ♖a4

Perhaps 25...a5!?

26 ♘xd7 ♘xd7 27 ♖xd7 ♖xa2

27...♖f7 would have been better.

28 ♖e8+ ♖f8 29 ♖xf8+ ♔xf8 30 ♖xh7 a5 31 c4 ♖a4

see following diagram

31...♖c2 32 ♖b7 a4 33 ♖xb6 a3 34 ♖a6 a2 35 ♔h2 ♖xf2 would have offered more drawing chances.

32 ♖c7 ♖b4 33 c5 bxc5 34 ♖xc5 a4 35 ♖c7 a3 36 ♖a7 ♖b3 37 g3 ♖c3 38 ♔g2

🜚b3 39 h4 🜚c3 40 g4 🜚b3 41 f3 ♔e8 42 ♔g3 ♔f8 43 ♔f4 🜚c3 44 ♔g5 🜚xf3 45 ♔xg6 🜚b3 46 g5 🜚b6+ 47 ♔h5 🜚b3 48 ♔h6 🜚b8 49 🜚xa3 ♔g8 50 g6 ♔h8 51 h5 🜚c8 52 🜚a5 🜚b8 53 ♔g5 🜚b1 54 🜚a8+ ♔g7 55 h6 mate 1-0

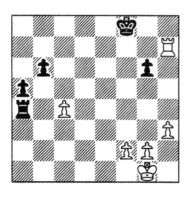

Black was doing fine in the ending; he only lost through poor technique. Not only that, I do not consider that Black is merely fighting for a draw in this kind of ending. With his superior pawn structure Black can play for a win, as the game Iskusnyh-Lempert in the notes demonstrates. The plan demonstrated in this game represents a solid way to counter 8 ♗g5. Now let's look at some less sound, but possibly more interesting methods.

> ### Game 30
> ### Grünfeld-Prie
> *Paris 1990*

1 c4 b6 2 ♘c3 e6 3 e4 ♗b7 4 d4 ♗b4 5 ♗d3 f5 6 ♕h5+ g6 7 ♕e2 ♘f6 8 ♗g5 fxe4 9 ♗xe4

Everything the same as the previous game so far, but here, just when White thought he was going to get some nice exchanges, Black chooses to sacrifice his queen.

9...♘xe4!? 10 ♗xd8 ♘xc3 11 bxc3 ♗xc3+ 12 ♔f1 ♗xa1 13 ♗xc7 ♗xd4

A dynamic balance has been reached:

Black has wonderful minor pieces, but his king could be better protected. Queens are superb pieces in situations where they have numerous targets to attack.

14 ♘f3 ♗c5

This way White's king comes under immediate fire. I prefer this move to 14...♗g7, though Black also has reasonable chances here too, e.g. 15 h4 ♘c6 16 h5 🜚c8 17 ♗d6 ♗a6 18 ♘d2 ♘d4 19 ♕g4 with a tense struggle ahead in Bick-Welling, Koop Tjuchem open 1996.

15 ♕e5 0-0

16 ♗xb8

It seems a pity to give up the bishop for a knight, especially a knight that hasn't even entered the game, but the prospect of the queen being hounded by the minor pieces was too worrying for White.

16...🜚axb8 17 h4 🜚bc8 18 h5 🜚f5 19

♕c3 ♗xf3

19...g5!? 20 h6 ♗f8 was worth a glance.

20 gxf3 g5 21 ♕d3 ♖c7

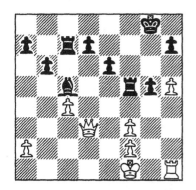

I am surprised that Black wishes to defend in such a painstaking and careful manner, though it has to be said that his strategy pays off in the game. 21...d6 with the idea of activating the rooks straightaway on the f-file appeals to me.

22 ♖g1 ♗e7 23 ♖g4

This was the moment to throw in 23 h6!? to confuse the issue. Black's rooks are not co-ordinated, so with the queen about the play is tricky.

23...♔f7 24 ♖d4 ♔e8 25 ♖g4 h6

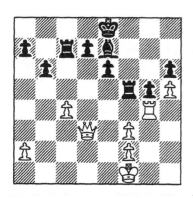

With a huge sigh of relief. Black's position is more secure and he can start to regroup for an attack in safety.

26 ♔g2 ♗f6 27 ♖e4 ♔e7 28 ♔g3 ♗e5+ 29 ♔g2 d6 30 ♖e2 ♔f7 31 ♖e4 ♔g7 32 ♖e3 ♖cf7 33 ♕e4 g4! 34 f4 ♗xf4 35 ♕xe6 ♗xe3 36 fxe3 ♖xh5 37 ♕xd6 ♖g5 38 e4 g3 39 e5 ♖f2+ 40 ♔g1 g2 0-1

The queen sacrifice is interesting, and most likely sound. That's not to say it gives Black a winning position; chances are balanced. It really depends on one's style of play – and one's opponent. It might be just the thing to shock the more gentle-minded player.

Game 31
Gamota-Karasev
Moscow 1996

---

1 d4 b6 2 c4 ♗b7 3 ♘c3 e6 4 e4 ♗b4 5 ♗d3 f5 6 ♕h5+ g6 7 ♕e2 ♘f6 8 ♗g5 h6

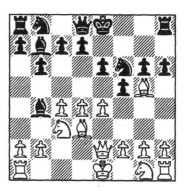

If you are looking for a 'sound' way to play for a win, then this is the move. 8...fxe4 is fine, but it releases the tension; and the queen sacrifice from the previous game is great fun, but can go wrong at a stroke. 8...h6 holds the tension but bags the bishop. It makes a virtue out of having the pawn on g6: the f5-pawn is bolstered, and the queen can slip back to g7 if necessary.

9 ♗xf6 ♕xf6 10 ♘f3 ♘c6

In most of the games played in this line Black has castled queenside, but there is nothing wrong with going the other way with 10...0-0, particularly as there is no dark-squared bishop to be concerned about; the queen also does a good job defending the king. I have found one game which follows this course: 11 0-0-0 ♗xc3 (11...♘c6!? is more challenging) 12 bxc3 fxe4 (likewise 12...♘c6!?) 13 ♗xe4 ♕f4+ 14 ♘d2 ♗xe4 15 ♕xe4 ♕xe4 16 ♘xe4 ♘c6, when a familiar ending has been reached and chances were equal in Ali-Freeman, Asian Team Championship 1995.

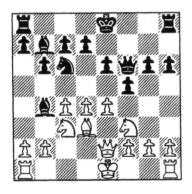

11 0-0

Alternatively, Hubert-Stanetzek, Porz 1989, continued 11 e5 ♕f7 (I prefer 11...♕g7; if White ever tries to play d4-d5, which can sometimes cause serious disruption, then it is nice to have the queen trained on the e5-pawn) 12 0-0 ♗xc3 13 bxc3 g5 (13...0-0 is stronger, and only then some action on the kingside) 14 c5! ♘e7 (or 14...bxc5!? 15 ♖ab1 with some compensation) 15 ♗a6! ♗c6 16 c4 ♕h5?! (it was better to play 16...0-0 with chances for both sides) 17 d5 exd5 18 e6 with the attack.

11...0-0-0

As I said above, I like 11...♗xc3 12 bxc3 0-0. For me, Black's king is safer on the kingside. But the big question here is whether Black can capture the pawn with 11...♘xd4!? 12 ♘xd4 ♕xd4:

a) 13 ♘b5 ♕e5 14 exf5 ♕xe2 15 ♗xe2 0-0-0 (not 15...♔d8 16 fxe6) 16 fxg6 ♖hg8

(or 16...♗e4) 17 ♘xa7+ ♔b8 18 ♘b5 ♖xg6 with compensation for the pawn.

b) 13 exf5 gxf5 14 ♗xf5 (but not 14 ♘b5? ♕g7) 14...0-0-0 with a complicated struggle ahead.

The verdict on 11...♘xd4...? Worth a try.

12 e5 ♕g7

12...♕f7 was tried in Schebler-Kalka, German Bundesliga 1985, and now the move which would worry me is 13 c5!? bxc5 14 ♗a6 with a vicious attack.

13 d5

Although this creates some confusion it destabilises the centre. As in the note above, I prefer 13 c5! when White gets a thumping attack. Here is a taste of what might happen: 13...bxc5 14 ♗a6 cxd4 15 ♘a4 g5 16 ♖fd1 d3 17 ♕xd3 g4 18 ♕b5 ♗xa6 19 ♕xa6+ ♔b8 20 ♘d4 ♘xd4 21 ♖xd4 and I cannot see Black's king surviving too long (though I must admit this was a co-operative variation).

13...♘e7 14 ♘b5 a6 15 a3 axb5 16 axb4 exd5 17 cxd5 ♘xd5 18 ♗xb5 ♕e7 19 ♖a7

see following diagram

Black's king is quite safe. The position reminds me of the Sicilian Dragon: the fianchettoed bishop holds the fort.

19...♘xb4 20 ♖fa1 ♕c5 21 ♖1a4 ♔b8 22 ♕e1 ♘c6 23 ♗xc6 ♗xc6 24 ♖a8

♖he8 25 b4 ♕d5 26 ♕a1 ♗b7 27 b5 d6
28 ♖xb7+ ♔xb7 29 ♖a7+ ♔c8 30 e6
♖xe6 31 ♘d4 ♕xd4 0-1

Game 32
Burger-Ehlvest
St Martin open 1993

1 d4 e6 2 c4 b6 3 ♘c3 ♗b4 4 e4 ♗b7 5 ♗d3 f5 6 ♕h5+ g6 7 ♕e2 ♘f6

And now, instead of 8 ♗g5 from the previous three games...

8 f3

...White attempts to maintain his big pawn centre. Speaking from Black's point of view, just what we want!

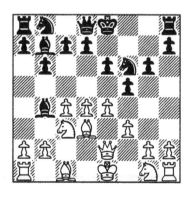

8...♘c6!

I like this move. White has bolstered the e4-pawn but it is now its d4-counterpart which is the sensitive spot.

After 8...fxe4?! 9 fxe4 ♗xc3+ (9...♘xe4 10 ♗xe4 ♗xc3+ 11 ♔d1! was good for White in Gillani-Williams, British Championship, Norwich 1994) 10 bxc3 ♘xe4 11 ♘f3 ♘f6 12 ♗g5 ♕e7 13 0-0 d6 14 ♘e5 0-0 15 ♘g4 ♘bd7 16 ♖f2 White had a winning position in Botvinnik-Wallis, simultaneous display, Leicester 1967.

9 ♗e3

9 e5? is an amusing blunder: 9...♘xd4! 10 ♕f2 ♘h5 and Black wins a pawn as 11 ♕xd4 ♗c5 traps White's queen. This was actually the continuation of Adorjan-Spassky, Toluca Interzonal 1982, which Black won in only 23 moves.

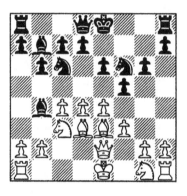

9...fxe4

Ehlvest has tried this twice (with success) but it is not Black's only option, as Plaskett has demonstrated:

a) 9...0-0 10 ♘h3 fxe4 11 fxe4 e5 12 d5 ♘d4 with advantage to Black in Crouch-Plaskett, Hitchin 1977.

b) 9...f4!? 10 ♗xf4 (10 ♗f2 e5!? is unclear – Plaskett) 10...♘xd4 11 ♕f2 ♘c6 12 ♘ge2 0-0 13 ♕h4 ♗e7 14 ♗h6 ♘e5 15 0-0-0 ♘fg4 0-1 Flear-Plaskett, Blackpool 1982.

10 fxe4 e5 11 d5 ♘d4 12 ♕d1

The following year, Gorbatov-Ehlvest, St Petersburg open 1994, continued 12 ♗xd4 exd4 13 a3 ♗xc3+ 14 bxc3 dxc3 (although White's centre appears impressive, it is difficult to do anything with it; it takes time to regain the pawn on c3, and in the meantime Black heaps on the pressure) 15 ♘f3 0-0 16 0-0 ♕e7 17 e5 ♖ae8 18 ♖ae1 ♕c5+ 19 ♔f2 ♕xf2+ 20 ♖xf2 ♘h5 21 ♖c2 c6 22 d6 c5 23 ♖xc3 ♗xf3 24 gxf3 ♖f6! 25 ♗e4 ♖xe5 26 ♗d5+ ♖xd5 27 ♖e8+ ♔g7 28 cxd5 ♖xd6 and this should have been a comfortable win for Black, but the game was drawn in 44 moves.

12...♘xe4!

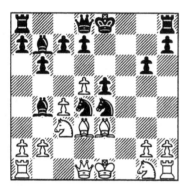

I have a feeling that White overlooked this. Black has a winning position.

13 ♗xe4 ♕h4+ 14 ♔f1 ♗xc3 15 bxc3 ♕xe4 16 ♗xd4 exd4 17 ♕xd4 0-0+ 18 ♘f3 ♖ae8 19 ♔f2 ♕e2+ 20 ♔g3 ♖e4 21 ♖he1 ♖xd4 22 ♖xe2 ♖xc4 23 ♖e7 ♗d5 24 ♖xd7 ♗xf3 25 gxf3 ♖xc3 26 ♖f1 ♖f7 27 ♖d8+ ♔g7 28 ♖f2 a5 0-1

Although I'm sure that 8 f3 isn't a poor move, in practice White has scored badly with it. There is so much pressure on the white centre that it is difficult to know where the next hit is coming from. What is encouraging about the position from Black's viewpoint is that he has several promising continuations at his disposal.

Game 33
Garces-Keene
Lausanne 1977

---

1 d4 e6 2 c4 b6 3 e4 ♗b7 4 ♘c3 ♗b4 5 ♗d3 f5 6 ♕e2

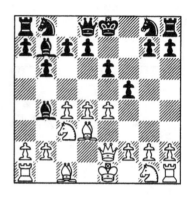

Instead of throwing in a check on h5, White plays the queen to e2 directly. Although this is less popular than 6 ♕h5+, I think it is stronger as the f5-pawn no longer has the protection of the pawn on g6. Nevertheless, Black has few difficulties as Keene demonstrates.

6...♘f6 7 ♗g5

7 f3 ♘c6! is very similar to the previous game.

7...fxe4

7...h6 is also playable here, when play will follow the lines of Game 31.

8 ♗xe4

Not 8 ♗xf6? as 8...exd3 9 ♕h5+ g6 10 ♕h4 ♗e7 11 ♗xe7 ♕xe7 12 ♕xe7+ ♔xe7 gave Black a winning ending in Razmyslov-Kengis, Bad Zwesten open 1997.

8...♗xc3+ 9 bxc3 ♗xe4 10 ♗xf6 ♕xf6 11 ♕xe4 ♘c6 12 ♘f3 0-0 13 0-0

13...♕f4!

Keene's improvement on one of his own games (13...♘a5?!, as in Sosonko-Keene, Haifa Olympiad 1976, could have been met by 14 ♘e5!). Compare the position after 13...♕f4 with Game 29 earlier in this chapter where the only difference is that the pawn is on g6 rather than g7. Keene's handling of the position is altogether more forthright than in that encounter.

14 ♖ae1 ♕xe4 15 ♖xe4 ♖f5 16 ♖d1

16...♖a5!?

Forcing White to 'do something' or he will fall into a passive position.

17 d5 ♘d8 18 ♘g5 ♖xa2 19 dxe6 ♘xe6 20 ♘xe6 dxe6 21 ♖xe6 ♔f7 22 ♖c6 ♖e8 23 ♖xc7+ ♖e7 24 ♖xe7+ ♔xe7 25 ♔f1 ♖a4 26 ♖d4 ♖a3 ½-½

Game 34
Zsu.Polgar-Speelman
Dutch League 1993

---

1 d4 e6 2 c4 ♗b4+ 3 ♘c3 b6 4 e4

After 4 d5 ♗b7 White has nothing better than a transposition to the main game with 5 e4, as 5 ♗d2 ♘f6 6 e4 0-0 7 e5 ♗xc3 8 ♗xc3 ♘e4 9 ♘f3 d6 was already very good for Black in Wohl-Lalic, Ubeda open 1998.

5...♗b7

And now for something a little differ-
ent. So far we have majored in 5 ♗d3 f5. Here we look at what happens if White blocks out the bishop with...

5 d5

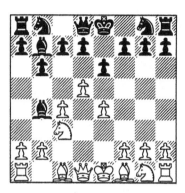

However, much to the chagrin of the unsuspecting, Black is able to upset White's plans straightaway with...

5...♕e7!

The threat is simply to take on d5, winning a pawn. So White must block the e-file.

6 ♗e2

If 6 ♗e3 then Speelman in his notes to this main game recommends 6...♘f6; while I favoured 6...f5 when faced with this position in one of my own games. The centre must crumble: 7 exf5 exd5 8 cxd5 ♘f6 9 ♗c4 (9 ♘h3 ♘xd5 10 ♕h5+ ♔d8 11 ♔d2 ♘xe3 12 fxe3 ♘c6 13 ♕g5 ♖f8 14 ♗d3 ♖f6 15 ♘f4 ♘e5 16 ♖he1 ♗e4 17 ♖ad1 ♘xd3 18 ♘xd3 ♗xd3 0-1 O.Ivanov-Chernyshov, Frydek Mistek open 1996) 9...♕e4 10 ♗e2 ♘xd5 11 ♗f3 and now in Castricum-King, Bunratty 1997, I played 11...♕xf5, which did the job, but 11...♘xc3! 12 bxc3 ♗xc3+ 13 ♔f1 ♕c4+ 14 ♗e2 ♕d5 15 ♕xd5 ♗xd5 would have left me with a winning ending.

Instead of 6 ♗e3 White may play 6 ♘ge2, though he still has problems developing his pieces after 6...exd5 7 exd5 ♘f6. Black is ready to batter down the d5-pawn with either ...b6-b5 or ...c7-c6.

6...♘f6

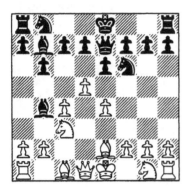

7 f3

White's pawn chain is extremely brittle. It is an easy task for Black to knock it down and in that case f2-f3 is not a helpful move: White's knight on g1 has its best square taken away and another diagonal is opened around the king.

Instead 7 ♕d4 exd5 8 exd5 ♕e4 gave Black the edge in Tartakower-Réti, Gothenburg 1920, but both 8...c6 and 8...c5 are more dynamic.

Finally, 7 ♗g5 is more solid, and if White wishes to limit the damage then after 7...h6 it is best to swap: 8 ♗xf6 ♕xf6 9 ♖c1 and White ought to be able to come out of the opening with his head on his shoulders – hardly a great achievement.

7...exd5 8 cxd5 c6 9 dxc6 ♘xc6 10 ♘h3 d5 11 exd5 0-0-0

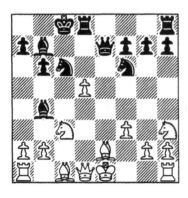

12 ♗g5

White's problem is that if she makes a normal move such as 12 0-0 then after 12...♗xc3 13 bxc3 both 13...♖xd5 and 13...♘xd5 are strong.

12...♖he8! 13 ♗xf6 gxf6 14 ♘f4 ♕e5 15 ♕d2 ♗xc3 16 bxc3 ♘b4

17 ♔f2?

Losing immediately, though White's position is unenviable. For a detailed analysis of this game I would direct you to *Jon Speelman's Best Games*.

17...♘xd5 18 ♘d3 ♘xc3 0-1

White resigned as, for instance, 19 ♖he1 ♕d4+ 20 ♔f1 ♖xe2 21 ♖xe2 ♘xe2 22 ♔xe2 ♗a6 wins material. An excellent example of how quickly an overextended centre can turn rotten.

Game 35
Rahman-Speelman
Calcutta 1998

---

1 c4 b6 2 d4 ♗b7 3 d5 e6 4 e4

It is a different story if White plays d4-d5 without the knight on c3. After the standard...

4...♗b4+

...White does not need to stick the knight on c3, but can play the more solid...

5 ♗d2

In Allen-Almeida, European Team

Championship, Haifa 1989, White played 5 ♘d2 ♕e7 6 ♕c2, and now I don't know why Black didn't play 6...exd5 7 cxd5 ♗xd5 8 ♕xc7 ♕xe4+ winning a pawn.

5...♕e7 6 ♗xb4 ♕xb4+ 7 ♕d2

7 ♘d2 is more combative, though Black can capture the pawn with impunity: 7...♕xb2 8 ♖b1 ♕f6 9 ♘gf3 ♘e7 10 ♗d3 ♘g6 11 0-0 ♘a6 12 ♖e1 (Milovanovic-Chernyshov, Djakovo open 1994) and now if 12...♘c5 Black stands well.

7...♕xd2+ 8 ♘xd2

Black has had few problems against 8 ♔xd2. Now it all depends on your style. Miles once played 8...f5 (while Spassky chose the calmer 8...♘f6 9 ♘c3 d6 10 ♗d3 0-0 11 ♘f3 c6 12 dxe6 fxe6 13 e5 dxe5 14 ♘xe5 ♘bd7 15 ♘xd7 ♘xd7 16 f3 ♖ad8 and a draw was agreed in Timman-Spassky, Tilburg 1983) 9 f3 ♘a6 10 ♘c3 ♘e7 11 ♗d3 0-0 12 exf5 exd5 13 ♖e1 ♘xf5 14 cxd5 ♘b4 15 ♘h3 ♘d6 16 ♗e4 a5 17 a3 ♘a6 18 ♗c2 b5 19 ♘e4 ♘c4+ 20 ♔c1 ♗xd5 21 ♖d1 ♘e3 22 ♖d2 ♗xe4 23 ♗xe4 ♘c5 with a clear extra pawn in H.Williams-Miles, BBC Master Game 1976.

8...f5!?

Thematic, though there are two decent alternatives:

a) 8...♘e7 (the advantage of this move is that Black can wait and see how White commits his pieces before deciding on a

method of attacking the centre) 9 g3 (horrible! White is making too many pawn moves) 9...♘a6! 10 dxe6 dxe6 11 0-0-0 ♖d8 12 f3 ♘c6 13 ♘h3 ♔e7 14 ♗e2 ♘d4 15 ♖he1 ♘b4 16 a3 ♘bc2 17 ♖h1 ♘e3 0-1 Hiebel-Lau, German Championship 1994. Another miniature. There is something about this opening that induces utter brainlessness in some players of the white pieces.

b) 8...c6 led to a slightly better position for Black after 9 dxe6 dxe6 10 e5 c5 11 f4 ♘e7 12 ♘gf3 0-0 13 ♗d3 ♘bc6 14 ♗e4 ♖ad8 in Sjodahl-Kengis, Vienna open 1996.

9 exf5?

This spoils White's structure. It would have been better to play 9 f3, which isn't as serious when the queens are off the board, though obviously White is under pressure.

9...exd5 10 ♘gf3 ♘e7 11 g4 h5! 12 ♖g1 dxc4 13 ♗xc4

13 h3!? hxg4 14 hxg4 b5 is good for Black.

13...hxg4 14 ♖xg4 ♘bc6 15 ♗d3

Or 15 ♖xg7 ♘xf5 and Black has a clear plus. Once he castles on the queenside his pawns are covered and safe, while White's pawns on h2 and f2 are bound to drop.

15...0-0-0 16 b4 ♖df8 17 b5 ♘d8 18 ♘h4

Or 18 ♘d4 ♖xh2.

18...♘f7 19 f4 ♘d6

Not 19...♘h6 20 ♖g5!

20 0-0-0 ♘dxf5 21 ♗xf5 ♘xf5 22 ♘g6 ♘e3 23 ♖dg1 ♘xg4 24 ♖xg4 ♔d8 25 ♘c4 ♗d5 26 ♘ce5 ♗e6 27 ♖g3 ♖hg8 28 ♖a3

28...d6?

Black gets there in the end, but he could have taken a shortcut to victory with 28...♖f5 29 ♖xa7 ♗d5! and wins. Black's opening has been a success and we can finish our analysis of the game. It was a hard slog to victory.

29 ♘c6+ ♔d7 30 ♘xf8+ ♖xf8 31 ♖xa7 ♖xf4 32 ♘b8+ ♔c8 33 ♘c6 ♖f1+ 34 ♔b2 ♖f2+ 35 ♔b1 ♗f5+ 36 ♔c1 g6 37 a4 ♖xh2 38 ♖a8+ ♔d7 39 ♖d8+ ♔e6 40 ♖e8+ ♔f6 41 ♖f8+ ♔g7 42 ♖e8 ♖c2+ 43 ♔d1 ♖c4 44 ♖e7+ ♔f6 45 ♖xc7 ♗c2+ 46 ♔d2 ♗xa4 47 ♖d7 ♔e6 48 ♖e7+ ♔f5 49 ♔d3 ♖c5 50 ♘d4+ ♔g5 51 ♖b7 ♗xb5+ 52 ♔d2 ♖d5 53 ♔e3 ♔g4 54 ♖xb6 ♗c4 55 ♖c6 ♗f1 56 ♖c1 ♖e5+ 57 ♔f2 ♖e4 58 ♖d1 ♗c4 59 ♖d2 d5 60 ♘c2 ♔f4 61 ♘e1 d4 62 ♘g2+ ♔g4 63 ♘e1 ♖f4+ 64 ♔g2 ♗f1+ 65 ♔g1 ♔g3 66 ♘g2 ♗xg2 67 ♖xg2+ ♔f3 68 ♔f1 ♔e4+ 69 ♔e2 ♔f5 70 ♖g1 g5 71 ♖a1 g4 72 ♖a5+ ♔e4 73 ♖a3 ♖f3 74 ♖a4 ♔f4 75 ♖xd4+ ♔g3 76 ♖a4 ♔h3 77 ♖e4 ♖f8 78 ♔e1 g3 79 ♖e7 g2 0-1

4...♗b4+ gives Black easy play, though if White plays sensibly he should be able to maintain equality. In the final game in this chapter we shall look at more dynamic attempts to break down d4-d5.

Game 36
Serper-Hodgson
Groningen 1993

---

1 c4 b6 2 d4 e6 3 e4 ♗b7 4 d5 ♘f6

If I were looking to embroil my opponent in wild complications in the hope of tripping him up then this is the move that I would choose in place of 4...♗b4+ – which is strong enough as we saw in the previous game. Apart from anything else, 4...♘f6 has the merit of developing a piece.

The other ways of having a go at White's centre are less reliable. Let's just have a quick run through these alternatives:

a) 4...b5 5 a3!? (5 cxb5 is worth a look) 5...bxc4 6 ♗xc4 c6 7 ♘c3 cxd5 8 exd5 ♘f6 9 ♘f3 exd5 10 ♗a2 ♗a6 11 ♘xd5 ♗e7 12 ♗f4 0-0 13 ♘c7 was good for White in Bagaturov-Chachibaia, Ml.Boleslav open 1993.

b) 4...♕h4?! just isn't appropriate here: 5 ♘d2 ♗b4 6 ♗d3 e5 7 ♘gf3 ♕e7 8 a3 ♗xd2+ 9 ♗xd2 ♘f6 10 0-0 with two bishops and a pleasant space advantage in Alexandrov-Simonenko, Ashkhabad 1990.

c) 4...f5?! is also a bit too gung-ho, as after 5 exf5 ♗b4+ 6 ♗d2 ♗xd2+ 7 ♕xd2 exd5 8 cxd5 ♕e7+ 9 ♗e2 ♘h6 10 ♘f3 ♘xf5 11 0-0 0-0 12 ♘c3 White had the freer game in Meister-Shabalov, Podolsk 1990.

5 ♗d3

If 5 e5 then Black's knight hops happily into the middle, 5...♘e4, and White's centre is seriously overextended.

5...b5!

This is the move that gives Black's position its kick. Having lured the bishop to d3, Black can gain a tempo when he captures on c4.

6 cxb5

White makes no attempt to hold his pawn centre together and grabs a pawn. It is a compromise, though looking at the alternatives it may well be a wise decision:

a) 6 ♘c3 (the most sensible move in the position, though Black has a good answer, which gives me faith in the system) 6...♗b4! (6...b4?! 7 ♘a4 takes the pressure off the centre and the bishop is prevented from moving to c5) 7 ♕f3 bxc4 8 ♗xc4 exd5 9 exd5 ♕e7+ 10 ♔f1 (if 10 ♘ge2 ♕c5) 10...0-0! 11 d6 ♕xd6 12 ♕xb7 ♗xc3 13 ♗e2 ♗a5 14 ♕xa8 ♕b4 15 ♘f3 ♘c6 16 a3 ♕b3 17 ♕xf8+ ♔xf8 18 g3 ♕c2 19 h3 ♗b6 and Black was well on top in Galliamova-Muhutdinov, Nabereznye Chelny 1993.

b) 6 ♕b3 looks extremely dodgy. Black has an excellent response: 6...♘a6! 7 ♘c3 (7 ♕xb5 ♘c5 8 ♗c2 c6 wins the queen) 7...♘c5 8 ♕c2 ♘xd3+ 9 ♕xd3 bxc4 10 ♕xc4 exd5 11 exd5 and Black's position is fine with two bishops and the isolated pawn on d5 to attack. It is possible just to play ...♗e7 and ...0-0, but in the game Kamp-Tischbierek, Bad Wörishofen 1996, Black played more ambitiously, aiming at the d-pawn straightaway: 11...♕e7+ 12 ♗e3 ♕b4 13 ♕e2 ♗e7 14 0-0-0 0-0 15 ♖d4 ♕d6 16 ♕d2 c5 17 ♖d3 ♘g4 18 ♗f4 ♕g6 19 ♘h3 (19 h3 ♘xf2 20 ♖g3 ♘e4 favours

Black) 19...c4 and Black held the initiative.

c) By the way, 6 e5 doesn't help too much: 6...bxc4 7 exf6 cxd3 White's centre has gone.

6...exd5

7 e5 ♘e4 8 ♘f3 a6 9 0-0 axb5 10 ♗xb5 ♗c5 11 ♘c3 0-0

11...♘xc3 12 bxc3 0-0 13 ♗d3 would only benefit White. By keeping the knight on e4 Black retains the initiative.

12 ♗f4

Not 12 ♘xd5? c6 and wins.

12...f6!?

Black is in a hurry to attack, and why not? It is best to use the knight on e4. The game plunges into a big mess.

13 exf6 ♕xf6

14 ♗xc7?

Serper thinks that 14 ♘xd5 is stronger as 14...♕xb2 15 ♗c4 ♘xf2 is met by 16

♘e3+ winning; but 15...♔h8 would be a better idea.

14...d6 15 ♘xd5 ♕xb2 16 ♗c4 ♘xf2 17 ♕b1 ♕xb1

Not 17...♘e4+? 18 ♘e3+! and wins.

18 ♖axb1 ♗a6

18...♘e4+ 19 ♔h1 ♗a6 is equal.

19 ♗xa6 ♘e4+ 20 ♔h1 ♘xa6 21 ♗b6 ♗xb6 22 ♘xb6

The position has stabilised and it is about equal, though that doesn't stop both sides from going for the win.

22...♖a7 23 ♘d4 ♖e8 24 ♖b2 ♘ac5 25 ♘d5 h6 26 ♘c6 ♖f7 27 ♖xf7 ♔xf7 28 g3 ♖c8 29 ♘d4 ♖a8 30 ♘b6?!

30 ♔g2 is stronger.

30...♖a3 31 ♘b5 ♖d3 32 ♔g2 ♖d1 33 ♔f3 d5 34 ♔e2 ♖h1 35 ♔e3 ♖e1+ 36 ♔d4 ♖d1+ 37 ♔e3 d4+ 38 ♔e2 ♖h1 39 ♘c4 ♖xh2+ 40 ♔f3 ♘g5+ 41 ♔g4 ♖xb2 42 ♘xb2 d3 43 ♔f4 d2 44 ♘c3 ♔e6 ½-½

4...♘f6 is a funky alternative to 4...♗b4+; not only that, there is a chance that White will find a way to go seriously wrong. When White plays his pawn to d5 his intention is to block out the bishop on b7 and in general to squash Black's counterplay. In practice, the opposite often occurs: pushing the pawn helps Black to get to grips with the white centre.

Summary

None of White's ideas in this chapter should cause Black problems; proof of which is the range of responses available. For instance, against 4 ♗d3, 5 ♘c3 and 6 d5 in Games 25-28, there are several solid and reliable moves (see Game 26), as well as the sharper 7...♕h4! in Games 27 and 28. Likewise 6 ♕h5+ can be met by the super solid endgame of Game 29, the queen sacrifice of Game 30, and the halfway house of Game 31. Game 32 only looks like good news for Black – in practical play the score is heavily in his favour; Game 33 does not differ significantly from 6 ♕h5+; and when the d4-pawn advances to d5, as in Games 34-36, Black can have a great time throwing stones at it and watching it crumble.

1 d4 e6 2 c4 b6 3 e4 ♗b7
4 ♘c3
    4 d5
        4...♗b4+ – *Game 35*
        4...♘f6 – *Game 36*
4...♗b4 5 ♗d3 *(D)*
    5 d5 – *Game 34*
5...f5 6 d5
    6 ♕h5+ g6 7 ♕e2 ♘f6
        8 ♗g5 *(D)*
            8...fxe4 9 ♗xe4
                9...♗xe4 – *Game 29*
                9...♘xe4 – *Game 30*
            8...h6 – *Game 31*
        8 f3 – *Game 32*
    6 ♕e2 – *Game 33*
6...fxe4 7 ♗xe4 ♘f6
    7...♕h4 8 ♕e2 ♘f6 9 ♗f3
        9...♗a6 – *Game 27*
        9...0-0 – *Game 28*
8 ♗f3 *(D)* **e5**
    8...♗xc3+ – *Game 26*
9 ♗d2 – *Game 25*

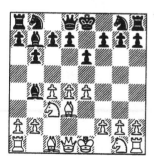
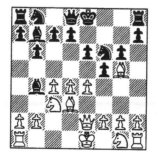
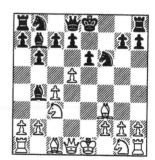

     5 ♗d3   *8 ♗g5*   *8 ♗f3*

CHAPTER FOUR

Main Line with 3 e4 ♗b7
4 ♘c3 ♗b4 5 f3 and 4 f3

1 d4 e6 2 c4 b6 3 e4 ♗b7

In this chapter White meets the attack on the e-pawn by the black bishop on b7 with the solid-looking f2-f3 either immediately (Games 37-38), or after the knight goes to c3 (Games 39-42). As we shall see, however, Black still has plenty of ways to upset his opponent.

Game 37
Babu-Miles
Sakthi 1996

---

1 d4 e6 2 c4 b6 3 e4 ♗b7 4 f3

Superficially, this gives White's centre a solid look: what can possibly go wrong

now that the bishop on b7 has been blunted by this little pawn move? Well, loads! The shift of the f-pawn opens more diagonals: there is a check on h4 to bear in mind; and White can also find himself embarrassed along the g1-a7 line. Black has a couple of ways to upset White's centre of which the most lively is...

4...f5

Miles first played this as long ago as 1979, so it is appropriate that we look at another of his games played nearly twenty years on. Another idea for Black is 4...e5, as in the next main game, where his other alternatives are also discussed.

5 exf5

5...♘h6

This was Miles's original idea. Black ambitiously sacrifices a pawn, speeding up his development and hoping to catch White's king in the middle of the board. It is possible to play more solidly just by recapturing, and results have shown that this is a reliable continuation. For example, 5...exf5 6 ♘h3 ♗b4+ 7 ♘c3 ♕h4+ 8 g3 ♕f6 9 ♗g5 ♕f7 10 ♕d3 ♘e7 11 0-0-0 0-0 12 ♘b5 ♘a6 13 ♗f4 ♘g6 14 a3 c6 15 ♘c3 ♘xf4 16 ♘xf4 ♗d6 with equal chances in Vukovic-Schussler, Smederevska Palanka 1979.

6 fxe6

Black was threatening to recapture the pawn on f5 with the knight, so something must be done. Alternatively, 6 ♗xh6 has been tried, though Black then has little to fear as this helps his development. For instance, 6...♕h4+ 7 g3 ♕xh6 8 ♕d2 (or 8 fxe6 ♗b4+ and ...0-0 with quick development) 8...♘c6!? so that if White exchanges on h6 the bishop can come to g7 to attack the d4-pawn. After 9 ♘e2 ♗b4 10 ♘bc3 ♕xd2+ 11 ♔xd2 ♘a5 12 ♘f4 ♗xf3 Black was already better in Semkov-Bricard, Sofia 1990.

6...♘f5!

A remarkable conception. Pawn number two is thrown in the pot – if White is foolish enough to accept it. Black threatens a big check on h4.

7 ♗f4

The best way to counter the threat, though two other moves have also been tried:

a) The original game with this idea continued instead 7 ♘e2 ♗d6! (the check is threatened again; in the notes to Game 39 we shall be looking at the same position but with the bishop already on b4 pinning the knight on c3 – in which case this possibility isn't open to Black) 8 h4 (an outrageous move, but how else can the check be stopped? 8 g3 allows 8...♗xf3; 8 ♗f4 gets hit by 8...♗xf4 9 ♘xf4 ♕h4+ 10 g3 ♘xg3; while Fritz suggests 8 exd7+ ♘xd7 9 ♔f2 – go on, make my day!) 8...0-0 9 ♘bc3 ♕f6 (9...dxe6 and 9...♕e7 have both been suggested as possible improvements over the game; in both cases I think that Black has a tremendous attack – what is that pawn doing on h4?) 10 c5! ♗e7 (10...bxc5? 11 e7! ♕xe7 12 ♕b3+) 11 exd7 ♕f7 12 ♕b3 ♕xb3 (12...♘xd7!) 13 axb3 ♘xd7 14 b4 ♗xh4+ 15 ♔d1 ♖fd8 and after more adventures the game Ree-Miles, Wijk aan Zee 1979, eventually ended in a draw.

b) It is interesting to see what happens if White does not prevent the check on h4 with 7 ♗d3? ♕h4+ 8 ♔f1 ♘xd4 9 ♗e4 ♗xe4 10 ♕xd4 ♗c5 11 exd7+ ♔f7 12 ♕d2 ♗d3+ 0-1 Pergericht-Boudre, Val Maubuee 1988. I can't guarantee that if you play the English Defence you are going to win as quickly as this, but let's just say your chances increase!

7...dxe6

A bit tame for Miles. Perhaps he was thinking back to his game against Ree where he went just a bit too far in the opening. I would prefer 7...♕h4+ 8 g3 ♕f6 when White is a long way from bringing his king to safety.

8 ♘e2 c5 9 d5!

A good move. Unusually, White keeps his head and prefers to return his extra pawn to speed up his development.

9...exd5 10 cxd5 ♕xd5 11 ♕xd5 ♗xd5
12 ♘bc3 ♗b7 13 ♘b5 ♘a6 14 ♘g3
♘xg3 15 hxg3 ♖d8

Black gives up a pawn to ease the pressure. A wise decision. 15...♗e7 16 0-0-0 would be wonderful for White.

16 ♔f2 ♗e7 17 ♖e1 ♔f8 18 ♗c4 ♗d5
19 ♗xd5 ♖xd5 20 ♖d1 ♘b4 21 ♖xd5
♘xd5 22 ♘xa7 ♗f6 23 ♘b5 ♔f7 24 b3
♘b4 25 a4 ♖d8 26 ♖b1 g5 27 ♗d6 ♘c2
½-½

White is still better, but Black timed his draw offer well as the position is still a bit murky. Nevertheless, I don't think the opening was at fault. Miles's sacrifice has more to it than shock value.

Game 38
Pytel-Piasetski
Buenos Aires 1978

1 c4 b6 2 d4 e6 3 e4 ♗b7 4 f3

In this position 4...f5, from the previous game, has a good (or perhaps I should say an 'interesting') reputation, but there are some alternatives to consider.

4...e5!?

To my knowledge this bizarre move has been played just once, though, curiously, I was recently flicking some pieces around on my chessboard and came up with the same idea independently. Before dealing with this move let's look at the

less interesting alternatives:

a) 4...♗b4+ has been played on a number of occasions but I find it uninspired. If White plays 5 ♗d2 then he takes the sting out of the position. The exchange of pieces robs Black's position of its dynamism.

b) A few games have been played with 4...d5, with some success from Black's point of view. However, in none of these games did White find a convincing answer. If he plays 5 cxd5 exd5 6 e5 c5 7 f4 cxd4 8 ♘f3 followed by recapturing on d4, then I think Black has a horrible position. White's kingside pawn majority is potent.

5 d5

Obviously this is not the most severe test of 4...e5. Let's take a look at what might happen if the pawn is taken with 5 dxe5 ♘c6:

a) 6 ♗f4 ♗b4+ (6...g5 7 ♗g3 ♗g7 also recovers the pawn) 7 ♘c3 ♕e7 and Black regains the pawn with a good position.

b) 6 f4 is critical. White hangs on to the booty. Black has several possible options:

b1) 6...d6 7 exd6 ♗xd6 8 ♘c3 ♕e7 (8...♕h4+ 9 g3 ♕e7 10 ♗g2 seems satisfactory for White; but 8...♗b4 9 ♕xd8+ ♖xd8 10 ♗d2 ♘f6 offers Black some compensation) 9 ♗d3 ♘f6 10 ♘d5 ♘xd5 11 cxd5 ♘b4 12 ♘e2 0-0-0 with excellent compensation for the pawn.

b2) 6...♗b4+ 7 ♗d2 ♕h4+!? 8 g3 ♕e7

ollowed by ...f7-f6 or ...d7-d6 depending on how White reacts.

b3) 6...f6 7 exf6 ♘xf6 8 e5 (or 8 ♘c3 ♗b4) 8...♘e4 9 ♘f3 ♗c5 with good attacking chances.

I don't suppose this analysis will get further until someone is silly enough to play 4...e5 again – and their opponent is mad enough to take the pawn.

5...♗c5

I rather like Black's position (though that doesn't mean he stands better). The queenside is secure and he can prepare to play the pawn break ...f7-f5 just like in a King's Indian; and before White can castle he must deal with that bishop.

6 ♘c3 a5

6...♗xg1!? 7 ♖xg1 ♕h4+ 8 g3 ♕xh2 9 ♖g2 ♕h1 would have been interesting! Apart from the immediate 10 ♘b5, causing a limited crisis, I imagine that White has good compensation for the pawn if he simply plays ♗e3, ♕d2 and 0-0-0.

7 ♘ge2 ♘a6 8 g3 ♘e7 9 ♗h3 0-0 10 ♘a4 ♗b4+ 11 ♘ec3 ♘c8

Obscure. Black is doing just fine if he sticks to more traditional strategy: 11...d6 12 a3 ♗xc3+ 13 ♘xc3 ♘c5 (or 13...♗c8) 14 ♗e3 ♗c8 (or 14...f5 15 0-0 ♗c8) 15 ♗g2 f5 16 0-0 (if 16 exf5 ♘xf5 17 ♗f2 ♘d4!?) 16...f4 17 ♗f2 ♘g6. I prefer Black. The immediate 11...f5 is also possible.

12 a3 ♗e7 13 0-0 ♘c5 14 ♗e3 ♗a6 15

b3 ♘xa4 16 ♘xa4 b5 17 cxb5 ♗xb5 18 ♖f2 ♗xa4 19 bxa4 ♗d6

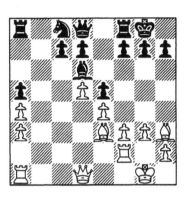

20 f4

This move merely leads to weaknesses on the kingside and centre. It would have been better to concentrate on the queenside with 20 ♕d3 ♘b6 21 ♕b5 ♕e7 22 ♖c2.

20...♘b6 21 fxe5 ♗xe5 22 ♖c1 d6 23 ♕b3 ♖b8 24 ♕b5 ♗f6 25 ♖fc2 ♗g5 26 ♗f4 ♗xf4 27 gxf4 ♕f6 28 ♖f2 ♕d4 29 ♕xa5 ♘xa4 30 ♕d2 ♕xe4 31 ♖xc7 ♘c5 32 ♗g2 ♖b1+ 33 ♖f1 ♖xf1+ 34 ♔xf1 ♕b1+ 35 ♔f2 ♘e4+ 36 ♗xe4 ♕b6+ 37 ♕e3 ♕xc7 38 ♕h3 g6 39 f5 ♕e7 40 ♕f3 ♕h4+ 41 ♔g2 ♖b8 42 ♗c2 ♕g5+ 43 ♔h3 ♖e8 44 ♗e4 h5 45 fxg6 fxg6 46 a4 ♕g4+ 0-1

Even though the 'modern' English Defence is now around 25 years old, much of the theory and many of the ideas are still very much in their infancy. I hope that 4...e5 isn't merely destined to be a footnote in history. Go on, play it! And if you do, you do so with my heartiest recommendation. Golly, I'm so impressed I might even play it myself.

Game 39
Sadler-Kengis
Koge 1997

1 d4 e6 2 c4 b6 3 e4 ♗b7 4 ♘c3 ♗b4 5

f3 f5

The standard move, but other moves are also seen from time to time. 5...♕h4+ is discussed in Game 41 and 5...♘e7 in Game 42.

6 exf5

The only testing move as 6 e5 ♘h6! is fine for Black.

6...♘h6

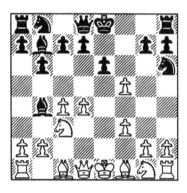

Compare this position with Game 37 after five moves. It is exactly the same apart from the bishop on b4 pinning the knight on c3. This sacrifice has been played on quite a few occasions – but the verdict remains wide open. Naturally, in place of 6...♘h6 Black can simply recapture the pawn, but that is not the reason why most of us play 5...f5. After 6...exf5 7 ♘h3 ♘c6 8 ♗g5 ♘g6 9 ♕e2+ ♔f7 10 0-0-0 White had a promising position in Piket-Timman, Wijk aan Zee 1999. The highly risky 6...♕h4+ is the subject of Game 40.

7 fxe6

7 ♗xh6 ♕h4+ 8 g3 ♕xh6 9 ♕d2!? (Sokolovs-Litus, Moscow 1992) is a safe option for White, though Black should be able to equalise. For instance, 9...♕xd2+ 10 ♔xd2 exf5 (or 10...♘c6!?).

7...♘f5

7...0-0 has been played on a number of occasions, and it is complicated, but I think White stands better. For instance, the game Arbakov-Mihalko, Budapest

1991, continued 8 ♘h3 ♕h4+ and now instead of 9 ♘f2 ♘g4!, White should have played 9 g3 ♕e7 10 ♗e2 ♕xe6 11 ♘f4 followed by 0-0 with a clear extra pawn.

8 ♗f4

This has become established as White's best move. The alternatives are less effective:

a) Hardly anyone goes the whole hog and takes the second pawn – and rightly so. The following is a blitz game, so I suppose we can forgive White, but it shows what Black can do with a massive lead in development: 8 exd7+?! ♘xd7 9 ♗f4 (9 ♕e2+ ♔f7 only encourages Black) 9...♕h4+ 10 g3 ♕e7+ 11 ♗e2 g5 12 ♕d3 ♖f8 13 ♗d2 0-0-0 14 0-0-0 ♘e5 15 ♕b1 ♘xd4 16 ♘d5 ♖xd5 0-1 Hager-Lempert, 'DataGeneral' 1992.

a) I have two games on my database with 8 ♘ge2 0-0. In both cases White lost, i.e. 9 ♕d3 (9 ♕b3?! c5! 10 exd7 ♘xd7 11 d5 ♘e5 with a massive attack in Ree-Morozevich, Tilburg rapidplay 1994) 9...♕h4+. As ever this is a useful 'destabiliser'. White can block the check with 10 g3, which weakens the long diagonal, or play 10 ♔d1 dxe6 11 ♔c2 ♘c6 with obscure complications in Gislason-Budnikov, Reykjavik open 1994, though with the king wandering all over the board the odds are in Black's favour.

8...dxe6

In view of the poor standing of this move (currently!), it is worth looking at alternatives:

a) 8...♕h4+!? 9 g3 ♕e7 (9...♕f6!?) 10 ♕d2 ♕xe6+ 11 ♗e2 d5 12 0-0-0 0-0 13 a3 ♗d6 14 ♗xd6 cxd6 15 ♘xd5 ♗xd5 16 cxd5 ♕xd5 17 ♘h3 ♘c6 18 ♕c3 (not 18 ♘f4?! ♕a2 19 ♕c3 ♘a5) 18...♘a5 19 ♔b1 ♖ac8 20 ♕d3 ♘c4 21 ♖c1 (it would have been better to play 21 ♘f4! ♕b5 22 ♕c3 ♘fe3 23 ♖c1) 21...b5 with counterplay in Szeberenyi-Czebe, Budapest 1997.

b) Sadler had faced 8...0-0 a year before the main game: 9 ♕d2 dxe6 10 0-0-0 ♘c6 11 d5 ♘a5 (or 11...exd5 12 ♕xd5+ ♕xd5 13 ♘xd5 and wins) 12 ♘h3! ♕e8 13 ♖e1 ♗xc3 14 ♕xc3 ♕a4 15 b4! ♕xa2 16 bxa5 exd5 (if 16...bxa5 17 ♗d3) 17 ♗d3 d4 18 ♕b2 ♕a4 (18...♕xa5 19 ♖e5 is no better) 19 ♘g5 bxa5 20 ♘e6 ♖fb8 21 ♘c5 ♕c6 22 ♕b5! ♕xb5 (or 22...♕f6 23 ♘d7; 22...♕g6 23 ♘xb7) 1-0 Sadler-Luther, Hastings 1995/96. 23 cxb5 ♘d6 24 ♖e7 is hopeless for Black.

9 ♕a4+

The original game with this line, Panno-Miles, Buenos Aires 1979, continued 9 ♘ge2 0-0 10 ♕d2 ♕h4+ 11 ♘g3 (or 11 g3 ♕h5) 11...♗d6 12 ♗xd6 cxd6 13 ♘ce2 ♘c6 14 0-0-0 ♘cxd4 15 ♘xd4 ♘xg3 16 hxg3 ♕xh1 17 ♘xe6 and Black was better, but the position is difficult. Miles eventually won on time. From a theoreti-

cal point of view this game isn't very relevant as the text move is so strong.

9...♘c6 10 0-0-0

10 d5 is also quite dangerous for Black.

10...♘fxd4

10...♗xc3 11 bxc3 0-0 12 ♘h3 ♘a5 13 ♗d3 ♕h4, as in Muhvic-Markovic, Croatian Team Championship 1995, is still a bit messy, but should be better for White.

11 ♘b5!

11 ♘h3 was successful in Conquest-Plaskett, Hastings open 1987, but Sadler's move is more direct and, above all, stronger.

11...0-0 12 ♗xc7

Not a random capture. White has calculated that he is winning material.

12...♕e7

12...♕g5+ (12...♕d7 13 ♘xd4 wins a piece) 13 f4 ♕g6 14 ♘xd4 ♘xd4 15 ♖xd4 ♗xg2 16 ♗d3 ♕e8 17 ♕xb4 ♗xh1 is winning for White.

13 ♘xd4 ♘xd4 14 ♖xd4 ♗c5 15 ♖d7 ♕g5+ 16 ♔c2 ♖ac8 17 ♘h3 ♕g6+ 18 ♔d2

Perhaps 18 ♔b3!?

18...♕e8 19 ♖xg7+

19 b3 ♖f7 20 ♖xf7 ♕xf7 must have looked rather terrifying from White's point of view. Instead, Sadler goes for the ending – a safe bet.

19...♔xg7 20 ♗e5+ ♔g8 21 ♕xe8 ♖cxe8 22 ♗d3

With two pawns for the exchange and a solid position White has a clear advantage.
22...♖d8 23 ♔c3 ♗xf3 24 ♗xh7+ ♔xh7 25 ♘g5+ ♔h6 26 ♘xf3 ♖g8 27 g3 ♖df8 28 ♗f4+ ♔h5 29 ♘e5 ♗d6 30 ♖e1 ♖f5 31 ♘d3 ♗xf4 32 ♘xf4+ ♔g4 33 ♖xe6

White should be winning, but it isn't easy and Black just manages to hang on in the end.
33...♖h8 34 ♖e2 b5 35 b3 bxc4 36 ♔xc4 ♖c8+ 37 ♔b4 ♔f3 38 ♖d2 a5+ 39 ♔a4 ♔e3 40 ♖e2+ ♔f3 41 ♖d2 ♔e3 42 ♖e2+ ♔f3 43 ♖b2 ♔e3 44 a3 ♔d4 45 ♖d2+ ♔c3 46 ♖d7 ♔c2 47 ♘d5 ♖f3 48 b4 axb4 49 axb4 ♖a8+ 50 ♔b5 ♖b8+ 51 ♔c6 ♖f2 52 b5 ♖xh2 53 b6 ♖h6+ 54 ♔c7 ♖bxb6 55 ♘xb6 ♖g6 56 ♘d5 ♖xg3 ½-½

Sadler's handling of the opening was powerful. If improvements aren't found

earlier then Miles's pawn sacrifice with ...f7-f5 and ...♘h6 appears dubious – at least against a well prepared opponent. As can be seen from the other games in the notes, those White players who aren't familiar with the theory often manage to go horribly wrong at a very early stage.

Game 40
Piket-Speelman
Andorra Zonal 1998

From a theoretical standpoint this next game is not particularly relevant, but I wanted to include it for its sheer verve. It was played in the last round of a Zonal tournament where Speelman absolutely had to play for a win to have a chance of qualifying for the next stage of the World Championship. His method was brutal, but successful. I'm grateful for his notes on which I have based my comments.
1 d4 e6 2 c4 b6 3 e4 ♗b7 4 ♘c3 ♗b4 5 f3 f5 6 exf5 ♕h4+

Never been seen before, and probably won't be seen again.

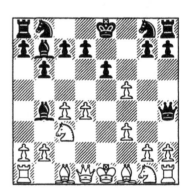

7 g3 ♕f6 8 fxe6 ♘e7 9 ♗h3 h5!?

Improvisation. Speelman realised that his original intention of 9...dxe6 would have just left him with a rotten position: 10 ♘ge2 (threatening to castle, when White has an extra pawn and a good position) 10...♕xf3 11 ♖f1 ♕h5 12 ♘f4 ♕xd1+

13 ♔xd1 when White wins the pawn on e6 with an excellent position to boot.

10 ♗f4

The point of ...h7-h5 was to discourage White from developing the knight: 10 ♘ge2 h4 with irritating pressure.

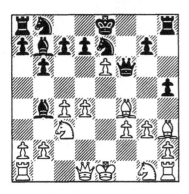

10...dxe6

Now if 10...h4 then 11 ♗e5 is strong.

11 ♕d2 ♘bc6 12 0-0-0 ♗xc3 13 ♕xc3

13 bxc3 ♘a5 14 ♕e2 ♗a6 gives Black some play.

13...g5 14 ♗e3

If 14 ♗xc7 then Black can create some confusion with 14...♖c8 15 ♗d6 g4, though I'm sure White is still better after 16 ♗g2.

14...g4!?

Tricky.

15 fxg4 hxg4 16 ♗xg4

If 16 ♗g2 ♘b4 17 ♕d2 ♕g6 18 b3?!

♘d3+ Black wins.

16...♘b4 17 ♕xb4 ♗xh1

At least Black has the exchange for his trouble but his position is a wreck.

18 ♘h3

After 18 h4 ♖g8 19 ♗h5+ ♔d7 Black is still in the game – just about.

18...♕g6 19 ♗g5 c5!

The only move to keep going. After this White misses several good continuations, but Speelman always manages to keep the position unstable enough to give himself chances.

20 dxc5

For what it is worth, 20 ♕d2 ♖d8 21 d5 ♗xd5 22 ♕f4 looks good for White.

20...♖xh3 21 ♕d2 ♖h7

22 ♖xh1

It might have been better to play 22 ♕d7+ ♔f8 23 ♖f1+ ♘f5 24 ♕d6+ ♔f7 25 h4 ♗e4 26 ♕e5 ♗d3 (26...♗g2 27 ♖xf5+ exf5 28 ♗xf5 wins for White) 27 ♗xf5 ♗xf5 (not 27...exf5 28 ♕d5+ ♕e6 29 ♕xd3) 28 g4 with an attack.

22...♕e4 23 ♖d1?

23 ♕d1 ♕xc4+ 24 ♔b1 is still messy. If White can organise himself then Black's king will be in trouble.

23...♕xg4 24 ♕d7+ ♔f8

25 ♗f4

25 ♗xe7+ ♖xe7 26 ♖f1+ ♔g8 27 ♕xe7 ♕xc4+ 28 ♔d2 ♕xf1 29 ♕g5+ ♔f7 30 ♕h5+ ♔e7 31 ♕h7+ ♕f7 32 ♕h4+ ♔e8 33 ♕h8+ ♕f8 34 ♕h5+ ♔d7 also wins for Black.

25...♖xh2 26 c6 ♕e2 27 ♗d2 ♕xc4+ 28 ♔b1 ♕e4+ 0-1

29 ♔a1 ♖h1 is the simplest. An inspiring game.

Game 41
Sashikiran-Speelman
British Ch., Torquay 1998

---

1 d4 e6 2 c4 b6 3 e4 ♗b7 4 ♘c3 ♗b4 5 f3

If one is going to play 5...f5 with the idea of sacrificing a pawn then I think one needs a special mentality: do or die. That's why it might not appeal to everyone. And that's the reason...

5...♕h4+

...has found more advocates over the

years. It has the merit of causing some confusion in White's position without the dangers which the ...f7-f5 pawn sacrifice implies.

6 g3 ♕h5

The check has created a weakness on the long diagonal, which Black would like to blast open with ...f7-f5 – as usual. Instead of retreating the queen there is an argument for throwing in the exchange on c3 first with 6...♗xc3+ 7 bxc3 ♕h5. Normally I would not advocate exchanging on c3 without being pushed by a2-a3 (the dark-squared bishop can be useful elsewhere) but here White can prevent the exchange, if he wishes, with 7 ♗d2 (see the next note).

7 ♘h3

The most forceful move, attempting to gain time on the queen. White has two main alternatives:

a) I once faced 7 ♗g2 but this hardly causes Black any problems. I was able to get on with attacking White's centre without delay by playing 7...♗xc3+ bxc3 f5 9 e5 ♘c6 10 ♘h3 ♘a5 (White's pawns are chronically weak and the position has great similarities to the Nimzo-Indian Defence) 11 ♘f4 ♕f7 12 c5 ♘e7 0-0 g5 14 ♘d3 f4 15 ♖f2 ♘f5 16 gxf4 gxf 17 ♗xf4 ♖g8 18 ♔h1 0-0-0 and White was getting done over on the kingside in Vaidya-King, Dhaka 1993.

b) The reason why I was suggesting that it might be more accurate to exchange on c3 a move before is that White can play 7 ♗d2. It doesn't look the most active move, and so perhaps for that reason it has only been tried once. Nevertheless, it is slightly irritating for Black, e.g. 7...f5 8 exf5 ♕xf5 9 ♘b5! (the point) 9...♗xd2+ 10 ♕xd2 ♘a6 11 0-0-0 ♘e7 12 ♗d3 ♕f6 (the knight on b5 is awkward for Black to deal with, but then again White has difficulties developing his kingside – unless he wishes to sacrifice a pawn) 13 ♘h3!? ♕xf3 14 ♘g5 ♕h5 15 ♖hf1 h6 16 ♘f7 (16 ♘e4!?) 16...0-0 with bizarre complications in Ree-Miles, Amsterdam 1978.

7...e5

Most people have tended to reach for the f-pawn in this situation, but Speelman has shown a penchant for this move in the English Defence. For instance, think back to his game against Lobron in the first chapter (Game 9), and check out the notes to move six to the next main game, Hodgson-Bischoff. Instead, here's an example of the f-pawn in action: 7...f5 8 ♘f4 ♕f7 9 d5?! (better was 9 exf5 ♕xf5 10 ♗d3 ♕f7 11 0-0 with an unclear position) 9...fxe4 10 fxe4 e5 11 ♘g2 ♘f6 12 ♗d3 ♗xc3+ 13 bxc3 d6 14 c5 bxc5 15 0-0 0-0 16 g4 ♕e8 17 ♖b1 ♗c8 18 h3 ♘bd7 19 ♗g5 ♕g6 20 ♗e3 ♘b6 with an extra pawn and the advantage in Borges Mateos-Arencibia, Ca-

pablanca memorial, Havana 1998.

8 d5

8 dxe5 ♗xc3+ 9 bxc3 ♕xe5 is good for Black. White's pawns are terribly weak.
8...♘e7 9 ♘f2 0-0 10 ♗e2 ♕g6 11 ♘d3 ♗xc3+ 12 bxc3 d6

The position is very similar to the Nimzo-Indian Defence: Black has the pawn on c4 to attack; while White has a space advantage and the bishops. Chances are balanced.

13 g4

Preventing Black from playing ...f7-f5.
13...♘d7 14 ♗e3 ♘c5 15 ♘f2!?

If 15 ♘xc5 dxc5 followed by ...♘e7-c8-d6, and ...a7-a5 and ...♗a6 to attack c4.
15...f6 16 h4 ♕e8 17 ♖b1 a5 18 ♖h2 ♗a6 19 ♕d2

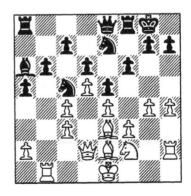

19...♘g6

I'm not sure why Speelman didn't just

go for the c-pawn straightaway with 19...♕a4.

20 h5 ♘f4 21 ♗xf4 exf4 22 ♕xf4 ♕a4 23 ♕d2 ♗xc4 24 ♗xc4 ♕xc4 25 ♖b2 a4 26 ♕d4 a3 27 ♖c2 ♕b5 28 c4 ♕a4 29 ♘d3 ♕e8 30 ♖he2 ♖a4 31 ♔f2 g5 32 hxg6 hxg6 33 ♔g2 g5 34 ♖e1 ♘xd3 35 ♕xd3 ♕e5 36 ♖h1 ♔g7 37 ♕b3 ♖aa8 38 ♕c3 ♖h8 39 ♖xh8 ½-½

The final position is about equal, though who knows what was going on earlier? Extremely complicated. Anyway, it is clear that Speelman's 7...e5 is a viable continuation for Black.

Game 42
Hodgson-Bischoff
Linares 1996

---

1 c4 b6 2 d4 e6 3 e4 ♗b7 4 ♘c3 ♗b4 5 f3

Because 5...f5 and 5...♕h4+ are such thematic 'English' moves, it doesn't seem entirely necessary to me to look any further. However, a little research has revealed that there is more than one player who has played the calm...

5...♘e7

...in this position. Black is treating the opening like a Nimzo-Indian. He might still go for ...f7-f5, hitting the centre, or he might play against the doubled c-pawns (if he manages to double them that is).

6 ♗d3

White can make an attempt to avoid the doubled c-pawns if he wishes with 6 ♕b3, for example, though he then runs the risk of falling behind with his development. I have seen one game where Black tried 6...♘a6 and then ...f7-f5, but I prefer 6...♘bc6 – there is more chance of a 'hit' against the queen. 6...c5 also isn't bad. Finally, 6 ♗d2 is less good as 6...f5 is a bit embarrassing.

6...♘bc6

Instead, twenty years ago Speelman tried his favourite move 6...e5!? 7 a3 (if 7 dxe5 ♘bc6 8 f4 d6 9 exd6 ♕xd6 Black has compensation for the pawn) 7...exd4 (I prefer 7...♗xc3+ 8 bxc3 ♘bc6 9 ♘e2 d6 followed by attacking the c4-pawn in traditional 'Nimzo' style with ...♕d7, ...♘a5 and ...♗a6) 8 axb4 dxc3 9 bxc3 ♘g6 10 ♘e2 ♘c6 11 0-0 ♘ce5 12 ♗c2 0-0 13 c5 d6 14 cxb6 axb6 15 ♖xa8 ♗xa8 16 f4 and White was a bit better in Christiansen-Speelman, Hastings 1978.

7 ♘ge2 ♗xc3+ 8 bxc3 d6 9 0-0 ♕d7

If we compare this position with one from the Sämisch variation of the Nimzo Indian, then Black is doing fairly well. He doesn't have to worry about his knight being booted away from f6, and his solid centre enables him to attack the c4-pawn.

10 f4

Or 10 ♗a3 ♗a6 11 c5 ♗xd3 12 ♕xd

dxc5 13 ♖ad1 ♘a5 14 ♕c2 ♕c6 15 d5 exd5 16 exd5 ♕d7 17 c4 0-0 with a clear extra pawn for Black in Gropp-Ruzele, Berlin 1997.

10...♘a5 11 f5 exf5 12 exf5 0-0-0

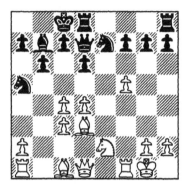

The only place to be now that the f-pawn has advanced.

13 d5

Perhaps White had missed earlier that 13 f6 gxf6 14 ♖xf6 ♘xc4 would be rather strong for Black. The g2-pawn is going to cave in.

13...♗a6 14 c5 ♗xd3 15 c6 ♕e8 16 ♕xd3 ♘xd5 17 ♕xd5 ♕xe2 18 ♕xf7 ♖hf8 19 ♕d5 ♖de8 20 ♗f4 ♕e4 21 ♕xe4 ♖xe4 22 g4 ♘xc6 23 ♔g2 ♖c4 24 ♖f3 h5 25 h3 hxg4 26 hxg4 g6 0-1

The loss of pawn number two is the final straw for White.

5...♘e7 is a respectable alternative to the (potential) madness of the alternatives we have already considered.

Summary

I relish games where my opponent plays f2-f3 – all those lovely open diagonals! Miles's sacrifice in Game 37 seems sound, though when repeated with the knight on c3 and the bishop on b4 (Game 39) it is less clear; Sadler's play in that game is convincing. But Black does not have to go in for this pawn sacrifice if he doesn't wish to, as proved by Games 38, 41 and 42.

1 d4 e6 2 c4 b6 3 e4 ♗b7

4 ♘c3
> 4 f3
>> 4...f5 – *Game 37*
>> 4...e5 – *Game 38*

4...♗b4 5 f3 (D) f5
> 5...♕h4+ – *Game 41*
> 5...♘e7 – *Game 42*

6 exf5 (D) ♘h6
> 6...♕h4+ – *Game 40*

7 fxe6 (D) – *Game 39*

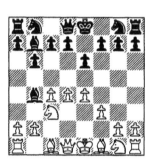

5 f3

6 exf5

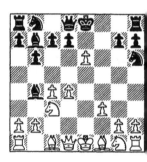

7 fxe6

CHAPTER FIVE

Main Line with 3 e4 ♗b7
4 ♘c3 ♗b4 5 ♕c2 and 4 ♕c2

1 d4 e6 2 c4 b6 3 e4 ♗b7

In this chapter we shall look at games in which White defends the e-pawn with ♕c2, either immediately (Games 43-46), or combined with ♘c3 (Games 47-49). Again, Black does not lack ways to create counterplay, though I must say that from a theoretical viewpoint the immediate 4 ♕c2 is perhaps the most solid way for White to play once he has advanced his three pawns into the centre.

Game 43
Remlinger-Rogers
Philadelphia 1986

1 d4 e6 2 c4 b6 3 e4 ♗b7 4 ♕c2

This solid move has the advantage, compared to 4 f3, of keeping the rest of the pawns intact and healthy – though the queen is sometimes open to a hit on c2; and the pawn on d4 is a little vulnerable. From this position, attention has centred on...

4...♕h4

...ever since it was first played in the Polugayevsky-Korchnoi Candidates match in 1977, and that is the move I shall be concentrating on. For alternatives to 4...♕h4, see Game 46.

5 ♘d2

The least troublesome method of defending the e-pawn – in theory. The alternatives are:

a) The thoughtless 5 ♗d3?! produced another miniature in Brunk-Berebora, Berlin open 1998: 5...♘c6 6 d5 (6 ♘f3 ♕g4 7 0-0 ♘b4 8 ♕e2 ♘xd3 9 ♕xd3 ♗xe4 is obviously good for Black) 6...♘b4 7 ♕e2 ♘f6 8 e5 ♘g4 9 ♔d2 ♕g5+ 10 ♔d1 ♘xf2+ 11 ♕xf2 ♕xc1+ and White could have resigned here.

b) 5 d5 engages prematurely, e.g. 5...f5 (or 5...♘f6!? 6 ♗d3 ♘a6!) 6 exf5 exd5 7 cxd5 ♗xd5 8 ♕xc7 with an unclear position in Koukolik-Tratar, Ceske Budejovice open 1995.

c) 5 ♘c3 allows a pin with 5...♗b4, though this isn't too bad (see Games 47-49).

5...♗b4

The pressure increases.

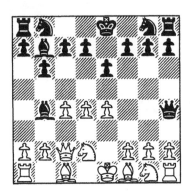

6 ♗d3 f5

6...♕g4 is a decent alternative – see Game 45.

7 ♘gf3 ♗xd2+

This was the move originally played in Polugayevsky-Korchnoi. For the alternatives, 7...♕h5 and 7...♕g4, see Game 44.

8 ♗xd2

By far the best move. Instead Polugayevsky played the ugly 8 ♔f1?! He must have been completely psyched out by Korchnoi's opening. After 8...♕h5 9 ♗xd2 ♘f6 10 exf5 ♗xf3 11 gxf3 ♘c6 12 ♗c3 Black has a pleasant choice

a) 12...0-0 13 ♖e1 ♕h3+ 14 ♔e2 ♖ae8 15 ♔d1 e5! 16 dxe5 ♘xe5 17 ♗e2 ♘xf3 18 ♕d3 ♖xe2 19 ♖xe2 ♕g2 20 ♖he1 ♘xe1 21 ♔xe1 ♕xh2 (21...♕h1+! 22 ♔d2 ♕xh2 is even stronger) 22 ♖e7 ♕g1+ 23 ♔e2 ♕g4+ 24 ♔e1 h5 25 ♕g3 ♕xg3 26 fxg3 and White had some drawing chances, though he eventually lost in Polugayevsky-Korchnoi, Candidates match 1977. The first time that the English Defence had succeeded at the highest level.

b) 12...0-0-0 13 ♖e1 ♖he8 14 ♖e2 ♕h3+ 15 ♔e1 ♕xf3 16 ♖g1 ♕f4 17 ♖xg7 exf5 18 ♕d2 ♖xe2+ 19 ♔xe2 ♖e8+ 20 ♔f1 ♕xh2

21 ♗xf5 ♘e7 22 ♗d3 ♘g6 23 f3 ♕h1+ 24 ♔f2 ♖f8 25 ♕g5 ♘h4 26 ♔e2 ♕xf3+ 27 ♔d2 ♘e4+ 28 ♗xe4 ♕xe4 29 ♕g4 ♖f2+ 0-1 Quinn-Speelman, Dublin Zonal 1993.

Finally, 8 ♘xd2 isn't very testing, as after 8...♘f6 White has problems on the long diagonal.

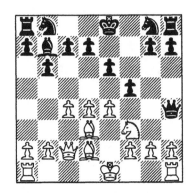

8...♕g4 9 ♘e5 ♕xg2 10 0-0-0 fxe4

The laudable attempt to exchange off some pieces with 10...♗xe4 unfortunately loses to 11 ♖hg1 ♗xd3 12 ♕xd3 ♕e4 (12...♕xf2 13 ♘f3 and Black must jump through hoops to save the queen) 13 ♕g3 g6 14 ♘xg6, as in Vujatovic-Le Blancq, Lloyds Bank open, London 1991.

11 ♗e2

This position was analysed by Korchnoi's team in the 1977 match immediately after the game against Polugayevsky (see above). According to

Messrs Keene, Tisdall and Plaskett in their book *The English Defence* Korchnoi was reluctant to repeat the whole line as he thought this position was too dangerous for Black. In that book some fairly detailed analysis of this position is given, though without any examples from actual play. Since then a few players have been brave enough to take on the black side (with mixed results) and those games help us to form an assessment of the variation.

11...♘c6

Recommended in the book above as one of the best continuations, but still doubtful. Alternatively, 11...♘f6 is a plausible move:

a) 12 ♗e3 ♕h3 13 ♖dg1 ♘c6 (13...h6 did not turn out well in Rogers-Lau, Wijk aan Zee 1989, after 14 ♖xg7 ♘c6 15 ♘g6! 0-0-0 16 ♘xh8 ♖xh8 and White ought to convert) 14 ♖g3 ♕f5 15 ♖g5 ♘xd4 16 ♕d1 ♘xe2+ 17 ♕xe2 ♕h3 18 ♖hg1 d6 19 ♖xg7 0-0-0 20 ♘f7 ♕xh2 when in Webster-Adams, Prestwich 1990, with so many pawns for the exchange, Black shouldn't be worse, but the position is still extremely complex.

b) 12 ♖hg1 was recommended in the above book as practically winning for White:

b1) 12...♕xf2 was the only move they analysed, and that is indeed good for White: 13 ♗h6! ♕xh2 (13...g6 14 ♖gf1 ♕xh2 15 ♗g7; or 13...gxh6 14 ♗h5+) 14 ♗xg7 ♖g8 15 ♗xf6 ♖xg1 16 ♗h5+ ♕xh5 17 ♖xg1 and White is winning – Keene, Plaskett and Tisdall.

b2) However, they failed to consider 12...♕xh2, when it looks like White should be able to win somehow, though it is difficult to prove conclusively, e.g. 13 ♖h1 (13 ♖xg7 ♘c6 14 ♗g5 0-0-0!) 13...♕xf2 14 ♗h6! (this is the trick that makes the difference) 14...e3 (not 14...gxh6? 15 ♗h5+) 15 ♖df1 (rather than 15 ♖hf1 ♗e4!?) 15...♕g3 (or 15...♗xh1 16

♖xf2 exf2 17 ♗xg7 ♗e4 18 ♕d1 ♖g8 19 ♗xf6 ♖g1 20 ♗f1 with a clear edge for White) 16 ♖hg1 ♕h2 17 ♗xg7 ♖g8 18 ♕d1 ♘e4 19 ♗h5+ ♔e7 20 ♖f7+ ♔d6 21 ♘f3 and White is winning. Some very 'Fritz'-inspired variations, I admit; but anyway, my gut feeling here is that Black is lost.

12 ♘xc6 ♗xc6 13 d5

13...♗b7

Perhaps 13...exd5!? 14 cxd5 ♗xd5! 15 ♖hg1 ♕xh2 (the lads above didn't consider this one, but 15...♕xf2 16 ♗h6 is hopeless) and Black is still in with a shout, e.g. 16 ♗c3 ♘f6 with an unclear position.

14 ♗h5+ g6

15 ♗c3

Instead, 15 ♕c3! looks like a winning move, e.g. 15...♘f6 (or 15...0-0-0 16 ♕xh8 gxh5 17 ♖hg1 and White is winning) 16

♕xf6 ♖f8 17 ♕g7 ♖f7 (if 17...0-0-0 18 dxe6) 18 ♕h8+ ♔e7 19 ♕e5 gxh5 20 ♗g5+ and wins.

15...♕g5+ 16 ♔b1 e5 17 f4 ♕xf4 18 ♖df1 ♕g5 19 ♕xe4 d6 20 ♗d1 0-0-0 21 ♖hg1 ♕e7 22 ♗d2 ♖f8 23 ♕g4+ ♔b8 24 ♗g5 ♕g7 25 ♕d7 ♕xd7 26 ♖xf8+ ♗c8 27 ♗g4 ♕g7 28 ♖xc8+ ♔b7 29 ♖f1 h5 30 ♖cf8 hxg4 31 ♖1f7 ♕xf7 32 ♖xf7 ♘h6 33 ♖g7 ♘f5 34 ♖xg6 ♖xh2 35 ♗c1 g3 36 ♖g5 g2 0-1

7...♗xd2+ is interesting but, if you play it, you (and your opponent!) must be tactically alert at all times. Before trying it out I would do some thorough research on the pawn sacrifice played in this game. My feeling is that it is good for White, though the evidence so far would suggest 'case not proven'.

Game 44
Remlinger-Kengis
Gausdal 1991

1 d4 e6 2 c4 b6 3 e4 ♗b7 4 ♕c2 ♕h4 5 ♘d2 ♗b4 6 ♗d3 f5 7 ♘gf3

This is all as in the previous game, but instead of 7...♗xd2+, Black plays:
7...♕h5

7...♕g4!? is also playable, e.g. 8 0-0 ♗xd2 9 ♘xd2 (not 9 ♗xd2? fxe4 10 ♘e5 exd3 and wins) 9...♘c6 10 f3 ♕h4 11 ♕c3 ♘f6 (11...♕f6!? 12 e5 ♕h4 13 f4 ♘h6 14

♘f3 ♕h5 15 b4 ♘e7 with counterplay wa… already quite strange in Wilson-Avni… Hastings Challengers 1995/96) 12 b4 fxe… 13 fxe4 0-0 14 d5 ♘g4 15 h3 ♘f2 16 ♗c… ♘d4 17 ♕xd4 ♘xh3+ 18 gxh3 ♕g3+ 1… ♔h1 ♕xh3+ 20 ♔g1 ♕g3+ 21 ♔h1 ½-½ Knechtl-Heilinger, Austrian Team Cham… pionship 1996.

8 a3

The critical 8 0-0!? ♘f6 9 exf5 ♗xd2 1… ♘xd2 ♕g4 is unclear according to Kengis.

8...♗xd2+ 9 ♗xd2 ♘f6 10 exf5 ♗xf3 11 gxf3 ♘c6

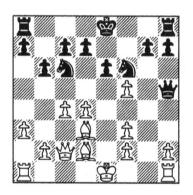

12 ♗c3

Or 12 ♗e3 e5 (12...♕xf3 is stronger, a… White's king is caught in the middle, e.g… 13 ♖g1 exf5 14 ♗xf5 0-0-0 with an attack… 13 dxe5 ♘xe5 14 0-0-0 ♘xd3+ 15 ♕xd… ♕xf3 16 ♖hg1 0-0-0 17 ♖xg7 ♖hf8 with… good counterplay in Webster-King, British… Championship, Eastbourne 1990.

12...♕xf3 13 ♖g1 0-0-0 14 ♕e2 ♕f4 1… ♕e3 ♕xh2 16 0-0-0 exf5 17 ♖h1 ♕d6… 18 ♗xf5

Black is a pawn up, but matters are… complicated by the presence of the two… bishops. However, the knights have soli… protection and weak squares to aim for, s… Black is already better.

18...♖de8 19 ♕g3 ♕xg3 20 fxg3 ♘a5… 21 ♗xa5

see following diagram

After 21 c5 ♘c4 Black also has the better game.

21...bxa5 22 ♖de1 g6 23 ♗c2 ♔d8 24 ♖e5 ♖xe5 25 dxe5 ♘h5 26 g4 ♘f4 27 ♔d2 h5 28 ♔e3 g5 29 gxh5 ♖xh5 30 ♖xh5 ♘xh5 31 ♔f3 ♘g7 32 ♔g4 ♘e6 33 c5 ♔e7 34 ♗f5 a4 35 c6 dxc6 36 ♗c2 ♘d4 37 ♗xa4 ♔e6 38 ♔xg5 ♔xe5 39 ♔g6 c5 40 ♔f7 ♔d6 41 ♔e8 ♘c6 42 ♗xc6 ♔xc6 43 ♔e7 c4 44 ♔e6 a5 45 ♔e7 ♔b5 46 ♔d7 ♔a4 47 ♔xc7 ♔b3 0-1

A successful game from Black's point of view, but 8 a3 is not the best move. 8 0-0 must be investigated.

Game 45
Parker-Sher
Copenhagen 1996

---

1 d4 e6 2 c4 b6 3 e4 ♗b7 4 ♕c2 ♕h4 5 ♘d2 ♗b4 6 ♗d3

Instead of 6...f5, in the past five years there have been some games with...

6...♕g4

...tempting White into weakening his structure with g2-g3, but in every game I have seen White has made the concession...

7 ♔f1

Although White cannot castle, he will gain time by attacking Black's queen. 7 g3 is met by 7...f5!

7...f5

Black must stir it up to get anything at all from the position.

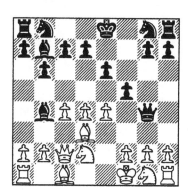

8 h3

White has two main alternatives here:

a) 8 ♘gf3 ♗xd2 and now:

a1) 9 ♗xd2 fxe4 10 ♘e5 exd3 and Black wins.

a2) 9 ♘xd2 and:

a21) 9...♘c6 10 f3 (not 10 ♕c3 ♕d1 mate!) 10...♕h5 (or 10...♕h4 11 ♕c3 ♘f6 with counterplay) 11 ♕c3 fxe4 12 ♘xe4 0-0-0 and Black has sufficient counterplay.

a22) 9...♘f6 10 h3 (or 10 f3 ♕h4 11 exf5 ♘c6 12 ♘b3 ♘b4 13 ♕c3 ♘xd3 14 ♕xd3 0-0 with counterplay) 10...♕h4 (perhaps 10...♕g6!?) 11 exf5 0-0 12 fxe6 ♕xd4 13 ♘b3 ♕e5 14 exd7 ♘bxd7 and again Black has enough counterplay.

a3) 9 ♘e5 ♕h4 10 ♘f3 ♕h5 11 ♗xd2 ♘f6 12 exf5 ♗xf3 13 gxf3 ♘c6 14 ♗c3, when via quite a different move order we have transposed to Game 43. Here Korchnoi played 12...0-0 and achieved a good position, while Speelman went the other way and achieved the same.

b) 8 f3 was, from a theoretical viewpoint, successful in the game Levitt-Ehlvest, New York 1994, so it is worthy of some close investigation. After 8...♕h4 9 exf5 we reach the first major crossroads:

b1) 9...♘c6. In principle, this is the move I would like to play, just developing quickly to get some attack, but it appears to fail: 10 fxe6 dxe6 11 ♘e2 0-0-0 12 a3 ♗xd2 13 ♗xd2 ♘xd4 14 ♘xd4 ♕xd4 15 ♗c3 ♕xd3+? (perhaps 15...♕d7! 16 ♗xh7 ♘f6 and Black has some compensation for the pawn, though for some people's taste it may not be sufficient! – DK) 16 ♕xd3 ♖xd3 17 ♗xg7 and White is winning – Jonathan Levitt.

b2) 9...exf5!? 10 ♗xf5 ♘c6 11 ♕e4+ (not 11 ♘b3 ♕e1 mate!) 11...♕xe4 12 ♗xe4 ♘f6 with some compensation in view of Black's superior development.

b3) And finally, the actual game, 9...♕xd4 10 ♘e2 (10 a3 ♗c5 11 ♘b3 is even stronger, according to Levitt) 10...♕h4 11 fxe6 ♘f6 12 ♘g3 0-0 13 ♘de4 ♗xe4 14 ♗xe4 ♘c6 15 exd7 ♘h5 16 ♗d5+ ½-½ Levitt-Ehlvest, New York 1994. Here, as Levitt himself points out, instead of agreeing a draw, he should have played 16...♔h8 17 ♗f4! with a clear advantage.

8...♕g6

The most sensible retreat, but 8...♕h5 9 exf5 ♘c6 (or 9...♘f6) is also possible.

9 ♘gf3 ♗xd2 10 ♘e5 ♕f6 11 ♗xd2 ♘e7 12 ♘f3 h6 13 ♖e1 0-0

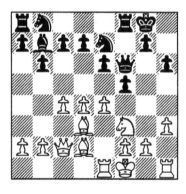

If White were castled then he would simply have a great position, but freeing the rook from h1 is not going to be easy.

14 d5! ♘a6 15 ♗c3 ♕f7 16 ♘e5 ♕e8 17 b4 c5 18 a3

Or 18 b5!? ♘b4 19 ♗xb4 cxb4 with counterplay.

18...cxb4 19 axb4 d6 20 ♘f3 fxe4 21 ♖xe4 e5 22 ♕e2 ♖f7 23 ♖h4 ♘f5 24 ♖h5 g6 25 ♗xf5 gxh5 26 ♗e6 ♘c7 27 ♘xe5 ♘xe6 28 ♘xf7 ♕xf7 29 dxe6 ♕g6 30 f3 ♖e8 31 ♔f2 ♖xe6 32 ♕d2 h4 33 ♖e1 ♕g3+ 34 ♔f1 ♖xe1+ 35 ♕xe1 ♕xe1+ 36 ♗xe1 ♗a6 37 b5 ♗c8 38 ♗xh4 ♗e6 39 ♗e7 ♗xc4+ 40 ♔f2 ♗xb5 41 ♗xd6 a5 42 ♗c7 a4 43 ♗xb6 a3 44 ♗d4 ♗d7 45 g4 ½-½

White played the opening sensibly (in general, quite rare in the English Defence) and it was Black who was struggling to counter White's initiative throughout the game.

Game 46
Levitt-Short
Calcutta 1998

1 d4 e6 2 c4 b6 3 e4 ♗b7 4 ♕c2 g6

A logical move. The d-pawn is now unprotected so Black aims to attack it. In the next chapter which deals with a2-a3 by White, we will see that the double fianchetto (hippopotamus system) has come into fashion again for Black.

Let's take a quick look at the alternatives to 4...♕h4 and 4...g6:

a) It is a pity that 4...♘c6 doesn't quite work due to 5 ♘f3 ♘b4 6 ♕e2 when White holds the e-pawn and next move boots the knight back.

b) 4...♗b4+ 5 ♘d2 ♘f6 6 ♗d3 c5 7 d5 b5 8 dxe6 bxc4 9 exf7+ ♔f8 10 ♕xc4 d5 11 ♕c2 dxe4 12 ♗e2 ♘c6 13 a3 ♘d4 14 ♕d1 e3 15 fxe3 ♗xd2+ 16 ♗xd2 ♗xg2 and Black was winning in the game Rogozenko-Teske, Dresden open 1996. That was jolly good fun, but after 4...♗b4+, life is far less interesting if White blocks with the bishop. In that case White is left with his big space advantage and Black's counterplay is less dynamic. Compare with 4 ♗d3 ♗b4+ from Chapter 2 – it is really rather similar.

5 ♘c3 ♗g7 6 ♗e3 ♘e7 7 0-0-0

If 7 ♘f3 0-0 and Black is ready for ...f7-f5.

7...0-0 8 f4 f5 9 e5

Or 9 ♘f3 b5!?

9...d5 10 c5 bxc5 11 dxc5 g5?!

This seems pointless as Black isn't going to use the kingside anyway. Instead, 11...♘bc6 doesn't look too bad for Black – compare with the game.

12 g3 ♘bc6 13 ♘f3 g4 14 ♘d4 ♘xd4 15 ♗xd4 ♘c6 16 ♗b5 ♘xd4 17 ♖xd4 c6 18 ♗d3 ♖f7 19 ♔b1 ♗f8 20 ♘e2 ♗c8 21 ♖a4

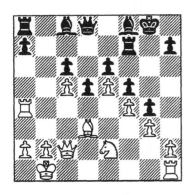

White has a clear advantage and his opponent lacks counterplay.

21...a5 22 ♘d4 ♖b7 23 ♖c1 ♗d7 24 ♕c3 ♕c7 25 ♘b3 ♖ba7 26 ♗e2 ♗c8 27 ♘d4 ♖b7 28 ♔a1 h5 29 ♘b3 ♖ba7 30 ♘d4 ♕d7 31 h4 ♗a6 32 ♗xa6 ♖xa6 33

♕b3 ♗e7 34 ♖c3 ♔f7 35 ♕c2 ♖6a7 36 ♖e3 ♕c8 37 ♖b3 ♗d8 38 ♕d3 ♔e7 39 ♔b1 ♔f7 40 ♔c1 ♔e7 41 ♔d1 ♖b7 42 ♔c2 ♖ab8 43 ♖xb7+ ♖xb7 44 a3 ♖b8 45 b4 ♕b7 46 ♘b3 axb4 47 axb4

47 ♖xb4! is winning according to Levitt, e.g. 47...♕a7 48 ♖xb8 ♕xb8 49 ♕a6 ♔d7 50 ♘d4 ♕c7 51 ♕a8.

47...♖a8 48 ♖xa8 ♕xa8 49 ♔b2 ½-½

4...g6 wasn't too successful here, but I don't think it was a true reflection of its worth. White players often underestimate this type of system.

Game 47
Ivanchuk-Sadler
Monaco (blindfold) 1998

---

1 c4 b6 2 d4 e6 3 ♘c3 ♗b7 4 e4 ♗b4 5 ♕c2

There have been quite a few games with the queen move in this position, though I don't think it is particularly good here.

5...♕h4!

Once again the best response. White faces immediate difficulties, and it is surprising that Ivanchuk went in for this line, though it wasn't a 'proper' game, as such.

6 d5

6 ♗d3 is the subject of Game 49.

6...♗xc3+

Sadler likes to go his own way. The majority of players have gone for 6...f5 here;

87

for that see the next game.
7 bxc3 ♘f6

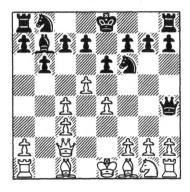

This treatment is more solid than 6...f5 (since the pawn structure is more intact) but it still has some bite. White's pawns on c4 and e4 are a cause of concern.

8 ♗d3

Not 8 e5? ♕e4+! 9 ♕xe4 ♘xe4.

8...♘a6 9 ♘f3 ♕g4!

If 9...♕h5 10 ♗a3! and the knight does not make it to the dream square.

10 0-0 ♘c5 11 h3 ♕g6 12 ♘e5 ♕h5 13 f4 ♘xd3 14 ♕xd3 d6 15 ♘f3 0-0-0

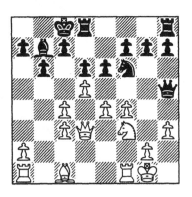

With the bishop on d3 gone the pawns become weaker.

16 ♗e3 ♖he8 17 ♖ae1 ♗a6 18 ♘d4?

Allowing a tactic, forgivable considering it was blindfold chess; in the same tournament Karpov left his queen 'en prise' to Sadler. Instead 18 a4 exd5 19 exd5

♖e7 followed by doubling is still more comfortable for Black than his opponent.

18...exd5 19 exd5 ♕xd5 20 ♕c2 ♗xc4 21 ♖f3 c5 22 ♘b3 ♖e7 23 ♘c1 ♖de8 24 ♔h2 ♕c6 25 ♕f5+ ♔d7 26 ♕g5 ♘d5 27 f5 f6 28 ♕g3 ♖xe3 29 ♖fxe3 ♖xe3 30 ♖xe3 ♘xe3 31 ♕xe3 ♕xf5 32 ♕e8+ ♔c7 33 ♕e7+ ♔d7 34 ♕f8 ♔b7 35 a3 d5 36 ♔g3 d4 37 cxd4 cxd4 38 ♕b4 ♕c7+ 39 ♔h4 ♕f4+ 40 g4 ♕f2+ 0-1

Game 48
Urban-Maciejewski
Lubniewice 1993

1 d4 e6 2 c4 b6 3 ♘c3 ♗b7 4 e4 ♗b4 5 ♕c2 ♕h4 6 d5 f5

More vigorous than Sadler's 6...♘f6.

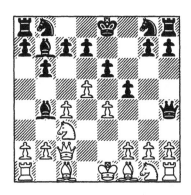

7 ♗d2

7 exf5 has been seen in several games and, while the situation is messy, there is no doubting that Black's position is fundamentally more sound than his opponent's due to his superior pawn structure. For instance, 7...exd5 8 ♘f3 (or 8 cxd5 ♘f6! 9 ♗d2 ♗xc3 10 ♗xc3 0-0 11 0-0-0 ♕f4+ 12 ♗d2 ♕xf2 13 ♘h3 ♕c5 14 ♕xc5 bxc5 15 ♗e3 d6 16 ♘f4 ♘bd7 17 ♗e2 ♖fe8 18 ♘e6 ♗xd5 19 ♖he1 ♗xe6 20 fxe6 ♘e5 and Black was clearly on top in Link-Kengis, Bern open 1995) 8...♕e4+ 9 ♕xe4+ dxe4 10 ♘d4 and now both 10...♘c6 and 10...♘e7 are strong. Black

...as a nice pawn structure and better development.

7...fxe4 8 0-0-0

Two other moves have been tried here:

a) 8 g3 as usual, is asking for trouble, e.g. 8...♕e7 9 ♗g2 ♘f6 10 0-0-0 exd5 11 cxd5 ♘a6 12 ♘xe4 ♘xd5 13 ♘c3 ♗xc3 14 ♗xc3 ♘db4 15 ♗xb7 ♘xc2 16 ♗xa8 c6 and Black was winning in Behrhorst-Birmingham, Hamburg 1986.

b) 8 ♘xe4 is reasonable, and after 8...exd5 9 cxd5:

b1) 9...♗xd2+ 10 ♘xd2 ♗xd5 (or even 10...♕e7+!?) 11 ♕xc7 ♘c6 is unclear.

b2) 9...♗xd5 10 ♗xb4 ♕xe4+ 11 ♕xe4+ ♗xe4 12 0-0-0 ♘f6 13 ♖e1 when White had some compensation for the pawn in Rotstein-Bricard, Cannes open 1992.

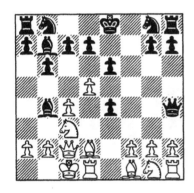

8...♘f6 9 ♗e2 ♕xf2

Considering that g2-g3 was a threat, why not?

10 ♘h3 ♕c5 11 ♘xe4 ♘xe4 12 ♕xe4 ♗xd5 13 ♗h5+ ♔d8 14 ♗xb4 ♕xb4 15 ♕h4+ ♔c8 16 ♖d4 ♗xg2 17 ♖hd1 ♗c6 18 ♘g5 ♔b7 19 ♘f7 ♖f8 20 ♘d8+

see following diagram

A slightly insane sequence, but Black's king is quite safe on b7, and he has taken lots of pawns.

20...♖xd8 21 ♕xd8 a5 22 ♖h4 h6 23 ♕h8 g5 24 ♖h3 ♕xc4+ 25 ♔b1 ♗e4+ 26 ♔a1 ♘c6 27 ♕xh6 ♘b4 28 b3 ♕c2 0-1

6...f5 is sound. That doesn't mean that Black stands better, but the pressure is already on White to prevent his centre from collapsing.

Game 49
Kryzius-Piesina
Radviliskis 1995

---

1 c4 b6 2 ♘c3 ♗b7 3 e4 e6 4 d4 ♗b4 5 ♕c2 ♕h4 6 ♗d3

This is seen more often than 6 d5 from the last two games, but it is not clear whether it is any better.

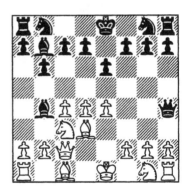

6...f5

...and the usual problems ensue on the long diagonal.

7 g3

Most players plump for this one, but the critical move has to be 7 ♘f3 ♗xc3+ 8

♕xc3 (not 8 bxc3? ♕g4 9 0-0 fxe4 and wins) 8...♕g4 9 0-0 (forced) 9...fxe4 10 ♘e5 ♕h4 (not 10...♕h5? 11 ♗c2 ♘f6 12 ♗d1 ♕h4 13 ♗e3 ♘c6 14 d5 ♘e7 15 dxe6 dxe6 16 ♗a4+ c6 17 ♕a3 and White was clearly better in Garcia-Gonzalez – Forintos, Montpelier 1985) 11 ♗e2! (11 ♗c2?, which was mentioned by Keene, Plaskett and Tisdall, is a dubious piece sacrifice; for instance, 11...d6 12 ♗a4+ c6 13 d5 dxe5 14 ♕xe5 ♕e7 15 dxe6 ♘f6 16 ♗g5 0-0 17 ♖ad1 ♘a6 and Black is winning) 11...d6! (11...♘f6? 12 ♗e3 0-0 13 ♕c1 is rather embarrassing) 12 ♘g4 ♘f6 13 ♘xf6+ ♕xf6 and Black is a pawn to the good.

Finally, I was once lucky enough to receive the following gift: 7 exf5?? ♗xg2 8 fxe6 ♗xh1 with a won position in Kachiani Gersinska-King, Oviedo rapidplay 1992.

7...♕h5

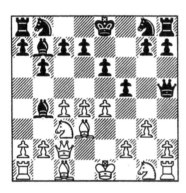

8 f3

The alternatives aren't terribly promising either:

a) 8 ♗e2 ♕f7 9 f3 fxe4 10 fxe4 ♘f6 11 d5 0-0 12 ♘f3 ♕g6! 13 ♗d3 ♕h5! 14 0-0 ♘a6 15 a3 ♗xc3 16 bxc3 ♘c5 17 ♗e3 ♘xd3 18 ♕xd3 exd5 19 exd5 ♘xd5 20 cxd5 ♖xf3 0-1 Farago-Miles, Hastings 1976/77. One of the first shocking games with the system on the international circuit (see the Introduction).

b) 8 ♘ge2? isn't too clever due to

8...♕f3 9 0-0 ♗xc3 10 ♘xc3 ♘c6 11 ♕d1 ♘xd4 and Black was winning in Chibukhchian-Lempert, Yerevan open 1996, although he messed it up and only drew.

8...♘c6

Fine, though I quite like the idea of playing very simply, as Miles did, with 8...fxe4 9 fxe4 ♘f6 10 ♘ge2 ♘c6 and now:

a) 11 a3 ♗xc3+ 12 bxc3 e5 13 d5 ♘a5 14 c5? (White probably wasn't expecting the fatal blow to come from this side of the board) 14...♘b3! 15 ♖b1 (or 15 ♕xb3 ♕f3) 15...♘xc5 and, a little prematurely, but understandably, White resigned here in Komarek-Chetverik, Policka open 1996. His kingside is a mess and he will probably lose his e-pawn.

b) 11 0-0 ♗d6!? 12 ♔g2 ♘b4 was good for Black in Wiedenkeller-Berg, Sollentuna open 1995. White's problem in these variations is that his kingside is so weak; the bishop on d3 can't return to cover the light squares.

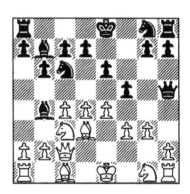

9 d5

Alternatively, 9 ♗e3 e5 (perhaps 9...fxe4!? 10 ♗xe4 ♘f6) 10 d5 ♘d4 11 ♗xd4 exd4 12 a3 fxe4 13 fxe4 ♗xc3+ 14 bxc3 dxc3 15 ♕xc3 ♘f6 and Black already had the initiative in Kharlov-Gretarsson, Leeuwarden open 1995.

9...♘d4 10 ♕f2 fxe4 11 ♕xd4

Hopeless. Black makes a simple sacrifice and it is all over. Instead, if 11 fxe4 e5 12

♗e3 ♘f6 with the initiative or 11 ♗xe4 exd5!? (11...e5 is reasonable) 12 ♕xd4 dxe4 13 ♕xg7 exf3! with a stonking attack.
11...exd3 12 ♕xg7 0-0-0

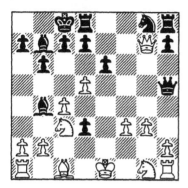

I love it when Black's king reaches the queenside in the English Defence – four pawns and a lump of rock on b7; it is *so* safe.

13 ♕xh8 exd5 14 ♗e3 ♖e8 15 0-0-0 ♘h6 16 ♕xe8+ ♕xe8 17 ♗xh6 dxc4 18 ♗d2 d5 19 ♘h3 d4 20 ♘e4 c3 21 ♘f4 ♗xe4 22 fxe4 ♕a4 23 ♘xd3 ♕xa2 24 ♔c2 ♕a4+ 25 ♔c1 cxd2+ 26 ♔b1 ♗a5 27 ♖hf1 ♕b3 28 ♘c1 dxc1♕+ 29 ♔xc1 d3 30 ♖f2 ♕c4+ 31 ♔b1 d2 32 ♖fxd2 ♗xd2 33 ♖xd2 ♕xe4+ 34 ♔c1 ♕c4+ 35 ♔d1 a5 0-1

There is no way that White would ever plan to go into positions like these after 6 ♗d3. He is already on the back foot.

Summary

The greedy idea of grabbing the pawns in Game 43 looks unsound. However, Game 44 is a more reliable way of playing the line, while 6...♕g4 of Game 45 seems a little dubious, though it is as yet relatively unexplored. The double fianchetto idea of Game 46 is yet another way of coping with 4 ♕c2 and seems reasonable. Games 47-49 are only fun for Black.

1 d4 e6 2 c4 b6 3 e4 ♗b7

4 ♘c3
    4 ♕c2
        4...♕h4 5 ♘d2 ♗b4 6 ♗d3
            6...f5 7 ♘gf3 *(D)*
                7...♗xd2+ – *Game 43*
                7...♕h5 – *Game 44*
            6...♕g4 – *Game 45*
        4...g6 – *Game 46*
4...♗b4 5 ♕c2 ♕h4 *(D)* 6 d5
    6 ♗d3 – *Game 49*
6...♗xc3+
    6...f5 – *Game 48*
7 bxc3 *(D)* – *Game 47*

7 ♘gf3

5...♕h4

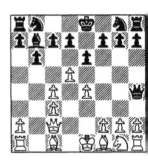

7 bxc3

CHAPTER SIX

White Plays an early a2-a3

1 d4 e6 2 c4 b6 3 a3

In this chapter I'm going to be looking at games where White plays a2-a3. A clever little move. In many of the games we have considered so far White's centre has come under enormous pressure from the bishop on b4; so why not prevent it from going there? The move has a respectable relation: the Petrosian variation of the Queen's Indian Defence (1 d4 ♘f6 2 c4 e6 3 ♘f3 b6 4 a3) which has the same aim. Indeed, a transposition is possible after 3...♘f6 4 ♘c3 ♗b7 5 ♘f3, so just on those grounds alone I'm not sure that 3 a3 represents a refutation of the system. But that's too gloomy an assessment! As ever Black has plenty of ways to stir up trouble.

The most modern method of dealing with a2-a3 is to play a double fianchetto, reaching a kind of 'hippopotamus' formation. Miles has championed this system, though I would say it takes skill to avoid being squashed (see Games 50-52).

In Games 53-58 Black instead prevents his opponent from occupying the centre with all three pawns by playing ...f7-f5, reaching an unusual kind of Dutch formation. This is probably the most respectable way of coping with a2-a3; at the very least

Black has several plausible options available if he plays in this way.

In Games 59 and 60 Black offers a transposition to the Queen's Indian Defence by playing ...♘f6, but White avoids this by playing his pawn to d5. However, Black does not suffer in these games, so White should just accept the transposition.

Let's start with a radical idea from the true master of the English Defence.

> ### Game 50
> ### Hellsten-Miles
> *Malmo 1996*

1 d4 e6 2 c4 b6 3 a3

Naturally 3 ♘c3 can be met by 3...♗b4, when 4 e4 ♗b7 transposes to Chapter 3 and 4 e3 (intending ♘e2) gives Black the option of either transposing to a Nimzo-Indian with 4...♘f6 or crippling White's pawns with 4...♗xc3+ 5 bxc3 ♗b7 followed by ...f7-f5.

3...g6

'I suspect that 3...g6 may well be best. 3 a3 really "wastes" a move to prevent ...♗b4 so Black instead aims for the best diagonal, hoping to get a little mileage out of ...e7-e6.' – Tony Miles. A simple argument, but in chess sometimes one has to 'take a view'. Previously Miles had experimented with a double fianchetto, but only after playing ...f7-f5 to reach a form of Leningrad Dutch.

4 ♘c3 ♗g7 5 ♘f3 ♘e7 6 e4 ♗b7 7 ♗e2 0-0 8 0-0

White has opted for sensible, straightforward development, and that can't be wrong, but I don't think it is the way to squash the system. Check out the next two games for attempts at a refutation.

8...f5

Miles writes here: 'Already it is hard to suggest moves for White. Hmm. I'm not so pessimistic about White's chances. Incidentally, 8...f5 isn't forced. Black may also play a hippopotamus formation: 8...d6 9 ♗e3 ♘d7 10 d5 ♘c5! 11 ♘d4 ♕d7 12 b4 ♘xe4 13 ♘xe4 exd5 14 cxd5 ♘xd5 15 ♗f3 ♖ae8 and, with the knight in the middle en prise and ...c7-c5 coming, Black had excellent compensation for the piece in Savchenko-Teske, European Cup, Bratislava 1996.

9 e5

White doesn't have to play this. For instance, 9 exf5 ♘xf5 10 d5 transposes into an old game of Plaskett's (he only fianchettoed his king's bishop after White had moved the pawn to d5):

a) 10...♗xc3!? 11 bxc3 ♘a6 (11...♕f6!?).

b) 10...♘a6 11 ♕c2 and Black has sufficient play.

c) 10...♕e7 11 ♗g5 ♕f7 12 ♕c2 ♘a6 13 b4 c5 14 dxc6 ♗xc6 15 ♖ad1 ♖ac8 16 ♘e4 ♘c7 17 ♘d6 ♘xd6 18 ♖xd6 ♗xf3 19 ♗xf3 ♘b5! with a tremendous attack in Akesson-Plaskett, Bergsjo 1981.

9...h6

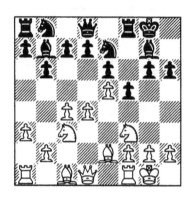

10 ♖e1

10 h4 d5 '...leaves the h-pawn looking silly' – Miles. That's as maybe. But one thing I am sure of is that it is best to prevent Black playing ...g7-g5, which, as we will see, gives Black a highly dangerous attacking formation on the kingside. Anyway, take a look at this, played a little later than the main game and see what you think. Miles's strategy is remarkable; it reminds me of the old Arabic formations. Although it appears that Black is cramped, in fact his co-ordination isn't too bad, and the central pawn majority a long-term asset: 11 exd6 cxd6 12 ♗f4 ♘c8 13 ♕d2 ♔h7 14 ♖ae1 ♘d7 15 ♗d1 ♖e8 16 ♖e3 ♘f8 17 ♖fe1 ♖e7 18 a4 a6 19 b3 ♖a7 20 ♖d3 ♖d7 21 ♗g3 ♗a8 22 ♘h2 ♘e7 23 ♗f3 ♗xf3 24 ♘xf3 e5 25 dxe5 dxe5 26 ♖xd7 ♖xd7 27 ♕c1 f4 28 ♗h2 ♘c6 29 ♘d5 ♔h8 30 ♕b1 ♖d6 31 g3 g5 32 hxg5 hxg5 33 ♕f5 ♖g6 34 gxf4 gxf4+ 35 ♔h1 when the situation was still unclear, but Black certainly wasn't worse in view of the bishop on h2 in Xu Jun-Miles, Tan Chin Cup, Beijing 1996.

10...g5!

White is definitely worse. His centre will crumble and his minor pieces are restricted.

11 d5 ♘g6 12 ♗f1 g4 13 ♘d4 ♗xe5 14 dxe6

Not 14 ♗xh6 ♖e8!

14...♛f6 15 ♗xh6 ♖e8 16 ♘db5 dxe6 17 ♛d2 ♘c6 18 ♛g5

18 ♗g5 ♛h8 19 ♖xe5 ♛xe5 20 ♖e1 ♛g7 is hopeless for White.

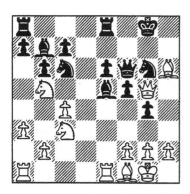

18...♖e7?

Miles thinks that White can resign after 18...♖ac8 19 a4 a6. That might be a little premature, but it certainly isn't very pleasant, e.g. 20 ♘a3 ♚f7 followed by ...♖h8 and it is difficult to see how White can defend on the kingside.

19 ♖xe5 ♚f7!?

Miles played this extraordinary move because his opponent was in time trouble, but objectively 19...♛xg5 20 ♗xg5 ♘cxe5 21 ♗xe7 ♘xe7 22 ♘xc7 ♖c8 23 ♘xe6 ♘xc4, with some compensation for the pawn, is stronger.

20 ♖ee1 a6 21 ♖ad1

21 ♘e4! fxe4 22 ♘c3 is much stronger, when Black is in trouble.

21...axb5 22 ♛xf6+ ♚xf6 23 cxb5 ♘ce5 24 ♗e3 ♘f7 25 ♗c4 ♖h8 26 g3 ♘d6 27 ♖a2 ♗f3 28 h4 ♘xh4 29 ♘d5+ ♚f7 30 ♗d4

see following diagram

Or 30 ♘xe7 ♘g6 31 ♗xe6+ ♚e8 and wins.

30...♖h6 31 ♖d3 exd5 32 ♖xe7+ ♚xe7 33 ♖e3+ ♚d7 34 gxh4 ♖xh4 35 ♖xf3 gxf3 36 ♗f6 ♖g4+ 37 ♚f1 ♚e6 38 ♗d8 ♘xb5 0-1

Amazing stuff. When anyone says that chess is being played out and that there is nothing new any more, I would direct them towards some of Miles's games. Nevertheless, White players have managed to come up with better replies to his system since this first try.

Game 51
Milov-Miles
Biel 1996

---

1 d4 e6 2 c4 b6 3 ♘c3

By the way, if White doesn't occupy the centre with his three pawns then Black gets a very easy game. For example, 3 a3 g6 4 ♘c3 ♗g7 5 ♘f3 ♘e7 6 e3 ♗b7 7 ♗e2 0-0 8 0-0 d5 9 cxd5 ♘xd5 10 ♗d2 ♘d7 11 ♖c1 c5 12 dxc5 ♘xc5 13 b4 ♘d7 14 ♘xd5 ♗xd5 15 ♗c3 ♗xc3 and a draw was agreed in Li Wenliang-Miles, Tan Chin Cup, Beijing 1996.

3...♗b7 4 a3 g6 5 ♘f3 ♗g7 6 e4 ♘e7 7 ♗e3

White does better to assume a more aggressive stance with his pieces than ♗e2 and 0-0, though this one might not be the best. The following year Milov tried something different – see the next game.

Alternatively, 7 d5 isn't convincing: 7...0-0 8 ♗g5?! f6 (surely 8...h6 – this is generally a move that Black would like to play, so I don't like ♗g5 at all) 9 ♗f4 c6 (too much) 10 d6 ♘c8 11 b4 with a clear plus for White in Sinanovic-Sandler, Yerevan Olympiad 1996.

7 ♗d3 is a sensible move, as the kind of King's Indian after 7...0-0 8 0-0 d6 (perhaps 8...f5!?) 9 ♖e1 ♘d7 10 ♗e3 e5 11 d5 is not what Black should be aiming for. Black is behind with his kingside attack, and is weak on the queenside (the c6-square). The course of the game Astrom-Sandler, Yerevan Olympiad 1996, demonstrates this: 11...h6 12 ♘d2 f5 13 f3 ♘f6 14 b4 f4 15 ♗f2 g5 16 c5 h5 17 ♖c1 ♘g6 18 ♗e2 ♗c8 19 ♕a4 ♖f7 20 ♗b5 g4 21 ♗c6 ♗d7 22 cxd6 cxd6 23 ♘b5 ♗xc6 24 dxc6 and White was clearly better.

7...f5 8 e5 h6 9 h4!

Milov appreciates how important it is to prevent ...g7-g5.

9...d6 10 exd6 cxd6 11 ♗f4 a6

Perhaps 11...0-0.

12 ♗e2 ♖a7

This looks bizarre, but if you think back to Xu Jun-Miles in the notes to the last game, then you will see what Black might be about. If 12...0-0 then 13 ♕b3!?

13 0-0

13 ♕d2!, preventing ...0-0 and preparing 0-0-0. would have been interesting. It would cut across Black's plans.

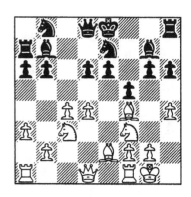

13...g5!?

Black could have just castled and played as in the game I mentioned above, but Miles obviously had good memories of his game against Hellsten, played just a few weeks before, and goes for ...g7-g5 again. It is just a bit too much here. Nevertheless, to refute it, White has to play with great energy and precision.

14 hxg5 ♘g6 15 ♗g3

White has plenty of ways to go wrong: 15 gxh6? ♗xf3! 16 hxg7 ♖xg7 17 ♗g3 ♗b7 and the rook on a7 comes good; and 15 ♗e3 ♗xf3 16 ♗xf3 hxg5 is also dangerous for White.

15...hxg5 16 ♖e1?

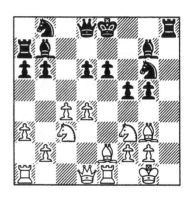

16 ♗d3! would have been a more precise move order. After 16...g4 17 ♖e1 play
transposes back to the game, but Black
could have exploited this inaccuracy
with...

16...g4?

...16...f4! 17 ♗d3 (not 17 ♗h2? g4 18
♘d2 ♕h4 and wins) 17...♘f8 18 d5 (or 18
♗h2 g4) 18...fxg3 19 fxg3 ♗c8 and Black
should survive the attack and win with his
extra piece. Once again the rook on a7
comes in handy.

17 ♗d3! ♔f7

After 17...gxf3 18 ♖xe6+ ♔f7 19 d5
White has a powerful initiative.

18 d5 ♗xc3 19 dxe6+

19 ♖xe6!? would also have been very
strong:

a) 19...gxf3 20 ♕xf3 ♗f6 21 ♕xf5 ♘f8
22 ♗xd6 and White is clearly on top.

b) 19...♗xb2 20 ♖xd6 ♕e7 (or 20...♕c8
21 ♘g5+) 21 ♖e6 ♕d8 22 ♗xf5 ♘f8
(22...♘e7 23 ♘g5+ ♔g8 24 ♕xg4 is winning for White) 23 ♘e5+ ♗xe5 24 ♗xe5
with a powerful attack.

b) 19...♗f6 20 ♗xf5 ♘f8 21 ♖xd6 ♕e7
22 ♘d4 and again White is on the attack.

19...♔g8 20 ♗xf5 gxf3

After 20...♗xf3 21 gxf3 ♗xe1 (or
21...♖ah7 22 e7 ♖xe7 23 bxc3 and wins) 22
♗xg6 White is also clearly better.

**21 ♗xg6 fxg2 22 ♗f7+ ♔g7 23 ♕g4+
♔f8**

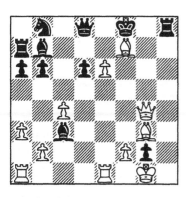

24 f3

24 ♗h5! is the simplest: 24...♗f6 25 e7+!
♗xe7 26 ♕f5+ ♗f6 27 ♗xd6+ ♔g8 28
♕g6+ and wins.

24...♗c8 25 bxc3 ♖xf7 26 ♕d4! ♕f6

Or 26...♖fh7 27 e7+.

27 ♗xd6+ 1-0

27...♔g7 is met by 28 ♗e5.

Miles went just a bit too far in this
game, but it does demonstrate the range of
Black's possibilities. I especially like the
way the rook on a7 is able to swing into
action.

Game 52
Milov-Miles
New York 1997

**1 d4 e6 2 c4 b6 3 a3 g6 4 e4 ♗g7 5
♘f3**

You might notice how Miles delays developing his queen's bishop, and there is a
subtle reason for this, which the following
game demonstrates: 5 ♘c3 ♘e7 6 ♗e3
(but now with the bishop on e3...) 6...d5
(...is possible, as the knight can move to f5
to hit the bishop) 7 cxd5 exd5 8 e5 0-0 9 f4
and in this kind of position the bishop is
better on c8, covering the f5- and g4-
squares. After 9...c5 10 ♘f3 ♘bc6 an unclear position was reached in Halldorsson-
Miles, Reykjavik 1998.

5...♘e7 6 ♘c3 ♗b7 7 h4

A year down the line from the previous game, Milov is better prepared. He knows that in certain positions ...g7-g5 can be a key part of Black's strategy, so he moves to prevent it from the outset (and h4-h5 can also be useful for White); and he positions his pieces so that he is ready to meet ...f7-f5 if necessary.

7...h6 8 ♗d3! d6 9 ♗e3 ♘d7 10 ♕e2 a6

This time Miles adopts a 'hippo' formation and awaits developments.

11 ♖c1 c5

11...0-0?! 12 ♕d2 ♔h7 13 h5! wouldn't be too good for Black.

12 d5 e5

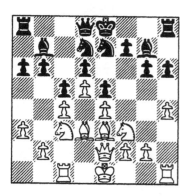

Another King's Indian type position and, again, not particularly good for Black as the bishop is misplaced on b7. It should be on c8 to cover the kingside. Milov has cleverly avoided committing his king

(which would have given Black something to aim for) but now it runs to the other side of the board.

13 h5! ♘f6

After 13...g5?! 14 ♘h2 the knight goes via f1 to g3 to look at f5.

14 hxg6 fxg6 15 ♘d2 ♗c8 16 f3 h5 17 ♔d1 ♗h6 18 ♔c2 ♗xe3 19 ♕xe3 ♘eg8 20 ♕g5

White has permanent pressure on the kingside.

20...♖h6 21 g4 ♕e7 22 ♕e3 ♖h7 23 gxh5 ♘xh5 24 ♘e2 ♖a7 25 f4 ♗g4 26 fxe5 ♕xe5 27 ♖cg1 ♘gf6 28 ♖h4 ♗xe2 29 ♗xe2 ♘g7 30 ♖xh7 ♘xh7 31 ♖xg6 ♘f5 32 ♕h3 ♘d4+ 33 ♔b1 ♘f8 34 ♖g8 ♔f7 35 ♖g2 ♔e8 36 ♕c8+ ♔e7 37 ♗h5 1-0

In this game Milov showed a good way to counter the Miles system, using containment and patience.

Game 53
Salov-Short
Madrid 1997

---

1 d4 e6 2 c4 b6 3 a3 f5

The most usual continuation for Black at this point has been 3...♗b7 (or 3...f5 4 ♘c3 ♗b7) 4 ♘c3 f5 5 d5 ♘f6 6 g3 ♘a6 and I'll be taking a look at this line later (Games 54-56). But first I thought it was worth looking at Short's individual treatment of the opening – he comes up with a subtle idea.

4 ♘c3 ♘f6 5 d5

If 5 g3, inviting a transposition to the 'main line' I mentioned above with 5...♗b7 6 d5 ♘a6, Black does have an alternative policy, as Short showed in another of his games: 5...c6!? 6 ♗g2 d5 (the game has transposed into a Stonewall Dutch where the extra moves a2-a3 and ...b7-b6 have been thrown in – not a bad deal for Black as his opponent can no longer trade bishops on a3, and Black's bishop stands well on b7, or sometimes a6) 7 ♘f3 ♗e7 8 ♗g5 0-0 9 0-0 ♗b7 10 ♖c1 h6 11 ♗xf6 ♗xf6 12 e3 ♘d7 and chances were balanced in C.Hansen-Short, European Rapidplay Championship, Cap d'Agde 1996.

5...♗a6!?

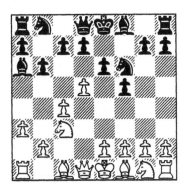

This reminds me of 4...♗a6 in the Queen's Indian (1 d4 ♘f6 2 c4 e6 3 ♘f3 b6 4 a3 ♗a6). However White defends the pawn he must make a small but significant concession which Black can exploit.

6 b3

If 6 ♕b3 Black could try 6...c5!? when the queen is stuck defending the pawn, while 6...♗c5 is also possible. 6 e3 doesn't present any difficulties either: 6...exd5 7 ♘xd5 (or 7 cxd5 ♗xf1 8 ♔xf1 with counterplay) 7...♗d6 with equality.

6...g6 7 ♗b2 ♗g7 8 g3 0-0 9 ♗g2

White could have prevented Black's next move with 9 ♕c2!?, but he is falling dangerously behind with his development on the kingside. For instance, 9...c6 10 ♗g2 (or 10 dxe6 dxe6) 10...cxd5 11 cxd5 exd5 12 ♘xd5 ♘c6 with the initiative.

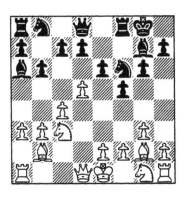

9...♘e4!

The exchanges free Black's position.

10 ♖c1 ♘xc3 11 ♗xc3 ♗xc3+ 12 ♖xc3 ♕f6 13 ♕d2 ♗b7

Work done, the bishop returns.

14 ♘f3 a5 15 0-0 ♘a6

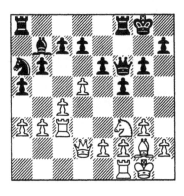

Chances are about equal. Black is solid on the queenside; the knight is about to leap into the beautiful c5-square; and the queen on f6 is well placed, a legacy of the exchanges a few moves ago.

16 ♕d4

Salov obviously didn't like the activity of Black's queen and hastens to exchange it. If 16 ♘d4 ♘c5 17 b4 axb4 18 axb4 ♘e4 19 ♗xe4 fxe4 20 dxe6 dxe6 21 ♕e3 ♖a2 Black is very active.

16...♖ae8 17 dxe6 ♖xe6

The pawn structure is very similar to a Queen's Indian; Black has no problems.

18 ♕xf6 ♖fxf6 19 ♘d4 ♗xg2 20 ♔xg2 ♖d6 21 e3 ♔f8! 22 h4 ♔e7 23 ♖b1 ♖f8 24 ♖c2 c6 25 ♔f3

Or 25 b4 axb4 26 axb4 ♘c7 27 c5 bxc5 28 bxc5 ♖d5, intending ...♘e6 with equality.

25...♘c5 26 ♔e2 ♖df6 27 ♘f3 h6 28 b4 axb4 29 axb4 ♘e4 30 ♖a1 c5! 31 bxc5 bxc5 32 ♘d2 g5 ½-½

The draw becomes inevitable with every pawn exchange: 33 hxg5 hxg5 34 ♖h1 ♖a8 is dead level.

Game 54
P.Cramling-Gulko
Pamplona 1996

---

1 d4 e6 2 c4 b6 3 a3 ♗b7 4 ♘c3 f5 5 d5

This is the most common move here, although the solid 5 ♘f3 ♘f6 6 g3 is also seen (see Game 57) and 5 f3 is also possible (see Game 58). Note that 5 ♘f3 ♘f6 6 d5 is less effective. In general, if White is going to play d4-d5, then it is best not to have the knight on f3, since the d-pawn needs protection. For example, 6...g6

(6...♘a6 is 'normal' with a likely transposition to the note to White's eighth move in the main game after 7 g3 ♘c5 8 ♗g2) 7 dxe6!? (7 g3 ♗g7 8 ♗g2 0-0 9 0-0 ♘a6 transposes to the note to White's eighth move in Game 56) 7...dxe6 8 ♕xd8+ ♔xd8 9 ♗f4 ♗d6 10 ♗g3 and now 10...♘bd7 would have been fine for Black in Petursson-Gretarsson, Reykjavik 1995.

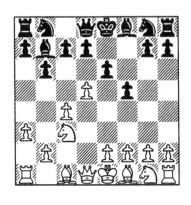

5...♘f6 6 g3 ♘a6

In these kinds of position, rather similar to the Queen's Indian and the Dutch, the problem piece for Black is the knight on b8, so it makes good sense to develop it while there is the opportunity. Nevertheless, the immediate 6...♗d6!? is worth more than a second glance: 7 ♗g2 0-0 8 ♘f3 (to prevent ...♗e5) 8...♕e7 9 0-0 a5 10 ♘d4 ♘a6 11 b3 ♘c5 12 ♗b2 ♘fe4 13 ♘db5 ♗e5 with good play in Apel-Lau Dresden open 1995.

However, 6...b5?! is less good due to 7 ♘f3 bxc4 8 dxe6 dxe6 9 ♕a4+ ♕d7 10 ♕xc4 ♘c6 11 ♗g2 ♗d6 12 b4 ♘e7 13 0-0 ♘ed5 14 ♗b2, as in S.Mohr-Bischoff German Bundesliga 1995/96. Black's pawn structure is a mess.

6...a5 is sometimes played (it is often useful to control White's queenside pawn structure) but it has been established that Black does best to develop as quickly as possible, and actually has no need for this preparatory move.

The other main alternative, 6...g6, is the subject of Game 56.

7 ♗g2

It is important to see what might happen if White attempts to trap the knight on the edge of the board. There are two possibilities after 7 b4:

a) 7...♘xb4!? 8 axb4 ♗xb4 9 ♗d2 (or 9 ♕b3) 9...exd5 and Black has three pawns for the piece and a solid position. Chances are balanced.

b) And for the less adventurous, 7...c5 and now:

b1) 8 b5 ♘c7 9 ♗g2 exd5 (9...♗d6) 10 cxd5 ♗d6 is fine for Black as the white d-pawn is a liability.

b2) 8 dxc6 dxc6 (8...♗xc6 9 ♘f3 ♗e7 10 ♗g2 ♖c8 11 0-0 ♘c7 is unclear) and now:

b21) 9 ♕xd8+ ♖xd8 10 ♗g2 ♖d4!? (10...e5) 11 b5 ♘b8 12 ♗f4 ♘fd7 and Black wins a pawn, though the game is just starting.

b22) 9 ♗g2 ♕xd1+ 10 ♔xd1 ♘g4 11 ♘h3 ♘e5 12 ♘g5 0-0-0+ 13 ♔c2 ♖e8 14 ♔b3 h6 15 ♘h3 ♘c7 16 ♗b2 ♘g4 17 e4 c5 18 b5 ♗e7 19 ♖ae1 ♗f6 20 f3 ♘e5 21 ♘f2 g5 22 ♘e2 ♖hf8 23 ♗c3 fxe4 24 ♘xe4 ♗xe4 25 fxe4 ♘g4 and Black was clearly better in Lazarev-Lempert, Bled open 1994.

Conclusion: Black has nothing to fear from 7 b4, so he does not need to waste a move with 6...a5 first.

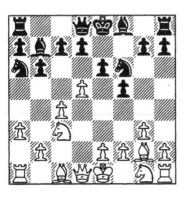

7...♘c5 8 ♘h3

8 ♘f3 isn't as good: 8...♘ce4! (the pawn on d5 is being rounded up) 9 dxe6 (or 9 0-0 ♘xc3 10 bxc3 ♗c5 with a free game in Apel-Blauert, German Bundesliga 1995) 9...dxe6 10 ♕a4+ ♕d7 11 ♕xd7+ ♔xd7 12 ♘xe4 ♗xe4 13 0-0 ♗d6 14 ♖d1 ♔e7 15 ♗e3 e5 with a slight plus for Black in Hoang Thang Trang-Czebe, Budapest 1998.

8...♗d6 9 0-0 ♗e5!

A clever manoeuvre. Black does best to set up pressure straightaway on White's centre.

10 ♕c2

There is a sharper move available to White: 10 ♘b5!? 0-0 (after 10...a6 11 f4 ♗xb2 12 ♘xc7+ ♕xc7 13 ♗xb2 0-0 14 ♘f2 the powerful bishop on b2 ensured White some advantage in Alexandrov-Matveeva, St Petersburg open 1994) 11 ♗f4 (11 f4!? ♗d6 12 ♘f2 is double-edged: the pawn on d5 could become weak and the e4-square already is, but White gets the two bishops) 11...d6 12 ♗xe5 dxe5 13 b4 ♘ce4 14 dxe6 ♕e7 15 ♕c2 a6 16 ♘c3 ♕xe6 was fine for Black in Shneider-Lempert, St Petersburg open 1993, as the knight on h3 is misplaced.

10...0-0

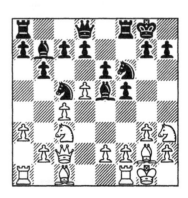

This has been the starting point for numerous games.

11 ♗e3

White has several alternatives here:

a) For 11 &d2, see the next game.

b) 11 ♖d1 ♕e7 12 &e3 ♘ce4 13 ♘xe4 ♘xe4 and now:

b1) 14 &xe4!? (White runs a great risk by exchanging off this bishop, but there are some strange tactics in the air) 14...fxe4 15 ♕xe4 &xb2 (not 15...exd5? 16 cxd5 ♖ae8 17 ♘g5 g6 18 d6 and wins) 16 d6!? &xe4! 17 dxe7 ♖fe8 18 ♖a2 &f6 19 ♖xd7 ♖xe7 and Black is fine.

b2) 14 ♖ac1 c5 15 dxe6 dxe6 16 &f4 &f6 17 ♖d3 e5 18 &e3 g5 19 ♖cd1 ♖ad8 20 ♖xd8 ♖xd8 21 ♖xd8+ ♕xd8 22 ♕d3 h6 23 g4 ♕xd3 24 exd3 ♘d6 25 &xb7 ♘xb7 26 f3 e4! was clearly better for Black in Sher-Lempert, Yerevan open 1996.

c) 11 ♘f4 ♕e7 12 &e3 ♘ce4 13 ♘xe4 ♘xe4 14 ♖ad1 (or 14 &xe4 fxe4 15 ♕xe4 &xb2 16 d6 &xe4 17 dxe7 ♖f7) 14...c5 (perhaps even 14...a5!? 15 &c1 ♖ae8 16 ♔h1 ♕f7 17 dxe6 dxe6 18 ♘d3 &d6 19 b4 axb4 20 axb4 c5 21 bxc5 bxc5 22 &b2 ♕c7 23 f3 ♘f6 24 ♕c3 e5 with counterplay in Franic-Doric, Croatian Championship, Porec 1994) 15 &c1 g5 16 ♘d3 &d4 17 e3 &g7 18 f3 ♘d6 19 e4 &d4+ 20 ♔h1 g4 with unclear chances in Naumkin-Lempert, Moscow 1994.

11...♘ce4!

As we have seen in the games above, this is a key move for Black, blocking out the bishop on g2.

12 ♘xe4 ♘xe4

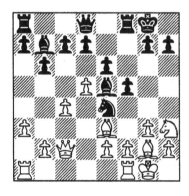

13 ♖fd1

Not 13 &xe4? fxe4 14 ♕xe4 &xb2 15 ♖a2 (if 15 ♘g5 ♖f5) 15...&f6 with a clear advantage for Black. White should only exchange the bishop for some tangible gain.

13...♕f6 14 ♖ab1 exd5

For tactical reasons 14...c5? isn't good due to 15 dxc6! &xc6 16 f3 ♘c5 17 f4 &c7 (not 17...&xg2? 18 ♕xg2! &c7 19 &xc5 bxc5 20 ♖xd7) 18 &xc6 dxc6 19 &xc5 bxc5 20 ♖d7 with a plus for White; while after 14...a5?! 15 f3 ♘c5 16 f4 &d6 17 b4 axb4 18 axb4 ♘e4 19 c5 Black has lost control.

15 cxd5 ♖ae8 16 ♕b3

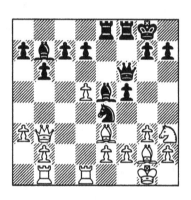

16...&d6

Perhaps 16...♔h8.

17 ♖bc1 ♕f7 18 &f4 c5 19 ♘g5!? ♕g6 20 ♘xe4 fxe4

Or 20...&xf4!? 21 ♘d2 &xd2 22 ♖xd2 d6 23 ♕a4!?

21 &xd6 ♕xd6 22 ♖c2 ♔h8?!

22...♖e5! would have been stronger.

23 ♕e3 ♕e5

23...&xd5? 24 ♖cd2 ♖e5 25 &xe4! ♖xe4 26 ♕xe4 wins for White.

24 ♖cd2 d6 25 b4 c4?

see following diagram

25...♖f6 would have been better. After the game move White holds a clear advantage.

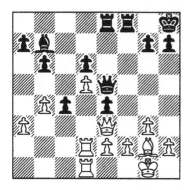

26 Rd4 Ba6 27 Rxe4 Wh5 28 Bf3 Rxe4 29 Wxe4 Wf7 30 Wd4 We8 31 Rc1 h6 32 Rc3 Wg6 33 Rc1 Wg5 34 Rc3 b5 35 Wxa7 Wd2 36 We3 Wb2 37 Wc1 Wa2 38 Rc2 Wb3 39 Rc3 Wa2 40 Kg2 Bc8 41 Rc2 Wb3 42 Rc3 Wa4 43 We3 Bf5 44 We7 Rf6 45 e4 Bg6 46 e5 Rxf3 47 Rxf3 Be4 48 exd6 Bxf3+ 49 Kxf3 Wd1+ 50 Kg2 Wxd5+ 51 f3 Wf5 52 d7 Wc2+ 53 Kh3 Wf5+ 54 Kh4 g5+ 55 Kh5 Wxf3+ 56 Kxh6 Wc6+ 57 Kxg5 Wd5+ 58 Kg6 Wd3+ 59 Kf7 Wh7+ 60 Ke6 We4+ 1-0

After 61 Kd6 Wd4+ 62 Kc6 White is winning.

The system with 4...f5 followed by ...Na6-c5 is quite good, but it is highly complex and requires a good understanding of the position. The next game is another example of the same set-up.

Game 55
M.Gurevich-Kengis
Bad Godesburg 1996

1 c4 b6 2 d4 Bb7 3 Nc3 e6 4 a3 f5 5 d5 Nf6 6 g3 Na6 7 Bg2 Nc5 8 Nh3 Bd6 9 0-0 Be5 10 Wc2 0-0

Everything as in the previous game, but now Gurevich tried something new and different.

11 Bd2

see following diagram

11...exd5

11...Nce4, as we have seen from some of the other games, is quite possible.

12 Nxd5

12 Wxf5 Bxc3 13 Bxc3 Nfe4 is equal; but not 12 cxd5? Bxc3 13 Bxc3 Nxd5 and Black is on top.

12...Nxd5 13 cxd5

13 Bxd5+ Bxd5 14 cxd5 Wf6 is balanced.

13...Wf6 14 Bg5

14 Bc3?! Bxc3 15 bxc3 Rae8 gives Black the initiative; while 14 Rab1 Ne4 15 Bb4 Rfe8 16 Rfd1 c5! 17 dxc6 dxc6 is unclear.

14...Wf7 15 Bf4 Bxf4 16 Nxf4 g5!? 17 Nh3

17 Nd3 Bxd5 18 Nxc5 Bxg2 19 Kxg2 Wd5+ offers Black good counterplay.

17...h6 18 b4 Ne4!?

18...♞a6?! 19 ♖ad1 would have been weird! Both knights are trapped at the edge of the board, but it is easier to activate the one on h3 with f2-f4 and ♞f2.

19 ♛xc7 ♝xd5

A complex position has arisen. Black's pawn structure isn't very pretty but his minor pieces are active, while White's knight on h3 is out of play.

20 ♖ad1 ♛e6!

Threatening ...♖fc8, trapping the queen.

21 ♛c1 ♖ac8 22 ♛e3 ♞c3! 23 ♝xd5 ♞xd5 24 ♛d3 ♞c3

25 ♖d2

Not 25 ♛xd7? ♛e4! threatening the rook and mate on e2.

25...♖fe8 26 ♖e1

26 ♛xd7 ♞xe2+ 27 ♔g2 g4 28 ♛xe6+ ♖xe6 29 ♞g1 is level.

26...♞e4

26...d5!? 27 f3 ♛e3+ 28 ♞f2 is unclear.

27 ♖c2 f4

White must force a draw.

28 ♖xc8

Not 28 ♔g2? ♛xh3+! 29 ♔xh3 ♞xf2+ 30 ♔g2 ♞xd3 and Black wins.

28...♖xc8 29 f3! ♛xh3

29...fxg3 30 ♛xe4 ♛xh3 31 ♛g6+ ♔h8 also draws.

30 ♛xe4 fxg3 31 ♛g6+ ♔h8 ½-½

32 ♛f6+ ♔h7 33 ♛f7+ with a perpetual check.

The system with ...♞a6-c5 has survived a severe test (Mikhail Gurevich is a decent player!), so we can conclude that it is fully viable.

Now we move on to Black's double fianchetto.

Game 56
Hjartarson-Gretarsson
Reykjavik 1995

1 c4 b6 2 d4 e6 3 a3 ♝b7 4 ♞c3 f5 5 d5 ♞f6 6 g3 g6

Instead of 6...♞a6, which we saw in the previous two games, Black fianchettoes the king's bishop, leading to a version of the Leningrad Dutch. This has been quite a popular way of handling White's opening so it is worth taking a look. On the surface of it, compared to the ...♞a6 systems where the bishop does a dance in the middle of the board (...♗d6-e5) and can be a little vulnerable in the process, the fianchetto has much to recommend it. The bishop reaches the crucial long diagonal and is quite safe on g7; moreover the f5-pawn gains some useful support. On the downside the knight on b8 doesn't get developed for some time, and that was Black's undoing in this game.

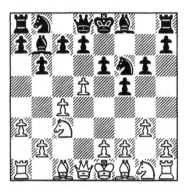

7 ♗g2 ♗g7 8 ♘h3!

The best way to develop the knight. Other routes are less effective:

a) 8 e3 0-0 9 ♘ge2 e5 10 0-0 d6 11 e4 fxe4 12 ♘xe4 ♘xe4 13 ♗xe4 ♘d7 14 ♘c3 ♗c8 15 ♗g2 ♘f6, as in Lautier-Topalov, Linares 1994, is more comfortable for White, but Black's position remains sound.

b) 8 ♘f3 0-0 9 0-0 ♘a6 10 ♗f4 (not 10 e4?! ♘xe4 11 ♘xe4 fxe4 12 ♘g5 exd5 13 cxd5 ♘c5 14 ♘xe4 ♘xe4 15 ♗xe4 ♕f6 16 ♖b1 ♕d4 with the initiative for Black in Fioramonti-Khenkin, Geneva open 1995) 10...exd5 11 cxd5 ♘c5 12 ♖c1 ♘fe4 13 ♗e5 ♗h6 14 e3 d6 15 ♗d4 ♗a6 16 b4 ♗xf1 17 ♗xf1 ♘xc3 18 ♗xc3 ♘e4, when White had some compensation for the exchange in Kharitonov-Morozevich, PCA open, Moscow 1994 (weak square on e6 and c-file), but I doubt whether it is really sufficient.

8...0-0 9 0-0

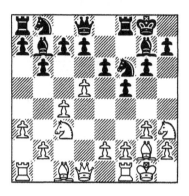

9...♘a6

9...a5 is possible, though Black must be prepared for 10 c5 (10 ♖b1 ♘a6 also slightly favours White), when he is fighting for equality: 10...♔h8 11 cxb6 cxb6 12 ♗f4 ♘xd5 13 ♘xd5 ♗xd5 14 ♗xd5 exd5 15 ♕xd5 ♘c6 16 ♖ad1 ♗xb2 17 ♖d3 ♗f6 18 ♖fd1 ♕e8 19 ♖e3 ♕f7 20 ♕b5 and White had the initiative in P.Cramling-Gulko, Spanish Team Championship 1996.

10 ♖b1

The immediate 10 b4 may be even better, as it appears that Black cannot exploit the position of the white rook on the long diagonal:

a) 10...♘e4 11 ♘xe4 ♗xa1 12 ♗g5 ♕e8 13 ♕xa1 fxe4 14 ♗h6 ♖f7 15 dxe6! dxe6 16 ♘g5 ♖e7 17 ♗xe4 and White is on top (Umanskaya).

b) 10...exd5 11 cxd5 ♘e4 12 ♘xe4 ♗xa1 13 ♗g5 ♕e8 14 ♕xa1 fxe4 15 ♗h6 ♖f7 16 ♘g5 ♗xd5 17 ♕d4! also favours White (Umanskaya).

c) 10...♘xd5!? 11 ♘xd5 exd5 12 ♗xd5+ ♗xd5 13 ♕xd5+ ♔h8 14 ♗g5! ♕e8 15 ♖ad1 with a clear edge for White in Farago-Varga, Pecs 1998.

10...♘c5 11 b4 ♘ce4 12 ♗b2 exd5?!

It would have been better to keep the position more fluid with 12...♕e7, for instance.

13 cxd5 ♘d6 14 ♕b3 ♔h8 15 ♖bc1 ♖e8

15...c5 16 dxc6 dxc6 17 ♘f4 and it lands on e6.

16 ♖fd1

White has a wonderful position; all his pieces are beautifully centralised. On the other hand, Black lacks space, the c-pawn is vulnerable, and opening the position merely unleashes the full force of White's army.

16...♘g4

16...♘fe4? 17 ♘xe4 ♘xe4 18 ♗xg7+ ♔xg7 19 ♗xe4 ♖xe4 20 ♕c3+ ♔g8 21 ♕xc7 is winning for White.

17 a4 a6 18 e3 ♖c8 19 ♘f4 ♘e5 20 ♘ce2 ♘e4 21 ♘d3

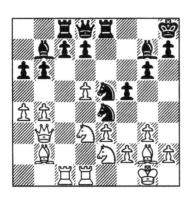

21...♕e7?

21...♘xd3 would have been a better try, but White still has a great position: 22 ♗xg7+ ♔xg7 23 ♕xd3 ♕e7 24 ♖c4 followed by doubling on the c-file.

22 ♘xe5 ♗xe5 23 ♗xe4 fxe4 24 ♖xc7! ♖xc7 **25 d6 ♕g7 26 ♗xe5 ♕xe5 27 dxc7 ♕xc7 28 ♕f7 ♖d8 29 ♘f4 1-0**

29...♕c8 30 ♘e6! dxe6 31 ♕f6+ is hopeless.

6...g6 is just about playable for Black (it is not necessary to get squashed like this) though still highly complex. Now we shall take a look at what happens if White delays playing d4-d5.

Game 57
Kislova-Minasian
Omsk 1996

1 c4 b6 2 d4 ♗b7 3 ♘c3 e6 4 a3 f5 5 ♘f3 ♘f6 6 g3

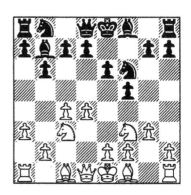

6...♘e4

Black does not have to leap in so quickly with the knight. Both 6...g6 7 ♗g2 ♗g7 8 0-0 0-0, as in Mednis-Plaskett, Luxembourg open 1990, and 6...♗e7 7 ♗g2 0-0 8 0-0 ♘e4, as in Rind-De Jager, Dieren open 1991, are perfectly playable. However, 6...♘e4 presents problems for White to solve at a very early stage in the game – and few players have been up to the challenge!

7 ♘xe4

This is the critical response. Others aren't nearly as testing, generally leading to positions with a strong resemblance to the Queen's Indian, but where White has wasted a move on a2-a3. For example:

a) 7 ♕d3 ♗e7 8 d5 ♘xc3 9 ♕xc3 0-0 10 ♕d3 ♗f6 11 ♗g2 ♘a6 12 ♘d2 ♘c5 with good play for Black in Bukic-Tratar, Slovenian Championship 1995.

b) 7 ♕c2 ♗e7 8 ♗g2 ♘xc3 9 ♕xc3 ♗f6 10 0-0 0-0 11 ♗e3 ♗e4 12 ♖ac1 ♘c6 13 b4 ♕c8 14 ♖fd1 ♕b7 15 ♕b3 ♘e7 16 ♗f1 a6! 17 ♘d2 ♗c6 18 f3 b5! with excellent control over the central light squares in Jakobsen-Rewitz, Esbjerg 1996.

c) 7 ♗d2 ♗e7 8 ♗g2 ♗f6 9 ♖c1 (or 9 0-0 ♘c6 10 d5 ♘a5 with counterplay) 9...♘c6!? 10 ♗e3 (10 d5 ♘a5 and 10 0-0 ♘xd4 11 ♘xd4 ♗xd4 12 ♘xe4 fxe4 both slightly favour Black) 10...0-0 11 0-0 ♘e7 12 ♘xe4 ♗xe4 13 ♕d2 ♖b8! with the idea of ...b6-b5, when Black had sufficient play in M.Gurevich-Kengis, Bonn 1995.

7...fxe4

If 7...♗xe4 White has an excellent response: 8 ♗h3! ♗e7 9 0-0 0-0 10 d5! ♗xf3 (not 10...exd5? 11 ♘d2! and wins) 11 exf3 ♗f6 12 ♖b1 ♘a6 13 ♖e1 ♘c5 14 b4 ♘b7 15 dxe6 dxe6 16 ♕b3 with a big advantage due to the white bishops and pawn structure and Black's poor knight in Adorjan-Miles, Gjovik 1983.

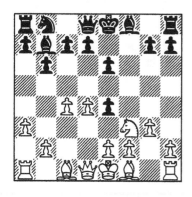

8 ♘h4

Also possible is 8 ♘e5 d6 9 ♘g4 '...intending ♗h3 and ♘e3 with a clear advantage.' – Keene, Plaskett and Tisdall. In fact this idea is rather similar to the game continuation. Black does not need to play ...d7-d6 however; 8...♗e7 is better.

8...♗e7 9 ♘g2 0-0 10 ♘e3 ♕e8 11 ♗g2

11 ♗h3 (as recommended by the gentlemen above) just doesn't have the same effect when Black hasn't moved the d-pawn: 11...♕h5 12 ♗g4 ♕f7 13 0-0 ♘c6 14 f3 (14 b4? ♘xd4 15 ♕xd4 ♗f6; 14 d5 ♘e5 15 ♗h3 ♗c5) 14...exf3 15 ♗xf3 ♗f6 and Black has the better development.

11...d5 12 0-0 ♘d7

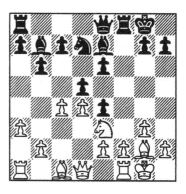

13 ♗h3

Black has to be a little careful of the pins after 13 cxd5 exd5 14 ♕b3, but 14...♕f7! holds.

13...♖f6 14 cxd5 exd5 15 ♕b3 c6 16 ♗g2

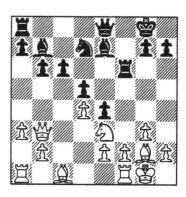

White has lost the plot somewhat with her to-ing and fro-ing. From now on she gets steadily outplayed. Around here, chances are still equal.

**16...⌖h8 17 f4 exf3 18 exf3 ⌓f7 19 ⌓d1
⌘f6 20 ⌘f1 ⌗d6 21 ⌗g5 h6 22 ⌗e3
⌓e7 23 ⌗f2 ⌒g6 24 ⌓d2 c5 25 ⌓c1 c4
26 ⌒c2 ⌒xc2 27 ⌓cxc2 ⌓ae8 28 ⌗h3
g6 29 ⌖g2 b5 30 ⌖g1 a5 31 ⌓c1 ⌗c6
32 ⌓dd1 b4 33 axb4 ⌗xb4 34 ⌓a1 ⌓e2
35 ⌓db1 a4 36 g4 a3 37 bxa3 ⌗c3 38
a4 ⌗xa1 39 ⌓xa1 c3 40 a5 c2 41 a6
⌓a8 42 a7 ⌓xa7 43 ⌓xa7 c1⌒ 44 ⌓c7
0-1**

Very few players have taken up the
challenge and captured the knight on e4.
However, I feel that Black's position is
strong enough; White is, after all, wasting
a lot of time by moving his knight around
the board, so he falls behind in his development. More practical tests are needed
(there was a large discrepancy in strength
between the players here) before a firm
conclusion can be reached. One thing is
certain: if White does not capture on e4,
and most players tend not to, then Black
should equalise.

Game 58
Suba-Plaskett
London 1991

---

1 c4 b6 2 d4 ⌗b7 3 ⌘c3 e6 4 a3 f5 5 f3

Here I'm going to be looking at games
where White plays with f2-f3. A dangerous move. Defensively, it blocks out the
bishop on b7 and prevents Black's knight
from moving to e4; and offensively White
can sometimes play for e2-e4, as he does in
this main game.

A similar idea is 5 e3 ⌘f6 6 f3 and now:

a) 6...c5!? is interesting.

b) 6...g6 is playable.

c) 6...⌗d6 7 ⌘h3 0-0 8 ⌘f2 ⌘c6 9 ⌗e2
⌘h5 10 f4 ⌘f6 11 ⌗f3 and White was
already better in Spraggett-Yewdokimov,
Oviedo rapidplay 1992.

d) 6...d6 7 ⌗d3 ⌘bd7 8 ⌘ge2 ⌘h5!? 9
d5 (9 0-0 ⌒h4) 9...g6 10 dxe6 ⌘c5 11 0-0

⌘xe6 12 e4 f4 13 ⌘d5 g5 14 g4 ⌘f6 15 b·
⌗g7 16 ⌗b2 c6 17 ⌘dc3 ⌘d7 18 ⌗c2 ⌘e·
with good play for Black in Galianina
Strutinskaya, Russian Women's Champi·
onship, Elista 1997.

e) 6...⌗e7 7 ⌗d3 c5 8 ⌘ge2 ⌘c6 9 0-
0-0 10 b3 ⌗d6 11 ⌗c2 ⌒b8 12 h3 ⌘e7 1.
⌖h1 ⌘g6 14 ⌓b1 cxd4 15 exd4 ⌒d8 1·
⌗e3 ⌓c8 17 ⌒d2 ⌗b8 18 c5 ⌒e8 19 b·
⌘h4 20 ⌓f2 h6 21 ⌗f4 ⌗xf4 ½-½ Piket
Adams, Linares 1997.

5...⌘f6 6 ⌘h3

6 e3 transposes to the previous note.

6...g6

I once tried 6...⌗e7, but with hindsigh·
I don't like this move: it is too passive·
After 7 e3 0-0 8 ⌗e2 a5 9 0-0 ⌘a6 10 b·
⌒e8 11 ⌘f4 ⌒f7 (if 11...g5 12 ⌘d3 d6 1·
b4 with a great position for White) 1·
⌗b2 d5 13 cxd5 ⌘xd5 14 ⌘cxd5 exd5 1·
e4 c6 16 exd5 cxd5 17 ⌘d3 White wa·
better in Murshed-King, Dhaka 1993.

7 ⌘f2 ⌗g7 8 e4

Suba is an uncompromising player: h·
is offered the chance to grab the centr·
with his pawns and takes it. If he wer·
safely castled then White would have ·
large advantage, but that is still some way·
off so Black has a chance to strike back.

**8...fxe4 9 fxe4 0-0 10 ⌗g5 h6 11 ⌗e·
⌘c6! 12 e5**

White must do something about hi·
pawns, and once the mass advances, Black·

can attack it more easily. However, 12 ♗e2 is met by 12...e5! 13 d5 ♘d4 14 0-0 c5.

12...♘h5 13 ♕g4 ♘e7 14 ♗d3 ♕e8 15 0-0 ♘f5 16 ♗d2 d6 17 exd6 cxd6 18 ♖ae1 ♕f7

The position is totally unclear: Black's pawns aren't in the best shape but, on the other hand, his minor pieces are extremely active.

19 d5 exd5 20 ♘xd5 ♗xd5 21 cxd5 ♗xb2 22 ♖e6 ♘f6 23 ♕c4 ♖ac8 24 ♕b3 ♗e5 25 ♗xf5 gxf5 26 ♗xh6 ♖c3 27 ♕b1 ♘xd5 28 ♖xe5 dxe5 29 ♗xf8 ♕xf8 30 ♘e4 ♖xa3 31 ♕b2 ♘e3 32 ♖f3 ♘c4 33 ♕c1 ♖xf3 34 ♕xc4+ ♔h8 35 gxf3 fxe4 36 ♕xe4 a5 37 ♔f1 ♕d6 38 h4 ♔g7 39 ♕g4+ ♔f7 40 ♕f5+ ♕f6 41 ♕d7+ ♔g6 42 ♕g4+ ♔h6 43 ♔e2 b5 44 ♕d7 b4 45 ♕b5 ♕f4 46 ♕e8 ♕c4+ 47 ♔e3 ♕d4+ 48 ♔e2 ½-½

Mad stuff. I feel that if White is going to play with f2-f3 he does better by hanging back with e3-e4 and seeing what formation Black adopts (as in the note to White's fifth move, for instance).

Game 59
Morovic-Speelman
Cala Galdana 1994

---

1 d4 e6 2 c4 b6 3 a3 ♗b7 4 ♘c3

I mentioned in the introduction to this chapter that if nothing else after White plays a2-a3, Black has the option of transposing back into a Queen's Indian Defence, Petrosian variation, with ...♘f6. But is that really so? In fact White can avoid that if he wishes to as the next couple of games demonstrate. White can also reach these positions by playing d4-d5 before a2-a3, so these positions have a direct significance for English Defence players.

4...♘f6

Black could also play 4...d5, when 5 cxd5 exd5 6 ♘f3 ♘f6 is one of the main variations of the Petrosian variation (which is outside the scope of this book). It is also possible to be crafty and delay the development of the knight on g8 with 6...♗d6.

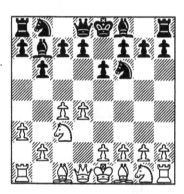

5 d5

A bold attempt to avoid the Queen's Indian. Instead, 5 ♘f3 would transpose directly.

5...exd5

For 5...♗d6 see the next game.

6 cxd5 b5!?

Very much in keeping with the wackiness of a great deal of the English Defence. Black has also tried:

a) 6...♗d6 7 g3 0-0 8 ♗g2 ♖e8 9 ♘h3 c5 10 0-0 ♗f8 11 ♖e1 d6 12 e4 ♘bd7, as in Lukacs-Ostojic, Budapest 1977, is a sensible set-up for Black. He threatens ...c5-c4 and ...♘c5.

b) 6...c6 is the most direct attempt to meet White's early (premature?) pawn push: 7 g3 (not 7 e4? ♕e7) 7...♘xd5 8 ♘xd5 cxd5 9 ♗g2 ♕f6!? 10 ♘h3 ♘a6 11 0-0 ♗d6 12 ♗xd5 ♗xd5 13 ♕xd5 0-0 14 ♖b1 ♕e6 15 ♖d1 ♕xh3 16 ♕xd6 ♕h5 17 ♕d3 ♘c5 18 ♕f3 ♕xf3 19 exf3 ♖fd8 20 ♖d5 ♖ac8 21 ♗e3 ♘a4 22 ♗d4 f6 23 ♖d1 ♖c2 ½-½ Lukacs-Regan, Budapest 1978. On the basis of this game Black has little to fear.

c) 6...g6 7 g3 ♗g7 8 ♗g2 0-0, as in Bischoff-Lau, Bad Endbach 1995, is also quite acceptable.

7 ♕d4

The most straightforward move is 7 e4, as Speelman has faced in another of his games: 7...b4 8 axb4 ♗xb4 9 ♗d3. Now I think Black should try 9...♕e7 10 ♕e2 c6 (10...0-0 and ...♖e8 is also possible). The actual game went 9...c6 10 dxc6 ♘xc6 11 ♘f3 0-0 12 0-0 ♗xc3 13 bxc3 d5 14 e5 ♘e4 15 ♕c2 ♖e8 16 ♗xe4 dxe4 17 ♕xe4 ♘a5 18 ♕b4 ♗xf3 19 ♕xa5 ♗e2 20 ♖e1 ♗c4 21 ♗e3 and White was somewhat better, though the game Baburin-Speelman, Copenhagen 1996 ended in a draw.

7...a6 8 ♗f4 ♗e7 9 e4 d6 10 a4 c5! 11 ♕d3 b4

see following diagram

Black's play on the queenside already gives him the advantage.

12 ♘ce2 0-0 13 ♘g3 ♖e8 14 ♗e2 ♗f8 15 ♘f3 a5 16 ♘d2 ♘bd7 17 ♘c4 ♘b6 18 ♘xb6 ♕xb6 19 f3 ♗a6 20 ♕b3 ♗xe2 21 ♘xe2 ♕a6 22 ♕c2 c4 23 0-0 c3 24 bxc3 ♘xd5 25 cxb4 ♘xb4 26 ♕d2 d5 27 ♘c3 dxe4 28 ♘xe4 ♖ad8 29 ♕f2 ♘d3 30 ♕g3 f5 31 ♘g5 ♖d4 32 ♗d2 h6 33 ♘h3 ♗d6 34 f4 ♗f8 35 ♗c3 ♖de4 36 ♕f3 ♕c4 37 ♗d2 ♖e2 38 ♗xa5 ♕c5+ 39 ♔h1 ♖2e3 0-1

6...b5 is fun, but perhaps one needs to be a special kind of player to get away with it.

When faced with d4-d5 preventing the Queen's Indian, most Black players have tried the system featured in the next game.

Game 60
Andreasen-Pedersen
Danish Championship 1988

1 d4 ♘f6 2 c4 b6 3 ♘c3 ♗b7 4 d5 e6 5 a3 ♗d6

By far the most popular way of dealing with White's system (but that doesn't mean it is necessarily the best).

6 ♘f3

White does best to prevent ...♗e5. For example, 6 e4 ♗e5 7 ♗d3 ♗xc3+ 8 bxc3 ♕e7 9 ♘e2 ♘a6 10 0-0 ♘c5 11 f3 ♗a6 12 ♗c2 ♗xc4 and Black was clearly better in Plachetka-Prie, Paris Championship 1989, though it is still complicated and Black

finally succeeded in losing this position.
6...0-0 7 e4 exd5 8 exd5 c6

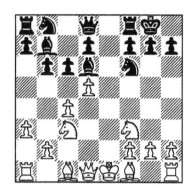

9 ♗e2

Or 9 ♗g5 h6 10 ♗h4 cxd5 11 ♘xd5 ♕e8+ 12 ♘e3 ♘e4 13 ♗e2 f5 with chances for both sides in Kindermann-Forintos, Reykjavik open 1982.

9...cxd5 10 cxd5 ♘a6 11 0-0 ♖e8 12 ♗g5

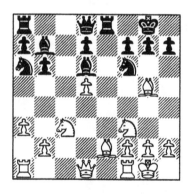

12...♘c5

Black probably ought to flick in 12...h6 as the option of ...g7-g5 is useful. After 13 ♗h4 we have two games:

a) 13...♘c5 14 ♘d4 ♗e5 15 ♗c4 ♕b8 16 f4 (16 ♗g3 ♗xg3 17 hxg3 ♘ce4 is fine for Black) 16...♗xd4+ (16...♗xf4 17 ♗xf6 ♗xh2+ 18 ♔h1 gxf6 19 ♕g4+ is too risky) 17 ♕xd4 ♘fe4 18 b4 ♘xc3 19 bxc5, and now instead of 19...♘e4, as in Knaak-Planinc, Polanica Zdroj 1979, I think Black should play 19...♘e2+ 20 ♗xe2 ♖xe2 with equal chances.

b) 13...♖c8 14 ♘d4 ♘c5 15 ♘f5 ♗f8 16 b4 ♘ce4 17 ♘xe4 ♖xe4 18 ♗d3 ♖e8 19 ♘e3 g5 20 ♗g3 ♘xd5 21 ♘xd5 ♗xd5 was also fine for Black in Petrosian-Planinc, Moscow 1975.

13 ♘d4 ♗e5 14 ♖a2

Not very clever. 14 ♗c4 h6 15 ♗h4 would transpose to Knaak-Planinc above.

14...♕b8 15 f4 ♗xd4+ 16 ♕xd4 ♘xd5 17 ♘xd5 ♖xe2 18 ♖f3 ♕e8 19 ♗h6 ♖e1+ 20 ♔f2 ♕e2+ 21 ♔g3 ♘e4+ 22 ♔h3 f6 23 ♘e7+ ♔h8 24 ♕xd7 ♘f2+ 25 ♖xf2 ♕xe7 0-1

This is a reliable system for Black; so if you are happy playing a Queen's Indian then after a2-a3 you can play ...♘f6 with confidence.

Summary

If you want to be one of the pioneers then I would recommend the double fianchetto in Games 50-52, but be prepared for reverses – even Miles hasn't scored that well with it. A reasonable alternative way of tackling a2-a3 is to play some kind of Dutch Defence. Short played excellently in Game 53 and the systems in Games 54-56 are all reliable. Personally, I have always found it rather irritating playing against f2-f3 (Game 58), probably because Black doesn't have the fun of knocking down a pawn centre, though this is still no refutation of the opening. And lastly, if you are content to play a Queen's Indian, then there is nothing to stop you transposing with ...♘f6, as Games 59 and 60 prove.

1 d4 e6 2 c4 b6 3 a3 *(D)*

3...g6

    3...f5 4 ♘c3
        4...♘f6 – *Game 53*
        4...♗b7 *(D)*
            5 d5 ♘f6 6 g3
                6...♘a6 7 ♗g2 ♘c5 8 ♘h3 ♗d6 9 0-0 ♗e5 10 ♕c2 0-0
                    11 ♗e3 – *Game 54*
                    11 ♗d2 – *Game 55*
                6...g6 – *Game 56*
            5 ♘f3 – *Game 57*
            5 f3 – *Game 58*
    3...♗b7 4 ♘c3
        4...f5 – see Games 54-58 above (by transposition)
        4...♘f6 5 d5
            5...exd5 – *Game 59*
            5...♗d6 – *Game 60*
4 ♘c3 ♗g7 5 ♘f3 ♘e7 6 e4 ♗b7 *(D)* **7 h4**
    7 ♗e2 – *Game 50*
    7 ♗e3 – *Game 51*
7...h6 – *Game 52*

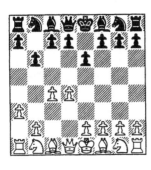

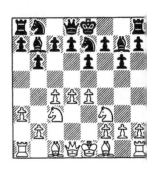

3 a3   *4...♗b7*   *6...♗b7*

CHAPTER SEVEN

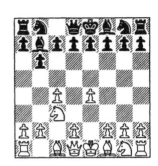

The Two-Pawn Attack
(1 c4 b6 2 ♘c3 ♗b7 3 e4)

1 c4 b6 2 ♘c3 ♗b7 3 e4

There are certain White players who open with 1 c4 and then play their next four pre-programmed moves without even looking up from the board. It is the equivalent of the second serve in tennis, designed not to score an ace, but just to get the ball safely over the net.

In these final two chapters I'm going to be examining games where White declines to occupy the centre with all three pawns in an attempt to refute Black's system, but instead attempts to play a more modest, and to them, more familiar English or Réti opening. Here we shall look at games where White advances two pawns, the c- and the e- pawns, but leaves the d-pawn at home.

Most of the games in this chapter contain some interesting ideas – generated by both colours. Although Games 62-66 are interesting enough, I don't think Black should experience any difficulties. The critical move is 4 ♘f3 followed by ♗d3 (Games 67-70).

But first, something a little out of the ordinary from Black. Short brings something new to the opening. (By the way I wouldn't put Korchnoi in the category of the 'second servers'; he has enough fight-

ing spirit for the rest of them put together!)

Game 61
Korchnoi-Short
Groningen 1997

1 c4 b6 2 e4 ♗b7 3 ♘c3 e5!?

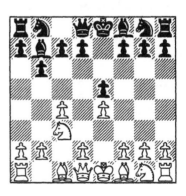

In a way, Black's fianchetto isn't particularly relevant to the position (though it can of course be useful in covering the d5- and e4-squares); what Black is aiming for is control of the central dark squares. This was the first time this move had been seen at such a rarefied level, though there are a couple of previous examples from less well-known players.

4 d3

Or ♘f3 ♘c6! (4...d6? is a horrible move, closing off the bishop's path to c5; after 5 d4 exd4 6 ♘xd4 ♘f6 7 ♗d3 White was already better in Endres-Oberem, Waldshut 1991) 5 d4 exd4 6 ♘xd4 ♗b4 7 ♘xc6 ♗xc6 8 ♗d3 ♗xc3+ 9 bxc3 and Black was already comfortably placed in Deubelbeiss-Horn, Swiss Team Championship 1993.

4...♘c6 5 g3 ♗c5 6 ♗g2 ♘ge7!

The knight is far better here than on f6: when its comrade leaps into d4 it can move over to c6 to lend support; moreover it might be useful that the f-pawn is free to move.

7 ♘f3 0-0 8 0-0 a5 9 ♗e3 d6 10 d4 exd4 11 ♘xd4 ♘xd4 12 ♗xd4 ♘c6! 13 ♗xc5 bxc5

White has absolutely nothing here. If he leaves the structure as it is, he must cover the d4-square with his knight (to prevent Black from occupying it with his own) but then he will be far too passive. Instead, Korchnoi explodes the position:

14 e5 dxe5 15 ♘a4 ♕d6 16 ♕d5 ♘d8 17 ♕xc5 ♗xg2 18 ♕xd6 cxd6 19 ♔xg2 ♘e6 20 ♖ad1 ♘d4 21 b3 f6 22 ♖d2 ♖ab8 23 ♘c3 ♖fc8 24 h4 h5 25 ♖fd1 ♖c6 26 ♘b5 ½-½

Wisely liquidating into a drawn endgame, as the knight on d4 was too strong. After 26...♘xb5 27 cxb5 ♖xb5 28 ♖xd6 ♖xd6 29 ♖xd6 the game is equal. Perhaps it is just a question of taste, but to me 3...e5 looks a sensible move. Certainly, Korchnoi failed to make any headway.

Game 62
Razuvaev-Barle
Maribor 1996

---

1 c4 b6 2 ♘c3 e6 3 e4 ♗b7

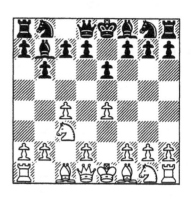

This is the 'normal' starting position for the two-pawn attack. Note that with certain move orders, like here, it is not always possible to go for Short's 3...e5 if you have already played ...e7-e6; at least, you'd be fairly silly to do so.

4 d3

White strengthens his centre, and waits to see what Black is going to do before committing his pieces, but this is rather tame. Alternatively, 4 ♘ge2 (Game 63), 4 g3 (Games 64 and 65) and the main move 4 ♘f3 (Games 66-70) are considered later in this chapter.

4...♗b4

Black continues in the spirit of the English Defence and pins. Instead, 4...c5, leading to a kind of 'Hedgehog' position, is quite acceptable. 4...g6 is more original: 5 g3 ♗g7 6 ♘ge2 ♘e7 7 ♗g2 d6 (7...c5!?) 8 0-0 0-0 9 d4 c5 10 ♗e3 a6 11 f4 and White was on top in Borek-Kirchmayr, Austrian Women's Championship 1996.

5 ♕g4

White is inspired by the opening to play something original, but considering the options, this was perhaps his best course of action:

a) 5 ♘ge2 d5 6 cxd5 (after 6 a3?! ♗xc3+ 7 ♘xc3 dxe4 8 ♘xe4 ♘e7 9 ♗e2 ♘bc6 Black's control of d4 already gave him the advantage in Eising-Hjorth, Amsterdam OHRA 1984) 6...exd5 7 ♕a4+ ♘c6 8 a3 ♗xc3+ 9 ♘xc3 ♘ge7 10 ♗g5 f6 11 ♗f4 0-0 12 ♗e2, as in McNab-Rowson, London Agency 1998, and now 12...f5 would have given Black a promising position, e.g. 13 exd5?! (13 ♗g5 is slightly better for Black according to McDonald) 13...♘xd5 14 ♕c4 ♘a5 15 ♕a2 ♔h8 with the initiative.

b) 5 ♘f3 ♘e7 6 ♗e2 0-0 7 0-0 f5 8 e5 ♘g6 9 d4 ♘c6 10 ♕c2 ♘h4, and after dreadfully stereotyped play from White, Black already held the initiative in Zlotnikov-Miles, Lloyds Bank open, London 1982.

c) 5 ♘h3 ♘e7 6 ♕g4 0-0 7 ♗d2 f5 was better for Black in Duckers-Forintos, Bozen open 1992.

5...♕f6

see following diagram

Anyone like to try the idea of 5...♔f8!? followed by ...♘f6 and ...d7-d5...? Black may be able to make something of his considerable lead in development.

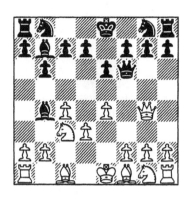

6 ♗d2 ♘c6 7 0-0-0 ♕g6 8 ♕h4 ♘f6 9 ♘h3 ♕g4 10 ♕xg4 ♘xg4 11 f3 ♘f6 12 ♘b5 ♗xd2+ 13 ♖xd2 0-0-0 14 d4 a6 15 ♘c3

It is curious how a position has been reached that is similar to the games where Black decides to check on b4 in Chapter 2 (Games 20-22); but in this case Black is better developed so his central strike has more effect:

15...e5 16 dxe5

Or 16 d5 ♘d4.

16...♘xe5 17 f4 ♘g6 18 e5 ♘h5 19 ♖f2 ♘e7 20 f5 ♘c6 21 ♗e2 ♘xe5 22 ♗xh5 ♘d3+ 23 ♔d2 ♘xf2 24 ♘xf2 g6 25 ♗f3 ♗xf3 26 gxf3 ½-½

Normally, with such a material balance I would prefer the knights, but as Black's pawns are so compact, the beasts have no good outposts. Here, instead of capturing on f5, I think Black should play 26...≌de8 and ...≌e5, with equal chances.

Game 63
Korchnoi-King
Oviedo rapidplay 1992

---

1 c4 e6 2 ♘c3 b6 3 e4 ♗b7 4 ♘ge2

I don't like this move. The knight goes to an inferior square without any provocation or justification. Black should have no difficulty in equalising.

4...♘f6!

Exposing the shortcomings of 4 ♘ge2. Alternatively, 4...♗b4 5 a3 ♗xc3 6 ♘xc3 ♘e7 followed by castling and ...f7-f5, was suggested by Keene, Plaskett and Tisdall, though no one has tried it to my knowledge, probably because 4...♘f6 is such a reliable choice. I wouldn't want to put you off the idea though; having played around with the pieces for a bit here I don't see an obvious way to control Black's counterattack, e.g. 7 d4 (or 7 ♗e2 d5!) 7...0-0 8 ♗d3 f5 with the usual counterplay. 4...c5 is, naturally, also quite acceptable, most probably leading to a 'hedgehog'.

5 ♘g3

The most straightforward, and the most sensible, move. If White gets too flashy he can end up in trouble. For example:

a) 5 f3 e5!? (like Short in Game 61;

5...d5!? appeals to me more though – i takes White a long time to develop with the knight on e2, and in the meantime the centre is exploding) 6 d4 exd4 7 ♘xd ♗b4 (perhaps 7...♗c5 or 7...♘c6) 8 ♗g! ♗xc3+ 9 bxc3 h6 10 ♗h4 d6 11 ♘f5 0-0 1: ♕d4 ♘bd7 was unclear in Jakobsen Keene, Aarhus 1976.

b) 5 e5, lurching forward, but it is only going to get beaten up: 5...♘g4 6 d4 ♕h 7 ♘g3 ♗b4 (or 7...d6!?) 8 h3 ♘h6 9 a ♗xc3+ 10 bxc3 ♘f5 11 ♕h5 ♕xh5 1: ♘xh5 0-0 13 a4 d6 14 exd6 cxd6 15 a5 ♖c 16 f3 bxa5 17 ♖xa5 ♘d7 18 ♔f2 ♘b6 and draw was agreed here in Plachetka-Kengis Viking open 1997, but Black is better.

5...c5

Since the knight no longer protects the d4-square it seemed like a good idea to fix it. Instead, 5...h5!? is good fun, e.g. 6 h4 (e5 h4!) 6...♗d6 7 d3 ♗xg3 8 fxg3, as in Byway-Smith, British Championship Southport 1983, and now 8...d5!? 9 e! ♘g4 is the most dynamic continuation.

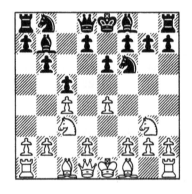

6 ♗e2 ♘c6 7 0-0 g6 8 f4 d6 9 d3 ♗g 10 ♗e3 0-0 11 ♗f3 ♕d7

With hindsight 11...♘d7 strikes me a far more sensible, increasing control ove the d4-square. My excuse is that this was rapidplay game.

12 ♘ge2 a6 13 ♗f2 ♖ac8 14 ♖c1 b5

see following diagram

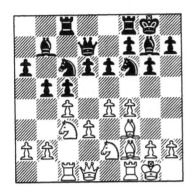

...nevertheless, Black is still doing fine. Up till now we had both been playing quite steadily, but now Korchnoi cracked off the pawn instantly, with a bang of the clock to boot.

15 cxb5 axb5 16 ♘xb5 ♘b4 17 a4

If 17 ♘ec3 ♘xa2 or 17 ♘bc3 ♗a6 with good compensation.

17...♗a6 18 e5 dxe5 19 fxe5 ♘fd5 20 ♖xc5 ♗xe5 21 ♖xc8 ♖xc8 22 d4 ♗g7 23 ♘ec3 ♘xc3 24 bxc3 ♘d5 25 ♕b3 ♘xc3 26 ♘xc3 ♗xf1 27 ♔xf1 ♗xd4 28 ♗xd4 ♕xd4

The position has finally settled. The a-pawn is potentially dangerous, but it is difficult to guide it down the board without the minor pieces; if the knight or bishop assists, then the king will become exposed. Black also has the long-term threat of advancing the f- and e-pawns.

29 ♘e2 ♕e5 30 h3 ♖c5 31 ♔f2 ♔g7 32 g3 ♕f5 33 ♔g2 e5 34 ♕b7

...here we stopped recording the moves as time was getting short. Korchnoi played recklessly and I mated him on the kingside. 4 ♘ge2 is not a move to trouble us.

Game 64
Smejkal-Kengis
Prague 1993

---

1 c4 b6 2 ♘c3 e6 3 g3 ♗b7 4 e4

A slightly unusual move order. Instead of 4 e4 White can play 4 ♘f3 which will often transpose to a 'hedgehog' system, after, for instance, 4...c5, but Black has the interesting option 4...♗xf3!? 5 exf3 c5, attempting to gain control over the d4-square, which is considered in the next chapter (Games 74-77).

4...f5 5 ♗g2

The system which White employs is quite common among a group of hardy 1 c4 players who have grown up playing the Botvinnik System (1 c4, 2 ♘c3, 3 g3, 4 ♗g2, 5 e4, 6 ♘ge2 and 7 d3) against almost anything. However, against the English Defence they have to do a little thinking for themselves.

5...♘f6

5...fxe4?! 6 ♘xe4 makes life a little too easy for White. Black should hold the tension for a bit longer.

6 d3

6 ♕c2 isn't too clever as White loses control over the d4-square. After 6...fxe4 7 ♘xe4 ♘c6 8 ♘xf6+ ♕xf6 Black was already better in Hort-King, German Bundesliga 1995.

6...fxe4

Black could have played 6...♗b4 here (and on the previous two turns) to increase the pressure on e4. That is the subject of the next game (by transposition).

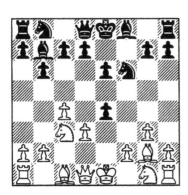

7 ♘ge2!

White does best to delay the recapture of the pawn. It keeps more options open, though 7 dxe4 has been played, e.g. 7...♗b4 (instead 7...♗c5!? is potentially rather dangerous for White) and now:

a) 8 ♗d2 0-0 9 ♘h3 ♘a6 (9...♕e7!? 10 ♕e2 ♘c6) 10 0-0 ♘c5 11 e5 ♗xg2 12 ♔xg2 ♘e8 13 ♘a4 ♘a6 14 ♘g5 ♗e7 15 ♘e4 d5

16 exd6 ♘xd6 17 ♕g4 and White was better in Libeau-Lau, German Bundesliga 1995.

b) 8 ♕c2 ♗xc3+ 9 ♕xc3 ♗xe4 (or 9...0-0) 10 ♗xe4 ♘xe4 11 ♕xg7 ♕f6 12 ♕xf6 ♘xf6. Here I prefer Black's position, but you should be aware of my prejudices: I always like centre pawns.

7...♗c5

7...♗b4 8 0-0 would transpose to the next game; but there is really no need to put the bishop on b4. I like the look of 7...♘c6!? – as Kengis played in a later game: 8 dxe4 ♘e5 (8...♗c5!? is also possible, e.g. 9 0-0 0-0 10 ♘a4 e5 11 ♘xc5 bxc5 12 ♘c3 ♘d4 13 f4 with complications in Cekro-Hausrath, Belgian Team Championship 1997) 9 b3 ♗c5 10 h3 ♕e7 11 f4 ♘f7 12 a3 a5 13 ♕d3 0-0 14 g4 (rather extravagant) 14...d5 15 e5 ♘e4 16 ♗xe4 dxe4 17 ♕g3 ♖ad8 18 ♗e3 ♗xe3 19 ♕xe3 ♘e5 0-1 Heinbuch-Kengis, Bonn GSK 1995. By the way, no one has tried 7...d5 – though it does look quite ugly, e.g. 8 dxe4 (8 ♘f4?! dxc4 9 ♘xe6 ♕d7 10 ♘xf8 ♖xf8 11 ♘xe4 ♘c6 12 ♕e2 0-0-0 with the initiative) 8...dxe4 9 ♕xd8+ ♔xd8 10 ♘d4 and Black is already under pressure.

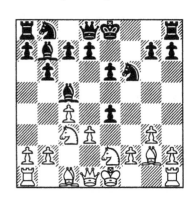

8 0-0 0-0 9 ♗g5!

Much stronger than 9 dxe4 ♘g4!; while 9 d4!? ♗b4 (9...♗e7) 10 ♕c2 ♗xc3 11 ♘xc3 d5 should be okay for Black.

9...♗e7 10 dxe4

10...♘g4

Not 10...d6? 11 ♘d4 and White has clear plus.

11 ♗xe7 ♕xe7 12 ♘d4 ♘e5 13 b3 ♘bc6 14 ♘c2 ♘b4 15 ♘xb4

According to Ribli 15 ♘e3!? a5 16 ♔h1 would have given White a slight advantage.

15...♕xb4 16 ♖c1 ♖ad8 17 f4 ♘f7 18 ♕d2 a6 19 ♖f2 ♕e7 20 ♖cf1 ♗c6 21 ♕d3 ♕c5 22 ♔h1 b5

White hasn't made the most of his pace advantage and after this move, chipping away at the structure, Black solves most of his problems.

23 cxb5 axb5 24 ♖c2 ♕b6 25 ♘e2 e5! 26 ♘c3 b4 27 ♘d5 ♗xd5 28 ♕xd5

28 exd5 exf4 29 ♖xf4 ♘e5 is unclear.

28...c6 29 ♕c5 ♕xc5 30 ♖xc5 ♖a8 31 h3 ♖fd8 32 ♖d1 ♖xa2 33 ♖xd7 ♖a1+

34 ♔g2 ♖a2+ 35 ♔f3 ♖xh2 36 ♖xc6 ♖xh3 37 ♖xd8+ ♘xd8 38 ♖c8 exf4 39 ♖xd8+ ♔f7 40 ♔xf4 h5 41 ♖d7+ ♔f8 42 ♖b7 h4 43 gxh4 ♖xb3 44 e5 ♖b1 45 e6 b3 46 ♔g3 ½-½

Although the game concluded satisfactorily from Black's viewpoint, it appears more promising to play 7...♘c6!? rather than 7...♗c5.

Game 65
Heinbuch-Spassky
German Bundesliga 1984

---

1 c4 b6 2 ♘c3 ♗b7 3 e4 e6 4 g3 f5 5 d3 ♗b4 6 ♘ge2 fxe4

Black could delay capturing on e4, though this has only been tested in one game: 6...♘f6 7 ♗g2 0-0 8 0-0 ♘a6!? 9 exf5?! (simply 9 a3 is stronger) 9...♗xg2 10 ♔xg2 exf5, as in Joksimovic-Bricard, Lyon open 1990. After the exchange of bishops Black is doing fine.

7 ♗g2 ♘f6

8 0-0 0-0

8...♕c8 is too passive: 9 dxe4 0-0 10 h3 ♘c6 11 ♗e3 ♘e5 12 b3 a5 13 ♖c1 ♘g6 14 f4 with advantage to White in Stulik-Bores, Czech Team Championship 1995.

9 dxe4

9 a3 ♗e7?! (9...♗xc3 10 ♘xc3 d5 is unclear) 10 dxe4 ♘c6 11 h3 e5 12 ♘d5 clearly favoured White in Sehner-Schmitzer,

German Bundesliga 1992.

9...♘c6

9...♘a6?! 10 e5 ♗xg2 11 ♔xg2 ♘e8 12 a3 ♗xc3 13 ♘xc3 was better for White in Schneider-Schonthier, German Bundesliga 1995.

10 h3

10...♖b8

10...♘e5 is more ambitious and, above all, tricky, e.g. 11 b3 ♗c5 12 ♘d4 (maybe 12 ♔h1) 12...♕e8 13 ♗f4 d6 14 ♗e3 ♕g6 15 ♘xe6 ♗xe3 16 ♘xf8 ♕xg3 17 ♘e2 ♘f3+ 0-1 Smejkal-Kavalek, Kettler Cup (rapidplay) 1997.

11 f4 a6 12 a3 ♗xc3 13 ♘xc3 d6 14 ♗e3 ♕e8 15 ♕e2 ♘e7 16 ♔h2 ♗a8 17 ♖ad1 b5

As in the previous game, once Black gets this move in, fighting White's central control, then he should equalise.

18 c5 d5 19 ♗d4

19 e5 ♘e4 is unclear.

19...♘xe4 20 ♘xe4 dxe4 21 ♗xe4 ♗xe4 22 ♕xe4 ♕c6 23 ♕xc6 ♘xc6

see following diagram

...and now if anyone is better, it is Black.

24 ♗c3 ♖bd8 25 ♔g2 ♖d5! 26 b4 ♖fd8 27 ♖xd5 ♖xd5

Perhaps 27...exd5!?

28 ♖e1 ♔f7 29 ♔f3 ♖d3+ 30 ♔e3 ♘d4+ 31 ♗xd4 ♖xd4 32 ♔e2 ♔f6 ½-½

Game 66
Laqua-Cording
OLNN 1997

1 c4 b6 2 ♘c3 e6 3 e4 ♗b7 4 ♘f3

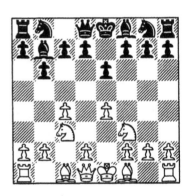

The most sensible, and I think the best move in this position. The knight belongs on f3!

4...♗b4

Applying the usual pressure on White's centre. In the early days of the English Defence (I mean in the late 1970s) attention was focused on...

5 ♕b3

...until Black came up with an excellent response:

5...♘a6!

The greedy 5...♗xc3?! 6 ♕xc3 ♗xe4 runs into 7 d3! ♗xf3 8 ♕xg7 ♕f6 9 ♗h6!

♕xg7 10 ♗xg7 and White picks up an exchange.

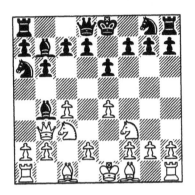

6 ♗e2

The point of 5...♘a6 is that if White now tries 6 a3 then 6...♘c5! is a good move as 7 ♕xb4?? loses the queen to 7...a5 8 ♕b5 ♗c6. Alternatively, 6 d3 f5! 7 exf5 ♗xf3 8 gxf3 ♕e7 9 ♔d1 ♗xc3 10 ♕xc3 exf5 11 ♗h3 0-0-0 12 ♗xf5 ♕f7 13 ♗e4 ♘f6 14 ♗e3 d5 gave Black a great attack in Ledger-Hodgson, Isle of Man open 1996.

6...♘e7 7 d3

7 a3 is still met by 7...♘c5! and if then 8 ♕c2 ♗xc3 9 ♕xc3 0-0, while after 7 0-0 0-0 8 e5?!, as in Uhlmann-Lau, Austrian Team Championship 1996, Black should have just played 8...♘f5, gaining control over the d4-square.

7...0-0 8 0-0 d5

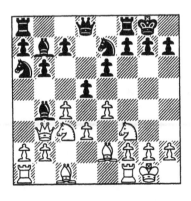

8...♘g6 is also strong, e.g. 9 ♗d2 d6 10

a3 (perhaps 10 ♕c2) 10...♘c5! (the same trick as before!) 11 ♕c2 (11 ♕xb4? a5 12 ♕b5 c6) 11...♗xc3 12 ♗xc3 f5! 13 exf5 ♖xf5 and Black had the initiative in Serper-Yermolinsky, Lucerne 1993.

9 cxd5

9 exd5 exd5 10 a3 ♘c5! (our familiar trick) 11 ♕c2 ♗xc3 12 ♕xc3 ♘f5 13 cxd5 ♖e8 14 ♖e1 ♗xd5 15 ♗f4 ♘b3 16 ♖ad1 c5 17 ♘d2 ♘bd4 18 ♗f1 ♕f6 19 ♘c4 ♘h4 20 ♖xe8+ ♖xe8 21 ♗g3 ♘xg2 0-1 Pastorini-Forintos, Forli open 1988.

9...exd5 10 ♗g5

After 10 exd5!? ♗xc3 (not 10...♘xd5 11 d4 and the knight on a6 is out of play) 11 bxc3 ♘c5 12 ♕c2 ♕xd5 (or 12...♘xd5) chances are balanced.

10...f6 11 ♗h4 ♔h8 12 ♖ac1 ♘g6 13 ♗g3 ♗xc3 14 ♕xc3 c5

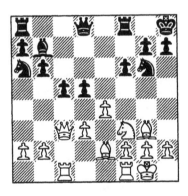

After this Black assumes control of the centre.

15 a3

15 exd5 is met by 15...♘b4!

15...♖c8 16 ♘d2 ♘c7 17 ♗g4 ♘b5 18 ♕b3 ♘d4 19 ♕a2 f5 20 exf5 ♘xf5 21 ♖fe1 ♕g5 22 ♗xf5 ♕xf5 23 ♖cd1 ♖ce8 24 ♕b3 ♘f4 25 ♗xf4 ♕xf4 26 ♘f3 d4 27 ♖xe8 ♖xe8 28 ♖e1 ♖f8 29 ♕d1 h5 30 ♖e5 ♗xf3 31 ♖xh5+ ♗xh5 32 ♕xh5+ ♔g8 0-1

5...♘a6 is a good response to 5 ♕b3; so much so that this move is hardly seen anymore compared to the main move, 5

♗d3, which we shall be concentrating on in the remaining games of this chapter.

Game 67
Krylov-Zak
Groningen 1994

---

1 c4 b6 2 ♘c3 ♗b7 3 e4 e6 4 ♘f3 ♗b4 5 ♗d3

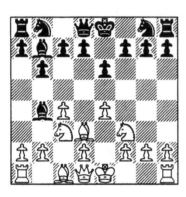

A strange move, blocking the d-pawn, but quite a good one too. If Black captures the knight on c3 then White immediately solves the problem of how to develop the bishop on c1; and if Black doesn't capture then he will have to lose time re-deploying the bishop on b4. So White's bishop manoeuvre, ♗f1-d3-c2 followed by moving the d-pawn, doesn't look so costly as Black also has to waste time. Generally Black's response to this is to play the knight to e7, castle and go for ...f7-f5, though in this first game with 5 ♗d3 I would like to look at some example where Black captures the knight on c3 and employs a different plan.

5...♘e7

After the immediate 5...♗xc3!? 6 bxc3?! (6 dxc3 is better) 6...d6 7 0-0 e5 8 ♗c2 ♘f6 9 ♗a4+?! ♘bd7 10 ♗xd7+?! ♕xd7 Black had no difficulties in Wulfmeyer-Rosch, G/RL-NO 1997.

6 0-0

6 ♘e2, preserving the knight, is the sub-ject of Game 70.

♗xc3!?

For 6...0-0 see the next two games.

7 dxc3

Naturally White takes the opportunit to open the diagonal for his bishop.

7...0-0

I prefer 7...d6. For one thing, Blac doesn't need to commit his king yet, bu also it is worth preventing the possibilit of e4-e5 – see the next note. For exampl 8 ♘d4 ♘d7 9 f3 0-0 10 ♖e1 e5 11 ♘c2 f 12 exf5 ♘xf5 13 ♘e3 ♘xe3 14 ♗xe3 wit equal chances in Johansen-Sandler, Austr lian Championship 1995.

8 ♗g5

This only helps Black to construct h ideal pawn formation. 8 e5!? is more dan gerous: 8...♘g6 9 ♖e1 ♗xf3?! (9...d6 an 9...f5 both spring to mind) 10 ♕xf3 ♘c 11 ♕g3 d6 12 ♗g5 ♕d7 13 ♗xg6 hxg6 1 ♖ad1 d5 and now 15 ♕g4 would hav given White a winning position in th game Roos-Haik, French Team Champi onship 1993.

8...f6 9 ♗h4 e5

With the pawn on e5 White's bishop are blocked in and it is difficult to see hov White can create play for them.

10 ♗g3 d6 11 ♕e2 ♘d7 12 ♘d2 ♘c5 1 b4 ♘e6 14 ♘b3 ♘g6 15 f3 ♘gf4 1 ♕e3 c6 17 ♖fd1 ♕c7 18 ♗f1 f5! 19 ♗f fxe4 20 fxe4 c5 21 ♖d2 ♘g5 22 ♖d5

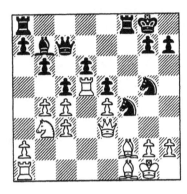

22...♗xd5 23 cxd5 ♖f6 24 ♗h4 ♖g6 25 ♔h1 h6 26 bxc5 bxc5 27 ♘d2 ♖b8 28 ♘c4 ♖f8 29 h3 ♕d7 30 ♔h2 ♘fxh3 31 gxh3 ♘f3+ 32 ♔h1 ♘xh4 33 ♗e2 ♖f3 0-1

The early capture of the knight on c3 is a solid alternative to the main continuations. Indeed, in view of the complexity of 6...0-0 and 7...f5, I can see 6...♗xc3 being employed more often.

Game 68
Fedorowicz-Flear
Wijk aan Zee 1988

---

1 c4 e6 2 e4 b6 3 ♘c3 ♗b7 4 ♘f3 ♗b4 5 ♗d3 ♘e7 6 0-0 0-0 7 ♗c2

This has to be the most sensible move – the first step to sorting out the queenside pieces. 7 ♖e1 has been played a few times, but not with great success, e.g. 7...f5

(7...♗xc3!? 8 dxc3 d6 – compare with the previous game) and now:

a) Not 8 e5? ♘g6 9 ♗f1 ♗xf3 10 ♕xf3 ♘c6 and Black was already clearly better in Hübner-Miles, Bad Lauterberg 1977.

b) 8 a3 ♗xc3 9 dxc3 fxe4 10 ♗xe4 ♗xe4 11 ♖xe4 ♘bc6 12 ♘d4 (or 12 ♕e2) 12...♕e8 with equality in Friedgood-Keene, Cape Town 1976.

c) 8 exf5!? ♘xf5 9 ♗e4 ♗xe4 and now:

c1) 10 ♘xe4 ♘c6 (10...♘h4!?) 11 a3 ♗c5 12 b4 ♗d4 13 ♖b1 ♘h4, when I prefer Black's position.

c2) 10 ♖xe4 ♗xc3? (10...♘c6! and Black is fine) 11 dxc3 ♘c6 12 ♗f4 ♖c8 13 ♕d3 ♕e8 14 ♖ae1 (preventing ...d7-d6) was a little better for White in Sunye Neto-Hoffman, Argentina-World 1994.

7...f5

Or 7...♗xc3!? 8 dxc3 d6 – once again, compare this position with Krylov-Zak. At this point White has a large range of options. Apart from those given below, the commonly played 8 ♕e2 is featured in the next game.

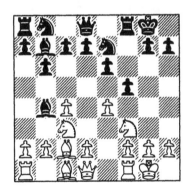

8 exf5

Alternatively:

a) 8 ♖e1 is sensible, e.g. 8...♗xc3 9 dxc3 h6 (or 9...fxe4 10 ♗xe4 ♗xe4 11 ♖xe4 ♘bc6 12 ♕e2 with a slight plus for White) 10 exf5 ♘xf5 11 ♘d4 ♕f6 12 ♘xf5 exf5 13 ♗f4 d6 14 c5! bxc5 15 ♗b3+ ♔h7 16 ♕h5 with a great attack in Rotstein-Sulava,

Geneva open 1996.

b) 8 d4 is, unsurprisingly, unpromising, e.g. after 8...♗xc3 9 bxc3 ♗xe4 10 ♗xe4 fxe4 11 ♘g5 ♕e8 12 ♘xe4 ♕g6 13 ♘g3 ♘bc6 Black was playing a good Nimzo-Indian Defence in Rahman-Speelman, Calcutta open 1996.

c) 8 e5 is a mistake due to 8...♗xf3 9 gxf3 (9 ♕xf3 ♘bc6 10 ♕e3 ♗c5 11 ♕g3 ♘g6 12 ♖e1 ♗d4 wins the e-pawn) 9...♘g6 10 d4 ♕h4 (10...c5 11 a3 ♗xc3 12 bxc3 ♕h4 13 ♔h1 ♘c6 is also strong, as in Contin-Vera, Saint Vincent open 1998) 11 ♘e2 ♘c6 12 f4 ♕g4+ 13 ♘g3 ♕h3 14 f3 ♘xd4 with a winning position in Zlotnikov-Shabalov, New York open 1997.

8...♘xf5 9 ♘e4

After 9 ♗e4 ♕c8!? (or 9...♗xe4 10 ♘xe4 ♘h4) 10 ♕b3 ♗c5 11 ♕c2 ♘c6 Black was already better in Uhlmann-Vera, Berlin 1982.

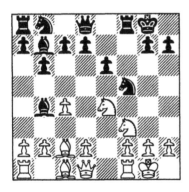

9...♗e7

Much too passive. I think the right move is 9...♘h4! with the following possibilities:

a) 10 ♘eg5? ♘xf3+.

b) 10 ♘fg5 h6 (10...♘xg2 is unclear) 11 ♘h3 d5 and Black has the initiative.

c) 10 ♘xh4 ♕xh4 when White doesn't have time to build a strong centre; Black has the attack going already.

d) 10 ♘e5 d6 11 ♘g4 d5 with a powerful initiative.

10 d4 ♘c6 11 d5

Black is getting pushed around, but his position remains fundamentally strong.

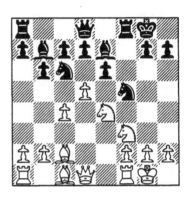

11...♘b4 12 ♗b3 ♘a6 13 ♘g3 ♘xg3 14 hxg3 ♘c5 15 ♗c2 ♗f6 16 ♖b1 a5 17 ♗e3 exd5 18 cxd5 ♕e7 19 a3 ♖ae8 20 ♖e1 ♕d8 21 b4 axb4 22 ♖xb4

After 22 axb4 ♘e4 23 ♕d3 g6 Black has enough counterplay.

22...d6 23 ♕b1 h6 24 ♗h7+ ♔h8 25 ♗g6 ♗xd5 26 ♗xe8 ♖xe8

Even here, Black shouldn't be worse his minor pieces are well placed.

27 ♗d4 ♗xf3 28 ♖xe8+ ♕xe8 29 ♗xf6 ♗e4 30 ♕c1 ♕g6 31 ♗d4 ♘d3 32 ♕xc7 ♘xb4 33 axb4 b5 34 ♕b8+ ♔h7 35 ♕xb5

It is unpleasant to play, but I don' think Black should lose. Anyhow, this ha nothing to do with the opening...

35...♗xg2 36 ♔xg2 ♕e4+ 37 ♔g1 ♕xd4 38 ♕f5+ ♔h8 39 b5 d5 40 ♕e6 ♕d1+ 41 ♔g2 d4 42 ♕e8+ ♔h7 43 ♕e4+ g6 44 b6 d3 45 ♕e7+ ♔h8 46 b7 1-0

Fedorowicz's opening play turned out well, but try 9...♘h4! Looking at all the eighth move alternatives, I think White does best by remaining 'solid' with 8 ♖e1 or 8 ♕e2 in the next game. The flashier ideas tend to give Black a good attack.

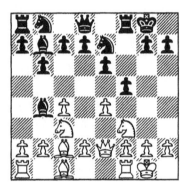

Game 69
Rayner-Plaskett
London (Lloyds Bank) 1993

1 c4 b6 2 ♘c3 e6 3 e4 ♗b7 4 ♘f3 ♗b4 5 ♗d3 ♘e7 6 0-0 0-0 7 ♗c2 f5 8 ♕e2

The most popular move in this position, for what that is worth.

8...♗xc3

In principle I would like to play 8...♘bc6 here, but it is difficult to 'make it work'. Koshy-Lovlu, Sakthi 1996, continued 9 d4 ♗xc3 10 bxc3 and now:

a) 10...♘a5 appeals to me, but White has a big space advantage, and that, combined with pins and threats on the kingside gives him the better chances, e.g. 11 ♗a3 ♗xe4 (after 11...♖e8 12 ♘d2 I would be worried about Black's king) 12 ♗xe4 fxe4 13 ♕xe4 ♘xc4? 14 ♘g5 ♖f5 (or 14...g6 15 ♕h4) 15 ♗xe7 and White is winning.

b) The actual game continued 10...♕e8 11 d5 ♘d8 12 ♘d4 ♗a6 13 ♗a3 f4 14 ♗a4 c6 15 dxc6 dxc6 16 ♖ad1 and Black's position is miserable – though he later won.

9 dxc3

9 bxc3 is less good after 9...♗xe4! 10 ♗xe4 fxe4 11 ♕xe4 ♘bc6 12 d4 reaching, once again, a kind of Nimzo-Indian position which presents few difficulties for Black, e.g. 12...♘f5 13 d5 ♘a5 14 dxe6 ♕e7 15 c5 ♕xe6 16 ♕xe6+ dxe6 17 ♖e1 ♖fe8 18 ♗f4 ♘b7 19 g4 ♘e7 20 ♗xc7 ♘xc5 21 ♖ad1 ♘d5 22 ♗e5 b5 23 ♘g5 ½-½ Ioseliani-Matveeva, European Women's Team Championship 1997.

9...♗xe4

9...♕e8 was played in Hjartarson-Lau, German Bundesliga 1990/91, resulting in a very similar position to the main game after 10 ♖e1 ♗xe4 11 ♗xe4 fxe4 12 ♕xe4 ♘bc6 13 ♗f4 ♖c8 14 ♖ad1 h6 15 h3 ♕f7 16 ♗h2. White has an excellent position with his heavy pieces bearing down on the centre pawns; they are a long way from rolling down the board, and in the meantime Black's pieces are seriously cramped.

Alternatively, 9...♘a6 doesn't help either due to 10 ♗g5 (10 b4!?) 10...fxe4 11 ♗xe4 ♘c5 12 ♗xb7 ♘xb7 13 ♖ad1 ♘d6 14 ♘e5 with similar pressure in Koshy-Shantharam, Indian Championship 1994.

10 ♗xe4 fxe4 11 ♕xe4 ♘bc6 12 ♗f4

This kind of position should be familiar

to you by now! I have a feeling that the Black players who went in for it just imagined that the centre pawns would give them a reasonable position. If the queens were off the board, enabling the king to march into the middle of the board, then I think Black would be better, but that is just a dream.

12...♘f5 13 ♖ad1 ♖c8 14 ♖d2 ♕e8 15 ♖e1!

Good move, preventing ...d7-d6 and ...e6-e5.

15...h6 16 h3 d6?

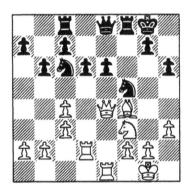

It is interesting that Black becomes frustrated with his position so quickly, and gives up a whole pawn just to free himself. Technically, he is lost, but in the end Plaskett pulls it off.

17 ♕xe6+ ♕xe6 18 ♖xe6 ♖ce8 19 ♖xe8 ♖xe8 20 g4 ♘fe7 21 ♔g2 ♘g6 22 ♗g3 ♖e4 23 b3 ♔f7 24 ♘d4 ♘xd4 25 cxd4 ♘e7 26 c5 ♔e6 27 ♔f3 ♖e1 28 cxd6 cxd6 29 ♖c2 ♔d7 30 ♗f4 ♘g6 31 ♗g3 ♖d1 32 ♖c4 b5 33 ♖b4 ♔c6 34 a4 a6 35 ♔e2 ♖b1 36 axb5+ axb5 37 d5+ ♔c5 38 ♖e4 ♔xd5 39 ♖e8 ♖b2+ 40 ♔d3 ♖xb3+ 41 ♔c2 ♖b4 42 ♖g8 ♖c4+ 43 ♔b3 ♖c7 44 ♖d8 ♘e5 45 ♖b8 ♔c5 46 ♗xe5 dxe5 47 ♖e8 ♔d4 48 ♔b4 ♖f7 49 ♖d8+ ♔e4 50 ♖d2 ♖f3 51 ♔xb5 ♖xh3 52 ♖d7 g5 53 ♖f7 ♖f3 54 ♖h7 ♖xf2 55 ♖xh6 ♔f4 56 ♖f6+ ♔g3 57 ♖e6 ♖e2 58 ♔c4 ♖e3 0-1

A solid approach by White has paid dividends in the example we have looked at. Black has to find an improvement early on after 8 ♕e2 to avoid falling into the kind of passive position we have seen too often.

Game 70
Agrest-Zviaginsev
Kazan 1997

---

1 c4 e6 2 ♘c3 b6 3 e4 ♗b7 4 ♘f3 ♗b4 5 ♗d3 ♘e7 6 ♘e2!?

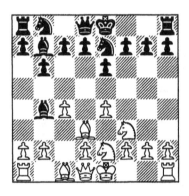

This can also be tried after both sides have castled. The knight runs over to the kingside, leaving the bishop on b4 stranded and looking silly. Then again, the bishop on d3 isn't too clever either, so it is going to take a few moves before everything straightens out and we will be able to see who is doing what to whom.

6...f5

6...0-0? loses to 7 a3 ♗d6 8 e5 ♗xf3 9 exd6 ♗xe2 10 dxe7 ♗xd1 11 exd8♕ ♖xd8 12 ♔xd1.

7 ♘g3

7 ♕c2 is sensible, e.g. 7...♗d6 (7...fxe4 8 ♗xe4 ♗xe4 9 ♕xe4 ♘bc6 10 a3 ♗d6 11 d4 0-0 also slightly favoured White in Eng-Wiemer, German Championship 1984; but not 7...0-0? 8 a3 ♗d6 9 e5 and wins) 8 a3 ♘g6 9 exf5 ♘h4 10 ♗e4 ♘c6 11 fxe6 0-0 12 d4 and White stood much better in

Mitenkov-Ivanov, Moscow open 1994.

7...♘g6 8 0-0 f4

After his game against Chernin (see later on) Speelman made the suggestion of 8...0-0!?

9 ♘e2 0-0

10 ♗b1

I don't see why White doesn't just put the bishop on c2. In effect he gains a move on the game when it comes to developing his queenside.

10...♗e7!?

10...♘h4 goes directly for the attack on the kingside, but it is just a bit too crude: 11 ♘xh4 ♕xh4 12 f3 e5 13 d4 ♘c6 14 a3 ♗e7 15 dxe5 ♘xe5 16 ♔h1 ♗d6 (perhaps 16...g5!?) 17 ♗xf4! ♖xf4 18 g3 ♖xe4!? 19 gxh4 and 1-0 a few moves later in Chernin-Speelman, European Club Cup 1997.

11 d4 c5 12 ♗d2

If White plays 12 d5?! then after the centre is closed with 12...e5 Black can go for it on the kingside. And if 13 d6 ♗f6 and the black knight lands on d4, cutting off the d-pawn.

12...♕c7 13 b3 ♘c6

13...e5!? 14 dxe5 (14 d5 is slightly better for Black) 14...♘xe5 15 ♘xe5 ♕xe5 16 ♗c3 ♕g5 17 f3 is unclear.

14 ♗c3

see following diagram

White does best to keep the centre fluid. Alternatively, 14 d5 ♘ce5 15 ♘xe5 and now:

a) 15...♘xe5 16 f3 (16 ♗c3 f3 favours Black; while 16 ♗xf4 ♘f3+ 17 gxf3 ♖xf4 18 ♘xf4 ♕xf4 19 ♕d3 ♗d6 is unclear) 16...g5.

b) 15...♕xe5 16 ♗c3 ♕g5.

In both cases Black has sufficient play.

14...e5 15 dxe5

Not 15 d5 ♘d4!

15...♘cxe5 16 ♘xe5 ♘xe5 17 f3

17...♘g6?!

What about 17...♗f6...? It is obviously more desirable than the text, the only question is whether it works tactically: 18 ♘xf4 ♘g4!? (18...♘xf3+ 19 ♖xf3 ♗xc3 20 ♘d5 ♗d4+ 21 ♕xd4; and 18...♘xc4 19 ♘d5 both win for White) 19 ♗xf6 ♖xf6 20 fxg4 ♖xf4. As extra pawns go, it is a pretty rotten one. I would even say that Black has the better chances. White is paying for putting the bishop on b1 and not c2 many moves ago.

18 ♕d2 d6 19 ♗c2 ♖ad8

19...♗f6 20 ♖ad1 ♗e5 would have been stronger.

20 ♖ad1 ♗f6 21 ♗xf6 ♖xf6 22 e5!

Giving the bishop some life; White has the better chances.

22...♘xe5 23 ♘xf4 ♕f7 24 ♘d5 ♗xd5 25 cxd5

25 ♕xd5 is better, e.g. 25...♕xd5 26 ♖xd5 ♘c6 27 ♗e4 ♘d4, though with that knight Black should hold.

25...♖f8 26 ♗e4 h6 27 ♕e1 g5 28 ♕e2 ♖f4 29 a4 h5 30 a5 bxa5 31 ♕a6 ♕c7 32 ♖a1 g4 33 ♕xa5 ♕xa5 34 ♖xa5 gxf3 35 gxf3 ♘xf3+ 36 ♗xf3 ♖xf3 37 ♖xf3 ♖xf3 38 ♖xa7 ♖f5 39 b4! cxb4 40 ♖b7 ♖xd5 41 ♖xb4 ♔f7 42 ♔f2 ♖d2+ 43 ♔g3 ♖e2 44 ♖h4 ♖e5 45 ♔f3 d5 46 ♖a4 ♔f6 47 ♔f4 ♖e2 48 ♖a6+ ♖e6 49 ♖a4 ♖c6 50 ♔e3 ♖c2 51 ♖f4+ ♔g6 52 ♖d4 ♖c3+ 53 ♔f4 ½-½

After 53...♖c4 (53...♖c5 54 ♔e5 is slightly better for White; and 53...♖h3 54 ♖xd5 ♖xh2 55 ♖d6+ is equal) 54 ♔e5 ♖xd4 55 ♔xd4 ♔f5 56 ♔xd5 ♔g4 57 ♔e4 the game is drawn. I am sure that we will be seeing more of 6 ♘e2. A couple of things strike me: first, that White could improve his position greatly by playing 10 ♗c2 instead of ♗b1; and that Black does not have to close the position in the first place – see Speelman's pawn sacrifice. Moreover, 7 ♕c2 is an unpretentious move that, at first glance, gives White an easy game.

Summary

I enjoyed looking at the games in this chapter – quite original positions often arise when White plays the 'two-pawn attack'. Short's solid idea in Game 61 reminds me a little of the game Pytel-Piasetski (Game 38) where Black also brought the bishop to c5: worth a try. White's fourth moves in Games 62-65 are not a cause for concern (I would prefer Black's treatment of 4 g3 in Game 64; in particular 7...⟋c6!?). 5 ♕b3 has been put out of business by 5...⟋a6 – Black equalises easily; which means that 4 ⟋f3 and 5 ♗d3 is the only proper test for Black. I would like to play as in Games 68-70 for Black, with ...0-0 and ...f7-f5, but if White players get wise and don't go too crazy (Game 68) then it might be time for a rethink. There could be a way to equalise here for Black, but it isn't immediately obvious to me. In which case I would recommend returning to Game 67. The capture on c3 is positionally desirable and, on the evidence of those games, a solid way to treat the position.

1 c4 b6 2 ⟋c3 ♗b7 3 e4

3...e6
> 3...e5 – *Game 61*

4 ⟋f3
> 4 d3 – *Game 62*
> 4 ⟋ge2 – *Game 63*
> 4 g3 f5 *(D)*
>> 5 ♗g2 – *Game 64*
>> 5 d3 – *Game 65*

4...♗b4 5 ♗d3 *(D)*
> 5 ♕b3 – *Game 66*

5...⟋e7 6 0-0
> 6 ⟋e2 – *Game 70*

6...0-0
> 6...♗xc3 – *Game 67*

7 ♗c2 f5 *(D)* 8 ♕e2
> 8 exf5 – *Game 68*

8...♗xc3 – *Game 69*

4...f5

5 ♗d3

7...f5

CHAPTER EIGHT

Systems with ...♗xf3

The first few chapters of the book dealt with White's most critical response to 1...b6: the occupation of the centre by three pawns. If Black fails to counter effectively then he could be squashed off the board. In that respect this chapter is far less important. White doesn't attempt a refutation of the opening, but merely continues with the standard 'Réti/Catalan' development, fianchettoing the king's bishop in the hope that Black will transpose into something 'normal'. Although there is nothing wrong with allowing a transposition, that would not be in the spirit of the pioneering English Defence. If you play this opening you have already accepted that you are doing something slightly offbeat so as to lure your opponent onto unfamiliar territory. And this is not the moment for orthodoxy. Instead Black can exchange the bishop on b7 for the knight on f3, doubling White's pawns, and so gaining a slight structural advantage. Whether this is enough to compensate for the 'loss' of the bishop remains to be seen.

Games 71-77 show Black playing ...♗xf3 against a Réti set-up; while the final two games feature Black trying ...♗xf3 to avoid the standard Queen's Indian Defence.

Game 71
King-Plaskett
London 1991

1 c4 b6 2 ♘f3 ♗b7 3 g3

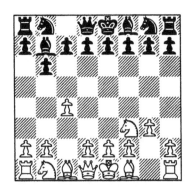

When I see my opponent bottle out of the three pawns challenge I feel provoked into doing something 'different' and, luckily, there are some interesting and reasonably sound methods of knocking White out of his complacency. Like this:

3...♗xf3! 4 exf3 c5!

Black must follow up in this manner or he will have just given up his bishop for no benefit. The aim is to seize control of the d4-square by playing ...♘c6 and ...g7-g6 followed by ...♗g7. It is a potent positional threat which White must counter immediately with...

5 d4!

By the way, here's a quick taste of the mess White gets into if he doesn't play 5 d4: 5 ♘c3?! ♘c6 6 ♗g2 g6 7 0-0 ♗g7 8 f4 e6 9 ♖e1 ♘ge7 10 d3 0-0 and Black already stood better in Buchegger-Schneider Zinner, Austrian Team Championship 1996. He has the d4-square firmly under control and is ready to break open with ...d7-d5. After 5 d4, most players capture on d4, and the majority of the games in this section concentrate on that move; but there are some who know better...

5...♘c6!? 6 d5

The most critical response. Instead, 6 dxc5 bxc5 7 ♗g2 g6 8 0-0 ♗g7 9 f4 ♖c8 should be okay for Black as the c5-pawn gives him control over d4.

6...♘d4

A wonderful square for the knight, though White can exchange it if necessary.

7 ♗e3 ♘f5

see following diagram

7...e5!? is possible, though it does give White something to aim at, which isn't quite in the spirit of the opening. Black's centre will be attacked by f2-f4.

8 ♗d2

I was impressed by Plaskett's idea and decided to try it myself at the next opportunity – which came about two years later. Instead of moving the bishop my opponent tried 8 ♘c3 g6 9 ♗h3 ♘xe3 (9...♗g7!?) 10 fxe3 ♗g7 11 ♕d3 ♘f6 12 d6 (12 0-0 would have been more sensible, with equal chances) 12...e6 and now:

a) 13 e4 was rejected by my opponent, though obviously it is critical, e.g. 13...0-0 14 e5 ♘e8 15 f4 f6 16 ♕e3 ♗h6! (but not 16...fxe5? 17 fxe5 and the bishop doesn't get out) and White's centre won't survive.

b) In the game he chose 13 ♘b5, but the d-pawn is doomed: 13...0-0 14 ♘c7 ♖c8 15 ♖d1 ♘e8 16 ♘xe8 ♖xe8 17 b3 ♖c6 18 f4 ♗f8 19 0-0 ♖xd6 with a clear extra pawn in Dunn-King, Dublin Zonal 1993.

8...g6 9 ♗c3 ♗g7 10 ♗xg7 ♘xg7 11 f4

Now I regain control over the d4-square.

11...♘h6

After 11...♘f5?! 12 ♘d2 ♘d4 13 ♘f3 Black is forced to exchange with 13...♘xf3+ 14 ♕xf3 ♘h6?! 15 ♗h3! and knight no.2 doesn't make it to d4.

12 ♘d2 0-0 13 ♗h3 e6 14 ♘f3 ♕f6 15 ♖b1 d6

15...exd5?! 16 ♕xd5 ♖fe8+ 17 ♔f1 followed by ♔g2 is simply good for White.

16 dxe6

Perhaps 16 0-0!? e5 17 fxe5 dxe5 18 ♖e1.

16...♕e7! 17 0-0 fxe6 18 ♖e1 ♘hf5 19 ♕e2 ♖ae8 20 ♕d2 ♕f6 ½-½

In the final position chances are about equal. Actually, I couldn't see what to do next, and neither could my opponent. For instance, doubling on the e-file is possible, but then what? And I didn't like the look of 21 b4 cxb4 22 ♕xb4 ♖c8 followed by ...♖c5 and doubling on the c-file.

5...♘c6 is chancing it, but there is no obvious refutation and it does have the advantage of making one's opponent think. In view of the popularity of 3...♗xf3, I'm surprised that it hasn't been played more often.

Game 72
Donchenko-Muhutdinov
Alushta 1993

---

1 c4 b6 2 ♘f3 ♗b7 3 g3 ♗xf3! 4 exf3

c5! 5 d4! cxd4 6 ♕xd4 ♘c6 7 ♕d2

By far the most popular retreat for the queen.

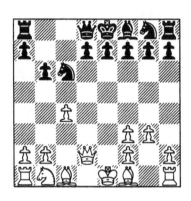

7...g6

In place of the standard 7...e6 (see the next game) this fianchetto has been tried in a few games, but it doesn't appeal to me. When Black plays ...e7-e6 the d5-square is covered; but in this case White's knight constantly threatens to land on d5.

8 b3

White decides to offer the exchange of bishop. This is okay, but not absolutely necessary as the following demonstrates: 8 ♘c3 ♗g7 9 b3 ♘f6 10 ♗b2 0-0 11 ♗g2 a6 12 0-0 ♖b8 13 f4 b5 14 ♘d5! ♘e8 15 ♘e3 ♗xb2 16 ♕xb2 ♘f6 17 ♖fd1 ♕b6 18 ♖ac1 ♖fd8 19 c5 ♕c7, as in Tonoli-Lau, Belgian Team Championship 1997, and now 20 h4 would have maintained White's excellent position.

8...♗g7 9 ♗b2 ♗xb2

In principle I think Black should be glad to exchange off a pair of bishops even though it makes his king draughty. Instead, 9...♘f6 10 ♗g2 0-0 11 f4 ♕c7 12 0-0 ♖ac8 13 ♘c3 d6 14 ♖fe1 gave White the usual space advantage in Egeli-Madsen, Norwegian Championship 1996. That game continued 14...♖fe8 15 f5 a6 16 ♖ac1 ♘e5 17 fxg6 hxg6 18 ♘d5 ♘xd5 19 ♗xd5 e6 20 ♗g2 ♘c6 21 h4 ♗xb2 22 ♕xb2 e5 23 h5 ♘d4 24 hxg6 fxg6 25 ♗d5+ ♔g7 26

♔g2 ♖h8 27 ♖cd1 ♖cf8, and now 28 ♖xd4 exd4 29 ♕xd4+ ♖f6 30 g4 wins for White.
10 ♕xb2 ♞f6 11 f4 0-0 12 ♗g2 ♕b8 13 0-0 b5 14 c5 b4 15 ♞d2 ♕b5 16 ♖fc1 ♖ac8 17 ♗f1 ♕b7 18 ♗g2 ♖c7 19 ♖e1 ♕b5 20 ♖ac1 ♖fc8 21 ♖c4 ♞e8 22 f5

With practically Black's entire army camped out on the other side of the board, White feels justified in exploiting his space advantage to launch a massive assault on the king. It isn't strictly necessary though as, for instance, the alternative 22 ♞e4 is strong.
22...gxf5 23 g4 ♞a5 24 ♖xe7 ♞xc4 25 bxc4 ♕xc5 26 ♖e5 ♕f8 27 ♖xf5 ♕g7 28 ♕xb4 ♕xg4 29 ♖f3 ♕d4 30 ♖g3+ ♞g7 31 ♗d5 ♔h8 32 ♞f3 ♕a1+ 33 ♔g2 ♞e6 34 ♕d6 f6 35 ♖g4 a5 36 h3 ♕c3 37 ♕e7 f5 38 ♞g5 ♞xg5 39 ♖xg5 ♖b8

40 ♕d6

40 ♔h2!? ♖cc8 41 ♖xf5 is still better for White.
40...♖cc8 41 ♖g3 ♕d4 42 ♖d3 ♖b6 43 ♕xd7 ♖g6+ 44 ♖g3 ♖xg3+ 45 fxg3 ♕d2+ 46 ♔f3 ♖g8 47 ♕xf5 ♕c3+ 48 ♔e4 ♖e8+ 49 ♔f4 ♕d4+ 50 ♗e4 ♕f2+ 51 ♗f3 ♕e3+ 52 ♔g4 ♖g8+ 53 ♔h4 ♕e7+ 54 ♔h5 h6 55 h4 ♖f8 56 ♕d5 ♕e8+ 57 ♔g4 ♕c8+ 0-1

The fianchetto of the king's bishop gives White a very easy game. Black does best to stick to a system with ...e7-e6, as we see in the next game.

Game 73
Moskow-Shabalov
New York 1993

1 c4 b6 2 ♞f3 ♗b7 3 g3 ♗xf3 4 exf3 c5 5 d4 cxd4 6 ♕xd4 ♞c6 7 ♕d2 e6 8 ♗g2

8 ♞c3 is more canny, leaving the bishop to defend the pawn on c4 for the time being – see Games 74-77 (by transposition).

8...♗b4! 9 ♞c3 ♕f6

In this way Black ensures that he doubles the c-pawns.

10 0-0 ♗xc3 11 bxc3 ♞ge7 12 c5

12 ♗a3 is a critical alternative:

a) 12...0-0?! 13 ♕xd7 ♖fd8 14 ♕b7 ♖db8 15 ♗xe7 ♞xe7 16 ♕a6.

b) 12...♞e5?! 13 ♖fd1 (13 f4 ♞xc4 favours Black) 13...♖d8 14 ♕e2 ♖c8 15 c5 bxc5 16 f4 ♘5c6 17 ♗xc5 and White is on top.

c) 12...♘a5! 13 ♕d3 (13 ♖fd1!? ♖d8) 13...♕f5 14 ♕d4 e5 15 ♕d6 ♕e6 16 f4 ♖c8 17 fxe5 ♘xc4 18 ♕xe7+ ♕xe7 19 ♗xe7 ♔xe7 20 ♖ad1 ♖c5 21 ♖fe1 ♖hc8 22 ♗h3 ♖8c7 and Black held the advantage in McNab-McKay, Scottish Championship 1988.

12...bxc5 13 ♗a3 0-0

Alternatively, 13...c4 14 ♗d6 0-0 15 f4 ♖fd8 16 ♗c7 d5 17 ♗xd8 ♖xd8 18 ♖ab1 ♘c8 19 ♕e3 ♘b6 and Black had good compensation for the exchange in Reschke-Cicak, OLO-C 1996.

14 ♗xc5 ♖fd8 15 ♖ab1 d6 16 ♗e3 h6 17 f4 d5 18 ♖b7 ♘f5 19 ♗c5 ♖ac8 20 c4 dxc4 21 ♖d7 ♘cd4 22 ♖xd8+ ♕xd8 23 ♕b4 c3 24 g4 ♘e2+ 25 ♔h1 c2 0-1

Game 74
Van Wely-Zviaginsev
New York open 1997

---

1 c4 e6 2 ♘c3 b6 3 g3 ♗b7 4 ♘f3 ♗xf3 5 exf3 c5 6 d4 cxd4

6...♘c6?! is not as successful here, with ♘c3 and ..e7-e6 thrown in, as it was in Game 71. For example, 7 d5 ♘d4 8 ♗e3 ♘f5 9 ♗h3 ♘gh6 10 ♕a4! g6 11 0-0 ♘xe3 12 fxe3 exd5 13 ♖ad1! with tremendous pressure for White in Davies-Plaskett, London 1991.

7 ♕xd4 ♘c6

This is the starting point for a great many games.

8 ♕d2

The usual retreat. 8 ♕d1 is the subject of Game 76 and 8 ♕d3 of Game 77.

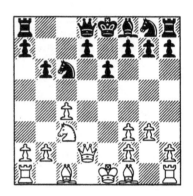

8...♕f6!?

Alternatively, 8...♗c5 isn't bad. Black develops sensibly and unpretentiously: 9 ♗g2 ♘f6 10 0-0 0-0 11 f4 ♕e7 12 b3 ♖ab8 13 ♗b2 ♖fd8 14 ♖ad1 a6! (it would be highly desirably for Black to play ...b6-b5, chipping away at White's centre) 15 a3 (cracking up) 15...♘a5 16 ♘e4 ♘xe4 17 ♗xe4 ♗xa3 and Black was on top in Reschke-Kulaots, Weilburg open 1995. 8...♖c8 is the subject of the next main game.

9 ♗g2 ♕e5+

There is nothing wrong with 9...♗b4 transposing to the previous game.

10 ♕e2 ♖c8 11 ♗d2 f5!?

Taking away an important square from White.

12 ♗e3 ♘f6 13 0-0 ♗e7 14 ♖fd1 0-0 15 h3 ♗c5 16 f4 ♕b8 17 ♖ac1 ♘d8 18 ♗d2 ♘f7 19 a3 ♖fe8 20 b4 ♗f8 21 ♗e3 ♖ed8 22 ♗d4 ♘e8

see following diagram

Black's set-up is a rather passive, but it is very solid and he manages to unwind successfully.

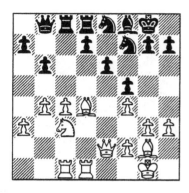

23 ♖b1 g6 24 ♖dc1 ♗g7 25 ♗e3 ♘c7
26 ♕d3 d6 27 a4 d5 28 cxd5 ♗xc3 29
♖xc3 ♘xd5 30 ♖xc8 ♕xc8 31 ♖c1 ♕d7
32 ♗xd5 exd5 33 ♕d4 ♖e8 34 b5 ♖e4
35 ♕f6 d4 36 ♗d2 ♖e6 ½-½

37 ♖c7 ♕xc7 38 ♕xe6 is dead level.

Game 75
Piesina-Kengis
Riga Zonal 1995

---

1 c4 b6 2 ♘c3 ♗b7 3 ♘f3 e6 4 g3 ♗xf3
5 exf3 c5 6 d4 cxd4 7 ♕xd4 ♘c6 8 ♕d2
♖c8

9 b3

Or 9 ♗g2 ♘f6 10 b3 ♗b4 11 a3 (11
♗b2 d5!) 11...♗xc3 12 ♕xc3 d5 13 ♗d2
(13 cxd5 ♘a5!) 13...dxc4 14 bxc4 ♘a5 15
0-0 0-0 16 ♖fd1 ♖xc4, pawn up, thank
you, Otto-Haubt, German Bundesliga

1994.

9...♘f6

In the light of experience...? In a game
five years previously Kengis had tried
9...♕f6 and now the best move is:

a) 10 ♗g2 when I imagine it must have
been Kengis's intention to play:

a1) 10...d5!? with the following possibilities:

a11) 11 cxd5 11...♗b4 12 ♗b2 ♘ce7 and
wins.

a12) 11 0-0 ♗b4 12 ♗b2 d4 13 ♖ad1
♕e7 and wins.

a13) 11 ♗b2 dxc4 (11...♗b4 12 a3) 12
0-0 ♗b4 is unclear.

a2) 10...♗b4 11 ♗b2 ♕e5+ 12 ♕e3 and
White's position is secure.

b) In the actual game White tried 10 f4?!
d5 11 ♗b2 d4 12 ♘e4 ♕g6 13 ♕e2 ♗b4+
14 ♔d1 ♘h6 15 ♕f3 0-0 16 ♗d3 f5 17 a3
♘g4 18 ♔e2 ♘ge5! and he was in big
trouble in Titz-Kengis, Vienna open 1990.

10 ♗b2 ♗b4!?

Clever; Black wishes to tempt a2-a3,
when the queenside pawn chain has been
weakened.

**11 a3 ♗e7 12 ♗e2 ♘a5 13 ♕d1 0-0 14
♘b5**

Perhaps 14 0-0!?

14...a6 15 ♘d4 d5

Kengis stirs it up while his opponent's
king is still in the middle of the board, a
decision which is justified in a practical

game, but isn't quite so sound when examined in the cold light of day.

16 cxd5 ♕xd5 17 ♗xa6 ♖cd8 18 b4 ♗c5!?

18...♘c4 19 ♗xc4 ♕xc4 20 ♖c1 ♕a2 21 ♕b3 ♕xb3 22 ♘xb3 is clearly better for White.

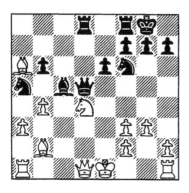

19 bxc5

19 bxa5? ♗xd4 20 ♕xd4 ♕xa5+ 21 ♕b4 ♕xa6 22 ♗xf6 gxf6 slightly favours Black.

19...bxc5 20 ♘c2 ♕b3 21 ♕c1 ♕b6 22 ♗xf6!

Not 22 ♗e2? ♘b3 and now:

a) 23 ♕b1 ♕a5+ 24 ♘b4 (24 ♔f1 ♘d2+ also wins) 24...♘xa1.

b) 23 ♕g5 ♘xa1 24 ♗xf6 ♕b1+.

In both cases with a winning position for Black.

22...gxf6

23 0-0?

23 ♗e2! is the move, though White needs steady nerves: 23...♘b3 24 ♕b2 ♖d2 (24...♕a5+!? 25 ♔f1 ♘xa1 26 ♕xa1 ♖d2 27 ♘e3 ♖xe2!?) 28 ♔xe2 ♕b5+ is fun, though I don't believe it) 25 ♖b1 ♕a5 26 ♕xb3 ♖d3+ 27 ♔f1 ♖xb3 28 ♖xb3 and with care White should be able to untangle and come out on top.

23...♕xa6 24 ♕f4 ♕d3! 25 ♘e3 ♕d4 26 ♕c7 ♘b3 27 ♖ad1 ♕e5 28 ♕xe5 fxe5 29 ♔g2 f6 30 ♖xd8 ♖xd8 31 ♖b1 ♖d3 32 a4 ♔g7 33 ♘c4 ♖c3 34 ♘d6 c4 35 ♖b2 ♖c1 36 ♘xc4 ♖xc4 37 ♖xb3 ♖xa4 ½-½

It is interesting to note that Kengis changed his mind and played 9...♘f6 instead of 9...♕f6 when faced with the same position in a later game. Having said that, I don't see anything wrong with 9...♕f6. Black has good counterplay.

Game 76
Appolonov-Lempert
Katowice 1992

---

1 c4 b6 2 ♘f3 ♗b7 3 ♘c3 e6

3...c5!? is worth a thought so that if 4 g3?! ♗xf3! 5 exf3 ♘c6 and Black already has control over d4. Naturally, 4 g3 is not the best move.

4 g3 ♗xf3 5 exf3 c5 6 d4 cxd4 7 ♕xd4 ♘c6 8 ♕d1 ♘f6

22 ♗g2 ♘h5

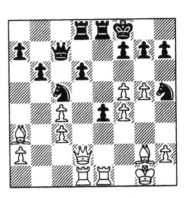

9 ♗e2

As we saw in the previous game, one of Black's idea's is a rapid assault on the c4-pawn, so White is understandably a little nervous about moving the bishop to g2.

9...♗b4 10 0-0

I don't see what is wrong with 10 ♗d2, preventing the doubling of the c-pawns.

10...♗xc3 11 bxc3

The play now becomes double-edged. Black has lots of weak pawns to aim for; while White has open lines for his rooks and bishops.

11...d6

11...0-0 is also possible. In fact I think I prefer it, e.g. 12 ♗a3 ♖e8 13 ♗d6 ♘a5 followed either by ...♖c8 or ...♘b7.

12 ♗a3 ♔e7 13 ♕d2 ♕c7 14 ♖ad1 ♖ad8 15 ♖fe1 ♘a5 16 f4 ♘b7 17 f5 e5 18 f4 ♘c5 19 g4 ♖he8 20 ♗f3 ♔f8 21 g5 e4

23 f6 g6 24 ♗f1 ♔g8 25 ♕e3 ♕c8 26 ♗c1 ♘d3 27 ♗xd3 exd3 28 ♕xd3 ♕g4+ 29 ♔h1 ♘xf4 30 ♕g3 ♖xe1+ 31 ♖xe1 ♕xg3 32 hxg3 ♘d3 33 ♖f1 ♘e5 34 ♗f4 ♘xc4 35 ♖e1 a5 36 ♖e7 ♖c8 ½-½

Exciting stuff, though I'm sure Black is doing fine (particularly after 11...0-0).

> ### Game 77
> ### Seul-Kengis
> *Bonn 1995*

1 c4 b6 2 ♘c3 e6 3 ♘f3 ♗b7 4 g3 ♗xf3 5 exf3 c5 6 d4 cxd4 7 ♕xd4 ♘c6 8 ♕d3 ♖c8

9 f4!

The best move, preventing ...♘e5. 9 b3? ♘e5 10 ♕e3 ♕f6 11 f4 ♘g4 12 ♕f3 ♗c5 13 ♗b2 ♘xf2 14 b4 ♗d4 favoured Black in Hagenbach-Bandza, Hessenliga 1994.

9...♗b4 10 ♗d2 ♘f6

If 10...♘a5 then 11 b3 holds White's position firm, e.g. 11...d5? 12 cxd5 ♕f6 13 ♕b5+.

11 ♗g2 ♘a5 12 b3 0-0 13 0-0

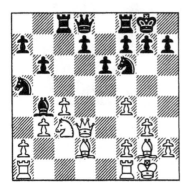

13...d5

Perhaps 13...♕e7!?

14 cxd5 ♗xc3 15 ♗xc3 ♘xd5 16 ♗xa5

16 ♖fc1!? ♘xc3 (maybe 16...♘c6) 17 ♖xc3 ♖xc3 18 ♕xc3 is better for White due to the poor position of the knight on a5.

16...bxa5

17 ♖fd1 ♘c3 18 ♕xd8 ♖fxd8 19 ♖xd8+ ♖xd8 20 ♔f1 ♔f8 21 ♔e1 ♔e7 22 ♗f1 a4 23 bxa4 ♘xa4 24 ♖c1 ♘b6 25 ♖c3 ♘d5 ½-½

White must take care when he plays 8 ♕d3 as the queen is a little exposed. How-ever, compared to the usual 8 ♕d2, it does stay out of the way of the bishop on c1 so development is smoother. On the basis of this game, Black has some work to do before he can equalise.

In the final two games of this book White invites a transposition to a Queen's Indian Defence instead of entering the usual fun and mayhem of the English. Here Black may also use ...♗xf3 (at the right moment!) to keep the game off the straight and narrow.

Game 78
Yermolinsky-Speelman
Hastings 1996

1 d4 e6 2 c4 b6 3 g3 ♗b7 4 ♘f3

4...♗b4+

The immediate 4...♗xf3 5 exf3, without the exchange of dark-squared bishops, is not as strong. For instance, 5...d5 6 ♘c3 c6 7 cxd5 exd5 8 ♗d3 ♗e7 9 0-0 ♗f6 10 ♗c2 ♘e7 11 ♕d3 ♘d7 12 ♖e1 a6 13 ♗f4, when although Black has an extra pawn on the queenside, without the light-squared bishop his structure is weak, and White's pieces are very active, as in Andersson-Ljubojevic, Monaco blindfold 1997.

5 ♗d2

The best block. The alternatives are:

a) Amazingly, 5 ♘bd2?! already lands White in difficulties. After 5...♗xf3 6 exf3 there are two decent moves:

a1) 6...♘c6!? 7 a3 ♗xd2+ 8 ♗xd2 (8 ♕xd2 ♕f6 is just good for Black) 8...♘xd4 9 ♗c3 c5 (or 9...e5 10 f4 with counterplay) 10 ♗xd4 cxd4 11 ♕xd4 ♕f6 12 ♖d1 ♕xd4 13 ♖xd4 ♖c8 14 b3 ♘e7 and Black is slightly better.

a2) 6...♕f6 7 ♗g2 ♕xd4 8 f4 ♘c6 9 0-0 ♗xd2 10 ♗xd2 ♕xb2 and Black was already well on top in Kraidman-P.Littlewood, Lloyds Bank open, London 1978.

b) 5 ♘c3 transposes to a kind of Nimzo-Indian Defence, although as Black has delayed the development of the knight to f6 he has more options so, in theory, he should have few difficulties. Here are some ideas after 5...♗xc3+ 6 bxc3:

b1) 6...♘f6 7 ♗g2 d6 8 0-0 ♘bd7 9 a4 a5 10 ♘d2 ♗xg2 11 ♔xg2 e5 12 e4 ♕e7 13 ♕e2 0-0 14 ♗a3 ♖ab8 15 f4 was better for White in Gyimesi-Bricard, Paris open 1995. Black's development was too routine.

b2) 6...♘c6!? 7 ♗g2 (7 e4 ♘ge7) 7...♘a5.

b3) 6...f5!? 7 ♗g2 ♘f6 8 0-0 0-0.

5...♗xf3!

Only now.

6 exf3 ♗xd2+ 7 ♘xd2

ops. It means, for example, that he may develop his queen safely on a dark square without fear of being hassled.

7...♘f6

7...♘e7 also has a good reputation. For example, 8 f4 ♘bc6 9 ♗g2 ♘xd4 (an enterprising sacrifice; Black gets a pawn for the exchange, and has excellent control due to the centre pawns) 10 ♗xa8 ♕xa8 11 0-0 c5 12 ♖c1 0-0 13 ♖c3 ♖d8 14 ♘f3 ♘ec6 with good compensation in Grabarczyk-Teske, OLO-B 1998.

8 f4

Or 8 ♗g2 0-0 9 f4 d5 10 0-0 c6, as in Relange-Degraeve, Cappelle la Grande open 1984. This is the most usual kind of structure that is reached when Black goes in for this line. Having got rid of the light-squared bishop, Black sticks his pawns on light squares to block out his opponent's bishop. Chances are about equal.

In the main game, Speelman does not go for this structure immediately, but maintains his flexibility and in so doing blocks out his opponent's minor pieces:

8...♘c6 9 ♘f3 ♘e7

To counter the threat of d4-d5, breaking open the position.

For 7 ♕xd2 see the next game. It makes a massive difference to the position for Black to have exchanged off a pair of bish-

10 ♗g2 0-0 11 0-0 c6 12 ♖c1 ♖b8 13 ♘e5 ♖c8 14 ♕e2 d6 15 ♘f3 ♕c7 16 ♗h3 ♖fe8 17 ♖c3 ♖cd8 18 ♖fc1 g6 19 ♕c2 c5 20 ♖d1 ♘c6 21 ♖e3 d5 22 dxc5 bxc5 23 cxd5 ♘xd5 24 ♖ee1 ♘cb4 25

♕c4 ♘b6 26 ♕b3 a5 27 ♘e5 a4 28 ♕f3
♘c2 29 ♖xd8 ♖xd8 30 ♖c1 ♘d4 31 ♕e4
♘d5

It is interesting to see how Black has
managed to find superb squares for the
knights.

**32 ♗g2 ♕b6 33 ♘c4 ♕a6 34 h3 ♘b6 35
♗f1 ♘xc4 36 ♖xc4 ♕a7 37 ♗g2 ♕b6 38
♖xa4 ♕xb2 39 h4?**

39 ♖c4 should still maintain the balance, but it is tricky with that knight on
d4.

39...♘e2+ 0-1

40 ♔h2 is met by 40...♘c3.

Game 79
Kempinski-Miles
Groningen 1996

**1 d4 e6 2 c4 b6 3 ♘f3 ♗b7 4 g3 ♗b4+
5 ♗d2 ♗xd2+ 6 ♕xd2 ♗xf3 7 exf3 d5**

Miles makes the logical move, playing
the pawn to d5 straightaway, but it is also
possible to wait for a move or two with
7...♘e7 or 7...♘f6. However, if you do,
you should be aware that White may try
d4-d5 to cut across your plans. For instance:

a) 7...♘e7 8 d5!? 0-0 9 ♘c3 a5 (not
9...c5?! 10 ♗h3 exd5 11 cxd5 d6 12 0-0
♘d7 13 ♖fe1 a6 14 a4 with advantage to
White in Rohde-Kengis, Tilburg 1992) 10
♗h3 ♘a6 11 0-0 ♘c5 12 ♖ad1 ♘g6 13 f4

e5 ½-½ Sloth-Hoi, Danish Championship
1983. Just when things were hotting up
White should play 14 f5 and now:

a1) 14...♘e7 15 d6 (or 15 f6!?) 15...cxd6
16 ♕xd6.

a2) 14...♘h8 15 d6 c6 16 f4.

In both cases with a promising position.

b) 7...♘f6 is the better of the two
moves as d4-d5 then has some drawbacks:

b1) 8 d5?! exd5 9 cxd5 0-0 10 ♘c3 ♖e8+
11 ♗e2 ♘a6!? (or 11...c6!?) 12 0-0 ♘c
allows Black good counterplay.

b2) 8 ♘c3 0-0 9 ♗g2 d5 10 f4 c6 11 b
♘a6 12 0-0 ♕d7 13 ♖ad1 ♘c7 14 ♖fe
♖fd8 15 ♕e2 ½-½ Ljubojevic-Speelman
PCA qualifier, New York 1995.

8 ♗g2

8 cxd5 would be a mistake due to
8...♕xd5 9 ♗g2 ♘c6 10 0-0 (or 10 ♘c.
♕xd4 11 f4 ♕xd2+ 12 ♔xd2 0-0-0+ with
an extra pawn) 10...♘xd4 11 ♕d3 ♖d8 an
Black was a pawn up in Bock-Czebe, Bu
dapest 1997.

8...♘e7

8...c6 is rather similar after 9 b3 ♘e7 1
♘a3 0-0 11 0-0 ♕d6 12 ♘c2 ♘d7 13 ♘e
a5 14 f4 g6 and Black's position was super
solid in Stanec-Loebler, Austrian Champi
onship 1995.

9 0-0 0-0 10 cxd5 ♘xd5

---

see following diagram

In general it is desirable to recapture on d5 with the knight so as to have a go at the pawn on d4 later on.

11 ♘c3 ♘c6!

It appears dangerous to put another piece on the same diagonal as the bishop, but Miles had calculated that by putting pressure on the d-pawn he can force a concession.

12 ♘xd5 ♕xd5 13 f4 ♕d6 14 ♖fd1 ♖ad8 15 ♗xc6 ♕xc6

The position is completely equal.

16 ♖ac1 ♕d6 17 ♕c2 ♖d7 18 ♕c6 ♕e7 19 ♖c4 ♖fd8 20 ♖dc1 g6 21 ♕a4 a5 22 ♕c2 ♖xd4 23 ♖xc7 ♕d6 24 ♖c8 ♖d2 25 ♖xd8+ ♕xd8 26 ♕c8 ♕xc8 27 ♖xc8+ ♔g7 28 b3 b5 29 ♖c5 ♖d5 30 ♖c7 h5 31 a3 ♖d3 ½-½

If Black doesn't want to allow it, then White cannot easily reach a Queen's Indian. Black's system, as played in the last two games, is fully viable.

Summary

5...♘c6 from Game 71 is fun, but objectively a bit dodgy; you need to pick your opponent well. If Black captures on d4 then he should definitely play with ...e7-e6 (Games 73-77) rather than fianchetto the bishop (Game 72). I see nothing wrong with Black's system in Games 78-79, so long as the dark-squared bishops are exchanged – but watch out for an early d4-d5 from White.

1 c4 b6

2 ♘c3

    2 ♘f3 ♗b7 3 g3 ♗xf3 4 gxf3 c5 5 d4 *(D)*
        5...♘c6 – *Game 71*
        5...cxd4 6 ♕xd4 ♘c6 7 ♕d2
            7...g6 – *Game 72*
            7...e6
                8 ♗g2 – *Game 73*
                8 ♘c3 – Games 74-77 below (by transposition)
    2 d4 e6 3 ♘f3 ♗b7 4 g3 ♗b4+ 5 ♗d2 ♗xf3 6 exf3 *(D)* ♗xd2+
        7 ♘xd2 – *Game 78*
        7 ♕xd2 – *Game 79*
2...♗b7 3 ♘f3 e6 4 g3 ♗xf3 5 gxf3 c5 6 d4 cxd4 7 ♕xd4 ♘c6 *(D)* 8 ♕d2
    8 ♕d1 – *Game 76*
    8 ♕d3 – *Game 77*
8...♕f6
    8...♖c8 – *Game 75*
9 ♗g2 – *Game 74*

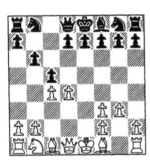  

     5 d4   *6 exf3*   *7...♘c6*

INDEX OF COMPLETE GAMES

CPSIA information can be obtained
at www.ICGtesting.com
Printed in the USA
BVHW030039280221
600953BV00002B/25

9 781857 442953